A Stranger is Calling

A Stranger is Calling

Jews, Christians, and Muslims as Fellow Travellers

Anton Wessels

Foreword by Charles Amjad-Ali
Translated by Henry Jansen

WIPF & STOCK · Eugene, Oregon

A STRANGER IS CALLING
Jews, Christians, and Muslims as Fellow Travelers

Copyright © 2017 Anton Wessels. All rights reserved. Except for brief quotations in critical publications or reviews, no part of this book may be reproduced in any manner without prior written permission from the publisher. Write: Permissions, Wipf and Stock Publishers, 199 W. 8th Ave., Suite 3, Eugene, OR 97401.

Wipf & Stock
An Imprint of Wipf and Stock Publishers
199 W. 8th Ave., Suite 3
Eugene, OR 97401

www.wipfandstock.com

PAPERBACK ISBN: 978–1-5326–0797–4
HARDCOVER ISBN: 978–1-5326–0799–8
EBOOK ISBN: 978–1-5326–0798–1

Manufactured in the U.S.A.   FEBRUARY 7, 2017

For Awraham Soetendorp and his exemplary role in the deepening mutual understanding, recognition, and compassion among Jews, Christians, and Muslims in the Netherlands and abroad.

Contents

Foreword by Charles Amjad-Ali | xi
Acknowledgments | xv
Abbreviations | xvi

Introduction | 1

    "Don't Jump on the 'Jew Bandwagon'"? | 1
    The Sources of the Qur'an Disputed? | 3
    Ban the Qur'an? | 4
    Jews, Christians, and Muslims: "People of the Way" | 4
    The Three Communities of the Way Go Their Separate Ways | 8
    Muhammad and the Christians of Najrân | 9
    The Qur'an and the One "Community" | 10
    Why Should We Read the Three Books Together? | 12

I   God as a Stranger | 13

    A Stranger Comes Calling | 13
    Do Jews, Christians, and Muslims Believe in the Same God? | 14
    The Silence of God? | 16
    Moses Was Not a Public Speaker?! | 18
    God is a Hidden God | 19
    God's Hiddenness and Revelation in the Qur'an | 20
    God's Name | 23
    "Water and Fire": "God Lives in the Thorn Bush" | 24
    The Parable of the Olive Tree | 25
    Two Names for God in the Psalter | 27
    Elijah's Confrontation with the Dumb Gods | 29
    Elijah and the Judgments in the Qur'an | 32
    Elijah in Baalbek | 33

        Elijah and the Gentle Whisper | 33
        Elijah's Ascension | 37
        Moses' Encounter with God in the Qur'an and Isaiah on Idolatry | 37
        Horses and Donkeys | 40
        Riding on a Young Donkey | 41
        Visitors Come to Ebenezer Scrooge | 42
        What does "Visit" Mean in the Bible? | 43
        Visits in the Qur'an | 45
        "It's all a parable with a more than earthly mystery" | 46

II   Abraham Visited by Three Strangers | 47

        Introduction | 47
        Gods as Strangers in Classical Literature | 49
        Odysseus as a Stranger in his Own House | 49
        Philemon and Baucis Visited by Two Strangers | 50
        The Stranger in the Torah | 52
        The Traveler as the Preeminent Stranger (the Qur'an) | 54
        Hospitality in the Bible and the Qur'an | 55
        God as the Host | 57
        Rembrandt and the Three Strangers | 58
        Abraham with the Three Angels (Marc Chagall) | 61
        Abraham Shows Hospitality | 62
        Lot's Story | 64
        Lot's Hospitality | 65
        Lot's Hospitality According to the Qur'an | 67
        Sodom's Destruction Because of Its Lack of Hospitality | 67
        The Destruction of Cities | 71
        Moses as a Stranger | 73
        Abraham as a Stranger—An Example for Jews, Christians, and Muslims | 74

III   The Language of Canaan and Foreign Tongues | 76

        Introduction | 77
        The Biblical ABCs | 78
        The Language of Canaan in the Prophet Isaiah | 78
        The Grammar of the Exodus | 86
        Overcoming the Confusion of Tongues | 90
        Maimonides and the Language of Canaan Spoken with Pure Lips | 92

CONTENTS   ix

        The Arabs in Northern and Southern Arabia | 93
        The Grammar of the Hijra | 96
        Clear Arabic | 98
        The Good News of the Tanakh, the Gospel, and the Qur'an | 101
        The Good News Has One Language | 103

IV   Foreign Powers and Religion | 105

        "The French 9/11" | 105
        "The Psalm against Fear" | 106
        Wise Men and Fools | 107
        The Human Being: Caliph or King | 108
        "I'm an Atheist" | 111
        No Separation of Church and State? | 112
        "Give to Caesar what is Caesar's" | 113
        "Bring me a denarius" | 116
        "Give to God what is God's" | 120
        Islam—Religion and State in One? | 121
        God's Religion | 122
        Abraham's Religion | 124

V   The Foreign King | 128

        Introduction | 128
        The Man Born to Be King | 129
        Joseph as a Stranger in a Strange Land | 131
        The "Joseph Drama" in the Qur'an | 132
        The Joseph Cycle in the Bible: His Dream and the Dreams | 134
        "God intended it for good" | 136
        The Nature of Joseph's Kingship | 138
        Joseph as the Interpreter of Dreams in the Qur'an | 140
        Jacob and his Two Sons Joseph and Benjamin in the Qur'an | 142
        Joseph's Shirt | 145
        Human Guile and Divine Guile in the Story of Joseph | 147
        Joseph as a Role Model for the Prophet Muhammad | 151
        Muhammad and Dreams | 151
        The Nightly Journey | 152
        The Moment of Truth (The Battle of Badr) | 153
        The Dream of Victory | 155

VI The Desert and the City | 157

   Introduction | 157
   Hagar and Ishmael in the Desert and at the Wells (Beersheba and Mecca) | 158
   Ishmael in the Desert: Paran and Mecca | 162
   Abraham's Prayer for the Dedication of the Ka'ba | 163
   The Theophanies on Three Mountains | 164
   The Lessons of the Cities that Have Been Destroyed | 166
   The Parable of the Arrogant Rich Man | 169
   The Unbelieving City | 171
   The Fate of the Cities | 172
   The City | 174
   The Macrocosm of the City and the Microcosm of the Human Being | 180
   Living Together in the One Community | 180

VII Humankind's Journey in the Wilderness | 183

   The Beginning of History: Cain and Abel | 183
   Cainites or Kenites? | 185
   Moses in the Desert | 187
   The Journey in the Desert as a Life Journey | 188
   The Three Masks of Cain | 189
   The Mask of Pharaoh: The Arrogance of Power | 189
   Human Arrogance | 191
   The Mask of Korah (Qârûn): "Money Rules the World" | 193
   The Mask of Balaam: The Spin Doctor | 195
   Political Satire | 196
   Two Talking Animals: The Serpent and the Donkey | 197
   Balaam in the Time of the Roman Empire | 199
   Serving the Beast | 204
   Food for On the Way | 207
   The Promised City, the Promised Land, the Promised World | 209

Bibliography | 211
Subject Index | 221
Bibliography | 231

Foreword

I AM DEEPLY HONORED to write this foreword to Prof. Anton Wessels' *A Stranger is Calling: Jews, Christians, and Muslims as Fellow Travelers*. This book covers issues which are closest to my heart, mind and intellectual vocation. I have known Anton for decades as one of those scholars who has always quested for the irenic, just and sustainable human dwelling and community along all the fractious borders of our time. He has been consistently working on the issues of Christian-Muslim encounters, relations and dialogue over his extensive career and has a comprehensive biographical history of consistent, critical, and significant texts on these issues starting with his dissertation *A Modern Arabic Biography of Muhammad: A Critical Study of Muhammad Husayn Haykal's Hayât Muhammad* (1972). He spent seven years as Associate Professor dealing with Christian-Muslim relations in the Near East School of Theology in Beirut, Lebanon from 1971 to 1978, teaching students from Syria, Lebanon, the West Bank, both East and West Africa in particular the South of the Sudan, as well as from Pakistan and Indonesia. Upon returning home to his native Holland, he was the professor of religious studies and cultural relationships, including those with non-Western cultures, at the Theological Faculty of the Free University of Amsterdam from 1978–2003.

Anton is not only a scholar eminently qualified to deal with the subject of this book, but he has already made highly significant contributions on these issues at some critical historical junctures of our time. He always enlightens and enriches us in the trajectories of his works, especially those of us who pursue these areas for biographical, existential, vocational, theological and intellectual purposes. As someone who has been involved in interreligious engagement for well over 40 years in Pakistan and the US, as well as in Asia more broadly, Southern Africa, and Europe, both in many actual dialogical and relational contexts as well as in the academic side of teaching, research and publications, I have the highest admiration for Prof. Wessels' work and his critical role in the field. *A Stranger is Calling* is no exception—I would go so far as to say that it is his *tour de force*. This book it is loaded with gems which should be mined wide and deep if we are to seek a world not marred by half-truths or post-truths-that being a word much in currency today.

Starting with his dissertation which I mentioned above, among his many significant books he has produced the following, covering the areas which concern him here

- *Images of Jesus: How Jesus is Perceived and Portrayed in Non-European Cultures* (1990);
- *Europe: Was it Ever Really Christian?* (1994);
- *Arab and Christian? Christians in the Middle East* (1996);
- *Understanding the Qur'an* (2000);
- *Islam in Stories* (2002);
- *Muslims and the West: Can They Be Integrated?* (2006);
- *The Torah, the Gospel, and the Qur'an: Three Books, Two Cities, One Tale* (2013)

If one even cursorily looks at Anton's work over the last five decades one is awe struck at the breadth of his academic and generative curiosity. Knowing these works, one sees the highly ethical and moral concerns that dominate them. They are always intellectually and academically creative and innovative and at times quite evocative because of the honest critical approach Anton has taken over the past decades. This has not always garnered him the high accolades he deserves, but rather they are often seen as a challenge to the accepted pervasive academic and cultural grammar. His work has thus at times generated biased controversy, hostility and prejudice. But this is their loss-for his work will always remain a deep reservoir for those of us who come to it for quenching our intellectual thirst in the often arid field of academic interreligious dialogue.

A Stranger is Calling: Jews, Christians, and Muslims as Fellow Travelers is by far his richest and most ambitious text yet. It weaves a very colorful and rich tapestry of multivalent and diverse traditions. Only an erudite and critical scholar like Anton Wessels could have brought such seemingly disparate elements together in such a brilliant and enlightening way. This coherent *tour de force* invites us to reevaluate our perspectives on truth, history, revelation, and even the divine. As always, Anton opens up new vistas for me. This book is both timely and pertinent to anyone interested in a peaceful and just world. It is intellectually stimulating and one of the most hopeful books in our current polarized context.

In the pages of this book, one encounters the issues of the common elements between the scriptures: from the original names of the three communities, to God the stranger and his silence, his hiddenness and his revelation, and their common thread in the *Tanakh* (the Jewish Bible), the New Testament/Gospels (in Arabic the *Injil*), and the *Qur'an*. Anton asks us to examine the parables, the stories and prophets in the Tanakh, and divine visitations, etc. In this context, he also makes reference to popular culture, taking a parabolic and metaphoric look at comic characters such as Donald Duck and Scrooge McDuck, and Dickens' Ebenezer Scrooge. We are encouraged to look seriously at God as a stranger-"stranger" being the major theme pursued from different angles through various lenses throughout the book. He approaches the theme of stranger from an aesthetic perspective, referring to "Rembrandt and the Three Strangers" and "Abraham with the Three Angels" in Marc Chagall, and even to Odysseus, the main protagonist of Homer's epic, who was a stranger in his own home. Anton explores Moses and Abraham who were both themselves Strangers, and the latter's hospitality to the three strangers. This then leads to the issue of language and foreignness. At this point Anton makes one of his bold moves, claiming that The Good News of the Tanakh, the Gospel, *and* the Qur'an has One Language.

He raises another controversial issue, especially in the context of the West, where the separation of church and state has been extended to the separation of religion and politics, and points out the common misreading of the biblical text of Luke 20:20–26, esp. vs 25, which demands "Give to Caesar what is Caesar's and to God what is God's" in the context of "Bring me a denarius." His hermeneutics of this much used and misused text is one with which I completely agree and have in fact written about. I was particularly fascinated by his section dealing with the strange power and religion and the commonality of the promised city, the promised land, and the promised world and humanity's relations to desert and wilderness.

Prof. Wessels not only raises these novel themes and makes you see their radical and critical role but also convinces you of their vital importance for genuine inter-religious work. There is so much more and so broad a vista covered that simply a foreword can never do full justice to the breadth of this book. Thanks Anton.

Charles Amjad-Ali, Ph.D., Th.D.
The Martin Luther King, Jr. Prof. & Director of Islamic Studies (Emeritus), Luther Seminary, USA
The Desmond Tutu Professor (Emeritus), University of Western Cape, South Africa
Author of *Islamophobia and Restorative Justice: Tearing the Veils of Ignorance*

Chicago, IL

Acknowledgments

I am grateful to Henry Jansen for his translation services and to De Stichting Zonneweelde for its financial support of this translation.

Abbreviations

Abbreviations of reference works listed in the bibliography and abbreviated in the footnotes

Bijbelse Encyclopaedie	Grosheide (1950).
B.W.	Reicke & Rost, *Bijbels historisch woordenboek*.
Dictionnaire	*Dictionnaire du Coran* (2007).
E.I.	*The Encyclopaedia of Islam* (1960).
E.Q.	Mc Auliffe (ed.), *Encyclopaedia of the Qur'ân*.
KBS.	Bible (Dutch): Willibrord translation (1995).
RGG	Von Campenhausen & Dinkler, *Die Religion in Geschich te und Gegenwart*.
Th.W.	Kittel (ed.), *Theologisches Wörterbuch zum Neuen Testament*.
Q	Qur'ân

Abbreviations of biblical books
(only the books that are actually abbreviated in the text are listed)

2 Bar	2 Baruch	Eph	Ephesians
1 Chron	1 Chronicles	Est	Esther
2 Chron	2 Chronicles	Ezek	Ezekiel
Col	Colossians	Exod	Exodus
1 Cor	1 Corinthians	Gal	Galatians
2 Cor	2 Corinthians	Gen	Genesis
Dan	Daniel	Hab	Habbakuk
Deut	Deuteronomy	Hebr	Hebrews
Eccles	Ecclesiastes	Hos	Hosea
En	Enoch	Isa	Isaiah

Jer	Jeremiah	2 Pet	2 Peter
Jon	Jonah	Prov	Proverbs
Josh	Joshua	Ps	Psalm
Jud	Jude	Pss	Psalms
Judg	Judges	Rev	Revelation
Lam	Lamentations	Rom	Romans
Lev	Leviticus	1 Sam	Samuel
1 Macc	1 Maccabees	2 Sam	2 Samuel
2 Macc	2 Maccabees	Sir	Wisdom of Jesus Sirach
Mal	Malachi	1 Thess	1 Thessalonians
Mic	Micah	2 Thess	2 Thessalonians
Nah	Nahum	1 Tim	1 Timothy
Neh	Nehemiah	Tob	Tobit
Num	Numbers	Wis	Wisdom of Solomon
Ob	Obadiah	Zech	Zechariah
Phil	Philippians	Zeph	Zephaniah
1 Pet	1 Peter		

Other

KBS	Katholieke Bijbelstichting
KJV	King James Version
NIV	New International Version
NRSV	New Revised Standard Version
RSV	Revised Standard Version

Introduction

Hebron—I like it there. That's where Abraham's tomb is, the father of believers, of Jews, Christians, and Muslims, and he's also the first hero of hospitality, of the right of asylum. I think that the problems that were present at the beginning of humankind will also be present at the end, especially those of the sacred right of asylum and of respect for the stranger.[1]

(LOUIS MASSIGNON)

Banner in Dresden: Goethe: "Das Land, das die Fremden nicht beschützst, geht bald under." (The country that does not shelter strangers will soon come to an end.)

(NRC, 14, 15 FEBRUARY 2015)

"Don't Jump on the 'Jew Bandwagon'"?

To make a case for reading and understanding the Bible together as Jews, Christians, and Muslims seems to be rather controversial. It certainly seems that the current political, secular, and religious climate is increasingly less favorable to such a project.

How difficult has it not been—and still often is—to have people truly read and understand both parts of the Bible together? Jews call the first part of the Bible the Tanakh (from the acronym of the Jewish terms for the Torah [T], the prophets [N], and the writings [K]), but Christians call it

---

1. Massignon, *L' hospitalité Sacrée*, 7.

"Old Testament," which often gives the suggestion of it being old and thus "outdated," "fulfilled," or even "replaced by the New." This is a serious matter because this view of the Jewish Bible has led to anti-Semitism or anti-Jewish readings of the New Testament. As a result, the Old Testament viewed as "law" is contrasted with the New Testament as "Gospel." "Law" is understood as "legalistic," as if it was only a matter of law after law and demand after demand (Isa 28:10).[2] Thus, Jews (and Muslims after them) are viewed as only having the law, whereas Christians have the Gospel, the Good News.

It is true that, since the Second World War, many people in Dutch churches have come to the realization that the New Testament cannot and should not be read without the Old. More attention, and rightly so, is being paid to the Jewish roots of Christianity and the fact that Jesus was a Jew—something that Martin Luther, by the way, emphasized. Although many Christians have been inspired by this approach, it has not by any means become common among church people nor has it remained undisputed. There still appear to be "orthodox" Christians in the Dutch Bible belt who see themselves reflected in a character from the novel *Mensen met een hobby* (People with a Hobby) by Désanne van Brederode (2001). That novel presents a character in his late 20s who feels very deeply connected with Jesus and has a very orthodox view of Jesus: you're either a Christian or you aren't, and if you are, then you don't jump on the current "Jew bandwagon" that teaches you to read the New Testament as an echo of the Torah and prophets. "The Old Testament is simply getting far too much attention nowadays. I think we should protest; we're not a people wandering in the desert, we're Christians. We can't understand the God of Abraham (Ibrâhîm) and Isaac (Ishâq) at all. It's not for nothing that God became man—that's the greatest thing he's done."[3]

If just reading the two parts of the Bible as a single whole is so difficult, why should we want to add the Qur'an to the mix as well? Isn't that book viewed as not very reliable? Hasn't it been asserted in recent years that the sources of the Qur'an themselves are disputed or even claimed that the book should be completely banned because it calls people to commit acts of violence?

---

2. Brueggemann, *Isaiah 1–39*, 223, calls this translation by the NRSV too cognitive. The rules, law, and precepts have more to do with sound than content. He speaks of a mocking "overstatement."

3. Cited (in Dutch) in Goedegebuure, *Nederlandse schrijvers*, 91.

The Sources of the Qur'an Disputed?

In recent decades the work of a few "revisionist" scholars has been subject to discussion. These scholars consider the sources of the Qur'an to be questionable for historical reasons.[4] A series of articles and then a book reported on the "scientific" discussion on the alleged origins of the Qur'an, the "tradition" (*hadîth*), the biography of the prophet Muhammad, and the early history of Islam. Making use of archeology, linguistics, inscriptions on coins and buildings (including texts about Jesus in the Dome of the Rock in Jerusalem) the revisionists demonstrate how a despised "ugly duckling" of Christianity developed into an independent world religion (Islam). The short chapter 97 of the Qur'an is said to be about Christmas night, rather than the revelation of the Qur'an to Muhammad!

All this goes contrary to the "orthodox" account that most Muslims and Western Islamic studies endorse. Professor Sjoerd van Koningsveld made some important points against the revisionists in his valedictory address, *Revisionisme en Moderne islamitische Theologie* (Revisionism and Modern Islamic Theology):

> Purely on scientific grounds, Muhammad was, is, and continues to be viewed as a historical person who, based on his belief in his status as prophet, proclaimed messages that were edited in codices[5] after his death and, around the year 650 of the Christian calendar—thus not two centuries later as the revisionists claim—set down in the official text of Caliph 'Uthmân (the second successor of the prophet Muhammad) that displaced the other editions. The Qur'an, along with the numerous documents written at Muhammad's request, constitutes the basis for the study of his biography, as do the philologically sifted poems by contemporaries, composed both for and against him, in addition to the data in the extensive tradition of literature verified by historical-critical research.[6]

---

4. Cf. Ohlig *and* Puin, *Die dunklen Anfänge*; Grosz *and* Ohlig, *Schlaglichter*; Grosz *and* Ohlig, *Vom Koran zum Islam*; Burgmer, *Streit um den Koran*; Mulder *and* Milo, *De omstreden bronnen*.

5. *mushafs*.

6. Van Koningsveld, *Revisionisme*, 12.

Ban the Qur'an?

The Dutch parliamentarian Geert Wilders caused quite a stir when he compared the Qur'an to Hitler's *Mein Kampf*. He argued that the Qur'an ("this awful book") should be banned, just like *Mein Kampf*.[7] One of his notorious claims—made without offering any evidence whatsoever—was: "If you take out all the rancorous texts from the Qur'an, you'd be left with a book about the size of a Donald Duck comic book." The comparison with Donald Duck shows, by the way, how much Wilders underestimates the significance of these comic books. Donald's uncle, one may recall, is called Scrooge McDuck, with a clear reference to Charles Dickens' notorious miser from his classic *A Christmas Carol*. McDuck ("Mc" = son of) is a reference to Scrooge McDuck's Scottish ancestry—and the Scots, just like the Dutch, are known for their proverbial frugality.[8] Isn't Scrooge McDuck, who is literally depicted as swimming in money, an appropriate way to denounce and ridicule the culture of the widespread chasing after bonuses we see so much of these days?

Jews, Christians, and Muslims: "People of the Way"

Jews, Christians, and Muslims stand in the same tradition of the prophets. They speak a common language, share many of the same stories. In any event, there is a close connection between the adherents of these three religions, which are usually called monotheistic: all three believe in one God, want to follow his way, which is characterized by the Torah, the Ten Commandments given to Moses, Mûsâ. The Jews can be called the people of the Torah. Similarly, the Qur'an speaks of the "people of the Book," i.e. the *Tawra* (Jews), and calls Christians the people of the Gospel (*Injîl*). The "Ten Commandments" are simply indicators in the desert to find the way of life. The image of the desert must be kept in mind: whoever loses his way, doesn't know the way, or can't find the way could die. The heart of the Torah is doing justice and loving one's neighbor. "It is not a question of law *or* love, but law conceived in love, love expressed in law. The two are a unity. To speak of one apart from the other is to produce a parody of the religion of Israel."[9] "The precepts of the Lord are right, giving joy to the heart" (Ps 19:8). "Your word is a lamp to my feet and a light for my path."[10] Just as the sun divides

---

7. *De Volkskrant* carried this story on 8 August 2007.
8. nl.wikipedia.org/wiki/Dagobert_Duck.
9. Levenson, *Sinai and Zion*, 77.
10. All quotes from the Bible are taken from the NIV, unless otherwise stated.

between the day and the night, between light and darkness, so the Torah guides and enlightens us.[11]

The Torah is how God "instructs sinners in his ways" (Ps 25:8, 9). Paul uses the image of walking (Rom 6:4; 8:1, 4, etc., KJV).[12] This Torah is not cast off by Jesus but instead fulfilled. He himself is the Torah become flesh (cf. John 1:14), the Torah itself in the flesh. Here we can see what the Torah is all about, and we can understand why Jesus' followers were called "people of the way."

Years ago I spoke with a Jewish woman, now living in the United States, who was from the same place in Holland where I was born. She became a "Christian" during the Second World War. When I met her while she was visiting the Netherlands, I asked her why she had done so. Her answer was: "Jesus gave me a better deal." When I asked her what she meant by that, she replied: "He talks about only two commandments instead of the 613." The 613 *mitswot* are a list of commandments God gave the Jews in the Torah. When he was asked what the greatest commandment was, Jesus answered: "'Love the Lord your God with all your heart and with all your soul and with all your mind.' This is the first and greatest commandment. And the second is like it: 'Love your neighbor as yourself.' All the Law and the Prophets hang on these two commandments." (Matt 22:37–40). What is striking about her answer is how properly "Jewish" I found it, for the summary of the Torah that the Jew Jesus provided is completely Jewish and borrowed from the Torah itself (Deut 6:5; Lev 19:18). In the discussion with the Pharisees it is not the "Christian" Jesus over against the "Jews"—Jesus ('Îsâ) himself was a Jew. Nor was it a question of being for or against the Torah; rather, what was at stake here was the content and meaning of the Torah.

In this connection, it is striking that the word "Christian" is only used three times in the New Testament, primarily by others. The first time followers of Jesus were called "Christians" was in the city of Antioch in Syria, now in Turkey, on the river Orontes. At that time, Antioch was the third city in "the world," after Rome and Alexandria. Thus, the term "Christian" was originally not used by Christians themselves but by others (Acts 11:26; cf. 26:28). Peter wrote in his letter: "[I]f you suffer as a Christian, do not be

11. *Katholic Bijbelstichting* (KBS) on Ps 19:1–14: Just as the sun gives light to the whole world, so the law gives light to all men (cf. Ps 19:8, 119:105; Wis 13:1–9). Cf. Brueggemann and Bellinger, *Psalms*, 102: "This divine revelation covers both day and night. . . . The heavens proclaim God, but there is no sound. This 'unheard sound' persists through all of creation and is open for all." "The *Torah* has a universal dimension reaching to all creation, as does the sun. The *Torah* renews or restores life. . . . God's upright precepts bring joy, and God's commandments bring light." See also Hossfeld and Zenger, *Die Psalmem*, 129.

12. Zuurmond, *God noch gebod*, 66, 82.

ashamed, but praise God that you bear that name" (i.e. "Christian") (1 Pet 4:16). The term was probably first used as a term of abuse and became a name they proudly called themselves.[13] This can probably be compared to the term *geuzen* in Dutch. The origin of this term is a saying by Margaret of Parma, Governor of the Netherlands under Philip II of Spain: "Ce sont que des gueux" (They're just beggars). She wanted to make clear that she could ignore the league of nobles who presented her with a petition. The opponents of the Spanish domination of the Netherlands took over that term of abuse in a positive sense and it became a *geuzennaam* (a badge of pride).

Another term for the "followers of Jesus" in the New Testament is Nazarene. After their stay in Egypt, where they had fled from King Herod, the murderer of innocents, Mary and Joseph returned to Nazareth with Jesus and settled down there. The New Testament adds: "So was fulfilled what was said through the prophets, that he would be called a Nazarene" (Matt 2:22-23; cf. John 18:5). Jesus is often called that in the book of Acts (Acts 2:22; 3:6; 4:10; 6:14; 22:8; 26:9). Nazareth had a poor reputation, certainly for the Jews faithful to the law in the leading circles in Jerusalem: "Galilee of the Gentiles" (Matt 4:15) was viewed as a socially and religiously underdeveloped backwater. At the end of the first century the term 'Nazarene" had become a common designation for these members of that "sect."[14]

The usual term in the New Testament for Jesus' disciples, however, was "people of the Way," which pointed to the way of life of Jesus' followers.[15] After Paul the Apostle was arrested in Jerusalem, the local Roman chiliarch, Claudius Lysias, had him transferred to Caesarea where he was tried by Felix, the procurator of Palestine. Felix and his wife Drusilla often sent for him to talk to him (Acts 24:24-26). When Felix was succeeded as procurator, he left Paul imprisoned as a favor to the Jews. Paul stated clearly to Felix: "I admit that I worship the God of our ancestors as a follower of the Way, which they call a sect. I believe everything that is in accordance with the Law and that is written in the Prophets" (Acts 24:14). That is, he acted entirely in line with what was appropriate for him as a Jew, as a follower of the Way (Acts 24:22). For him, being a follower of Jesus meant being a follower of the Way. Jesus demanded discipleship (Matt. 8:19-22), and his words clearly indicated how seriously he intended this discipleship: "Whoever does not take up their cross and follow me is not worthy of me" (Matt 10:38). "The way" is specified as the way of Jesus, the way of the cross, the way of suffering, the *via crucis*. It means: not being content with a way of life that does not

---

13. *B.W.*, s.v. "Christenen."
14. Nieuwenhuis, *Johannes de ziener*, 348-49.
15. *Hodos*; cf. *KBS* on Acts 9:2; 19:9, 23; 22:4; 24:14, 22.

entail doing justice and showing love, a way of life that is at cross purposes with the false ways of self-confidence.[16] Other names are: "the way of the Lord" (Acts 18:25; cf. 13:10), "the way of God" (Acts 18:26), "the way to be saved" (Acts 16:17; cf. 1 Cor 4:17; 2 Pet 2:2, 21). The "Way," without any further specification, becomes the characteristic term for the followers of Jesus (Acts 9:9, 23; 24:14, 22).

It is striking, by the way, that the followers of Jesus in the Qur'an are called *nasârâ* (pl. *nasrâni*).[17] This term only appears in passages from the time of Muhammad's activities in Medina and, apart from one exception (Q 3:67), only in the plural. The expression is or was derived from Jesus's birthplace, al-Nâsira, or from the *ansâr*, helpers, the name for Jesus' disciples (cf. Q 3:45). Muhammad's supporters in Medina, where he moved after the *hijra*, the emigration, were also called "helpers."[18] Jewish Christians who confessed Jesus as the Messiah, Masîh, but remained Jews were called Nazarenes.[19]

In fact, the same image was used with respect to "Muslims." They also follow the way. The idea or notion of the way[20] of God can be found throughout the Qur'an and is connected with fundamental ideas such as right guidance.[21] The opening prayer of the Qur'an, which has the same function for Muslims that the Lord's Prayer has for Christians, prays for guidance on the straight path (Q 1:6; cf. 28:56, 42:52–53). "This is the path of [Muhammad's] Lord" (Q 6:126; cf. 14:12, 16:15). Those who dedicate themselves to doing God's will be led by him on his way (Q 29:69): the way of righteousness (Q 40:29; 40:38),[22] the straight path of the Lord (Q 6:126, 153). The way of God is equated with the sunna and the law (Q 5:48).[23]

The way of God is contrasted with the way of the idols (Q 4:76),[24] the way of the ignorant (Q 10:89) and the wicked (Q 6:55). The way of error stands over against the way of righteousness (Q 7:146).[25] Whoever exchanges belief for unbelief has strayed from the straight path (Q 2:108; 5:12).

16. Brueggemann, *Genesis*, 122.
17. Q 2:111, 113, 120, 135, 140; cf. 3:67; 5:14, 51, 69, 82; 9:30; 22:17.
18. Jeffery, *The Foreign Vocabulary,* 280–81: "The most probable origin, however, is the Syric which represents the Nazoraens (of Acts XXIV, 5 and was a commonly used designation of Christians who lived under Persian suzerainty."
19. *E.I.*, s.v. "Nasârâ."
20. *sirât, tarîq, minhâdj.*
21. *hûda, hidâya.*
22. *sabîl al rushd of rashâd.*
23. Cf. *shirî'a.*
24. *taghût.*
25. *E.Q.*, s.v. "Path or Way."

Believers are charged with calling others to the way of their Lord through wisdom and proper exhortation, and to exchange ideas with each other in the best way. For God knows best who is straying from his path and who is being rightly guided (Q 16:125).

The word that is used in Arabic for "way" is *sharî'a*. This presents a similar problem to that connected with the translation of Torah. Just as Christians often view "Torah" in a legalistic way, so *sharî'a* is often similarly misunderstood. That is why *sharî'a* is often negatively understood by Christians and also by Muslims, by the way, as "law" in the legalistic sense in a way comparable to the Torah. But *sharî'a* must be understood as an equivalent of the word "Torah" in which the "way" one must follow is indicated (cf. Q 5:48).

When I was working in Cairo, I lived close to Tahrir Square, on a street called Sharî'a Abû Allam. This did not, of course, mean Abû Allam Law but Abû Allam Street or Road. The street led to Tahrir Square, which means "Liberation Square": like the Torah, the *sharî'a* is intended to be the way to liberation. Originally, *sharî'a* meant "the way to the well," the water necessary for living and surviving in the desert.

In summary, one could say that "Jews," "Christians," and "Muslims" are all, on the basis of and according to their Scriptures, people of the way. And, just as Jesus fulfilled the Torah, so the Qur'an confirms both the Torah that was given to Moses and the Gospel, the *Injîl*, given to Jesus (Q 3:50; 5:46; 61:6).

The Three Communities of the Way Go Their Separate Ways

It is, of course, very clear that three separate communities—leaving aside their various internal divisions—have come into existence: the Jewish, the Christian, and the Islamic. But it is good to understand that the separation or, as it is usually called, "the schism between the Jews and the Christians," did not happen all at once at a certain point in time. Neither Jesus nor the apostle Paul founded a Christian church in the form we know today. It was not the intention for Jesus' followers to set themselves up as a separate church or *ecclesia*, separate from and over against the Jewish "congregation" (*qahal*), the later synagogue. There were groups of Jewish followers of Jesus who continued to participate in and be part of the Jewish congregations. The "congregations" mentioned in the New Testament were still largely Jewish-Christian, while the "Gentile Christian" part of the congregation began to develop under the influence in particular of the Apostle Paul but were still part and parcel of the one community.

The later painful separation did occur, but it had not yet happened in a complete and definitive way at the end of the first century, as is often thought. In places in what we call the Middle East, it sometimes took centuries for it to happen. That was true to a certain extent even in the time of the Prophet Muhammad in Arabia! A considerable number of the first people the prophet addressed were "Jews" and "Christians," and some of the "Christians" would also have been Jews who followed Jesus.

Muhammad and the Christians of Najrân

There were certainly Christian communities in the Arab Peninsula. They were known in the north primarily as Syrian Orthodox and in the south as Nestorians. They were the ones Muhammad knew and dealt with. The prophet Muhammad cannot be called the founder of the Islamic community in the sociological sense of the word any more than Jesus can be called the "founder" of the church.

The extent to which the situation was still open is apparent from the fact that in the tenth month of the year 630 a Christian delegation from Najrân, in the south of the Arab Peninsula, came to visit Muhammad in the city of Medina. Muhammad permitted his guests to pray in his mosque (literally: "the place where one bows before God"). He then made a covenant with the Christians that guaranteed their freedom to practice their own religion, although the Christians did have to pay a yearly tax. This was the first treaty of this kind, a prototype for later.

Najrân was a caravan city in the southern part of Arabia, where the famous Silk Road split into two, one branch going to Mesopotamia and the other via Yemen to Syria. The flourishing city had connections to Judaism as well as to Christianity and Islam, which changed the course of their lives and history. Christianity had reached Najrân in the fifth century, and the most powerful Christian (probably Nestorian) center in the Arab Peninsula was established, with its own basilica. Around 520, Dhû Nuwâs, a king in southern Arabia who had converted to Judaism, attempted to force the Christians to abandon their faith for Judaism as well. When they refused, he had about 400 Christians killed and thrown into a burning pit. The phrase people "of the Pit" that the Qur'an mentions (Q 85:4–7) is said to refer to those Christian martyrs.[26]

The Ethiopian Christians came to Najrân's aid, which led to a golden period lasting about a hundred years for "the city of martyrs," the holy city for Arabs. The church was called the Ka'ba Najrân, just like various other

---

26. But this is also disputed; cf. Paret, *Der Koran: Übersetzung*, on Q 85:4–7.

shrines in Arabia were called *ka'ba*, such as, of course, the Ka'ba in Mecca, the cube-shaped "house of God" Abraham built with his son Ishmael (Ismâ'îl) (Q 2:125, 127). The Ka'ba Najrân became a pilgrimage center for Christian Arabs.

The bishops of Najrân came to the large markets in and around 'Ukâz. The market in 'Ukâz was located strategically on the "spice route" of Western Arabia and flourished particularly in the sixth century. This was just before the rise of Islam. At that time, the Byzantine-Persian wars were raging, which led to shifts in the Mesopotamian trade route. This had a favorable effect on trade in Mecca and Muhammad's tribe, the Quraysh, profited well. Literary competitions were also held in 'Ukâz.[27]

It was entirely possible that, before his call to be a prophet, Muhammad heard Quss, the bishop of Najrân, preach at the market while sitting on a camel as his pulpit. The Qur'an alludes to Najrân as one of the blessed or clearly visible cities (Q 34:28),[28] whereas the tradition views it as one of the "protected" cities. Najrân was a center for tailoring businesses, and the *kiswa* or cover for the Ka'ba in Mecca was originally made there every year.[29]

The Qur'an and the One "Community"

It is indeed true that the Qur'an clearly views Jews and Christians as having gone their own separate ways and that differences of opinions arose, especially among Christians. The Qur'an speaks of one community[30] of humankind, of which God is Lord (Q 23:52)—thus not only of the *umma* of the Muslims but also of the "community" or *umma* of all other prophets. There is a messenger for every community (Q 10:47). God sends a messenger to every people (Q 16:36; cf. 4:41; 16:89; 28:75; 39:69). The community of prophetic messengers is seen as one community: "Surely this community of yours [Jesus] is one community" (Q 21:92). But it was the various schools of thought among the Jews and the primarily Jewish followers of Jesus that caused divisions among them (Q 21:93).[31]

"Abraham' himself is called a "community" in the Qur'an. He, Ishmael, Isaac, and Jacob (*Ya'qûb*) are called one community, and Abraham has consequently become the prototype of the true community of people who obeyed

---

27. *E.I.*, s.v. 'Ukâz'.
28. Cf. Paret, *Der Koran: Übersetzung*, for other interpretations.
29. *E.Q.*, s.v. 'Najrân' and Glassé, *The Concise Encyclopaedia*, s.v. 'Najrân'.
30. *umma*.
31. It could be that the followers of Jesus had split up into various sects. Cf. Paret, *Der Koran*, on Q 21:93.

God (Q 16:120).[32] The word *muslim* is used for the word "obey," but it should be noted that this word in the Qur'an did not yet have its current sociological meaning. According to the Qur'an (Q 2:140; 3:67) Abraham was not a Jew and not a Christian but a "Muslim." That is not to say that Abraham can be claimed by the "Muslims" but precisely that Abraham is the father of all believers and, for "Jews," "Christians," and "Muslims" alike, is the true person who was obedient to God, a "muslim" in the original sense of the word that it still has in the Qur'an. People were originally one single community or *umma*. After they fell out, God sent the prophets as proclaimers of the good news and as warners. And He sent the Scripture with the truth with them so that it would help people decide on matters they disagreed about (Q 2:213; cf. 10:19). Eventually, however, those who dedicate themselves, submit themselves to God will form one community that will call others to what is good, what is right, and forbid what is reprehensible (Q 3:104; cf. Q 3 110, 114; 9:71, 112; 22:41; 7:157; 31:17). If the message of the Qur'an points then in a certain context to different communities—the people of the Torah (Jews), the people of the Gospel (the Christians), and the those who have been called by the message given to Muhammad (the Muslims)—it reads: "If God had willed, He would have made you one community [*umma*]" (Q 5:48). One is sometimes inclined to think: that would have been handier, given all the terrible things that have occurred and still occur between the three individual communities. But the answer of the Qur'an is that God's intention here was to test all three communities (Q 5:48). Apparently, God does not want to use compulsion: there is no compulsion in religion (Q 2:256; Q 10:99, 100),[33] Rather, God allows people to make their own choices. But if it is a matter of the relations that need to exist between the three communities, the advice is: "Compete in good works, and you shall all return to God together" (Q 5:48).

Presupposing that Jews, Christians, and Muslims do take their own Scriptures seriously, the question remains: How do each of them deal with the other two groups? There are Jews who view the New Testament as not relevant for them or superfluous or look at it in a negative way. There is, as already indicated, a long Christian tradition of anti-Semitism whereby the Old Testament is viewed as superseded and replaced. There is also an Islamic reading of the Qur'an whereby it is viewed as the final, definitive revelation and has come to replace both the Torah and the Gospel (the Old and New Testaments).

Such a way of reading and understanding has taken shape under the influence of, respectively, Rabbinic Judaism, church councils, and the

---

32. Paret, *Der Koran*, on Q 16:120; see also the chapter below "The Strange Powers and Religion."

33. For the opposite stance, cf. Q 9:67.

generally accepted Islamic interpretations. All three, Judaism, Christianity, and Islam, have been organized as individual and separate communities: "I am taking an ecclesial agenda because for too long, so it seems to me, christological certitude in the church has much of the time been permitted to silence, trump, and give closure to the Old Testament. I have wanted to suggest that faithful Christian exposition could do otherwise."[34] Edward Schillebeecks once commented to the effect that Christians have often praised Jesus "to the skies" in order to be rid of him as prophet. Everyone has tried to be able to justify themselves exegetically and theologically in all kinds of ways. They built their own walls and fortresses and formulated dogmas with—sometimes especially among Christians and Muslims—their own "replacement theology" or "ideology." There are examples of times and places where there was a peaceful and fruitful symbiosis (Jews, Christians, and Muslims living together in Andalusia, the Balkans, North Africa, and last but not but least in the Middle East, as in Baghdad). But there is an abundance of historical examples, especially with respect to Christians and Muslims, of polemics or, even worse, crusades and holy wars.

Why Should We Read the Three Books Together?

Rather than continue to explore or rehash any further the countless discussions and polemics about the Bible and the Qur'an that have been and are still being conducted,[35] I want to show how exciting and important it is for Jews, Christians, and Muslims to learn to read and understand these three books together from the perspective of their great mutual connection with each other.

The title I chose for an earlier book was *The Torah, the Gospel and the Qur'an* (2103). The subtitle concisely articulated its intention and purport: *Three Books, Two Cities, One Tale*. This does not, of course, suggest that there is only one story but that the prophetic stories of Abraham, Moses, Jesus, and Muhammad revolve around one single message, one narrative, directed at all three—at all people.

Individually, the three books stand in a wide tradition with three different approaches. It is high time we search together into common lectionaries and approaches so we can travel the one road to justice and love in this world.

---

34. Brueggemann, *The Word Militant*, 73.
35. Cf. my *De moslimse naaste*.

I

God as a Stranger

God does not die on the day when we cease to believe in a personal deity, but we die on the day when our lives cease to be illumined by the steady radiance, renewed daily, of a wonder the source of which is beyond all reason.[1]

(DAG HAMMARSKJÖLD)

A Stranger Comes Calling

Someone's Coming, Children
Someone's coming, children,
Someone's knocking, children,
Someone's tapping at the window frame.
It's a stranger, I guess,
Who is wandering, I guess,
I shall check and ask him for his name.

Saint Nicholas, Saint Nicholas,
Will you please make a stop at our door,[2]
And throw in some candy,
All around the floor.

(Fragment from a well-known Sinterklaas song)[3]

---

1. Hammarskjöld, *Markings*, https://www.goodreads.com/author/quotes/946904.Dag_Hammarskj_ld.
2. I.e., pay us a visit.
3. "'t Is een vreemd'ling zeker...."

THE SONG QUOTED ABOVE is one of the many songs sung to and by children during the Sinterklaas feast celebrated annually in the Netherlands. The "stranger," of course, is St. Nicholas himself come to give presents and candy to good children and carrots to bad ones. Despite the associations that Sinterklaas or Santa Claus might have for children, the word "stranger," even for adults, awakens feelings of fear or even hate. Those feelings discourage people from attempting to discover who the stranger is. I can still remember an article in a local paper in the 1970s about garbage collectors who did not want to take the trouble to remember the name of their Moroccan coworker. They found names like Ahmad or Mahmoud too complicated to remember, not to mention pronounce: "We'll just call you 'Jack.'"

In the Sinterklaas song the singer expressly asks who the stranger is, and the answer that is immediately given is: "Saint Nicholas! Saint Nicholas!" followed by the explicit request that Saint Nicholas pay them a visit: "Will you please make a stop at our door."

This is not the place nor is it my intention to explore the history of this song or its origin, although that would certainly be interesting. I suspect that, somewhere behind that question about the stranger, we can find the Eternal One—the Stranger with a capital S—whom so many cultures and traditions speak about.[4]

This chapter deals with the question of who the Eternal One is, who that "God" is. Do Jews, Christians, and Muslims believe in the same God? Wouldn't we be better off not saying anything at all about God? Didn't God himself keep mum about himself? Isn't he a God who conceals more than he reveals about who he is? What is the nature and being of that "Stranger" who, again and again, has stopped in to visit human beings and the world?

Do Jews, Christians, and Muslims Believe in the Same God?

Whether Jews, Christians, and Muslims believe in the same God is a question I have never heard Muslims ask. It is usually, in my experience at least, Christians who claim that Muslims believe in a different God: Muslims believe in "Allah" while Christians believe in God, the "Father of our Lord Jesus Christ." Many Christians, by the way, used to think there was a major difference between the God of the Old Testament and the God of the New— but is that really only something in the past? The first part of the Muslim

---

Translated into English by Ruben 't Lam, Dutch Saint Nicholas songs translated into English; http://www.stnicholascenter.org/pages/hoor-wie-stapt-daar-kinderen/.

4. See Wessels, *The Torah*, 119–22.

confession of faith declares: "There is no god but God (*lâ illâha illa 'Allâh*)." The Qur'an leaves no doubt that the message Muhammad brings is inspired by and descended from the same God who revealed himself to Moses and Jesus.

In a television program some years ago,[5] Tiny Muskens, the Roman Catholic bishop of Breda, suggested using "Allah" as a general name for God. He explained that the name "Allah" is an Aramaic word that means "Lord." In Arabic-speaking countries, this is the name that is used the most by Muslims, Jews, and Christians for God. The Aramaic origin of the word means that it existed before the Qur'an was written. Eastern Christians were familiar with this name for God prior to the advent of Islam. Bishop Muskens talked about this on the basis of his personal experiences during the eight years he lived and worked in Indonesia, the largest Islamic country in the world, where Catholics also use the word "Allah" to address God in their liturgy. "If Muslims and Christians can use the same name to address God, this contributes to both religions living together in harmony."[6]

Linguistically, the name Allah is explained as a contraction of *al-ilâh* ("the God"). It is not a proper name but a term for the nameless God beside whom there is no other. Allah is the one and only God. Muhammad proclaimed the Qur'an in the name of "Allah." Well before the time of Muhammad, the Arabs and Muhammad's fellow townspeople, the Meccans, worshipped a great deity and supreme being they called "Allah": "Say: 'Who is the Lord of heaven and earth?' Say: 'God'" (Q 13:16; cf. 29:61; 31:25; 39:38). They called on him in times of need: "And when the waves cover them like shadows they call upon God" (Q 31:32).[7]

The most striking and definitive proof that this name of God was pre-Islamic is the name of Muhammad's father himself, who died before Muhammad was born. His name was 'Abdallâh, which means "servant (*'abd*) of Allah." Hebrew, a sister language of Arabic, also contains the phrase "servant (*'ebed*) of the LORD (YHWH). Both terms derive from their respective words for the verb "to serve."

Incidentally, Bishop Muskens also stated later that, although he still felt the same way about the common use of the one name for God, Allah, he had become aware that now was not the right time for this: "If people constantly hear extremists with big guns crying Allâh u akbar ('God is greater'

---

5. Netwerk, Monday, 13 August 2007.
6. Bisdomvanbreda.nl/nieuwsbericht.php?entry=archive*and*id=263. See interview.
7. *E.Q.*, s.v. "God and His Attributes," 316-17.

or 'God is the greatest'), then the time has not yet arrived for a worldwide acceptance of Allah."[8]

In fact, the opposite has even been argued recently. Namely, Muslim organizations, such as the Malaysian government, are forbidding Christians from using the name "Allah" for God. This caused a great deal of unrest among Christians because God is called "Allah" in the Malaysian Bible. The Minister of Islamic Affairs informed the public that the Cabinet felt that the word "Allah" referred to the god of Islam and could only be used by Muslims. "The use of the word Allah by non-Muslims could be a sensitive issue and lead to confusion among Muslims in the country."[9]

The Silence of God?

Blaise Pascal,[10] the famous French mathematician, physicist, and Christian philosopher and theologian, was deeply struck by the silence of the universe: "The eternal silence of these infinite spaces fills me with dread."[11] But he was also deeply struck by the voice of God that broke through that silence.

Hans Alex Keilson (1909–2011), a German-Dutch writer, physician, and psychiatrist whose parents were killed in Auschwitz, makes some very striking comments about "literature and keeping silent." His words are particularly relevant when contemplating the silence of God. He cites the Dutch poet Jan Hendrik Leopold (1865–1925), who felt that he could not praise P.C. Boutens more than by saying that his poems were "almost silence." This "almost silence" contains something of the *unio mystica*, contact with a deity so intense that it is experienced as a merging or identification with the deity. "Contemplation, meditation, and ascesis are only practices along that road. The redemptive experience of a true unity of the 'self' with the goal striven for, they are all embedded in the silence, in the deepest hush that seems to be inherent to the essence of existence."[12]

One needs to be silent first, however, before one can speak about God.

Prophets speak of the command to be silent: "Be still before the LORD, all mankind, because he has roused himself from his holy dwelling" (Zech

---

8. *Friesch Dagblad*, 14 August 2007. This article refers to the daily newspaper *BN De Stem* of November 2004.

9. The article can be found on the website of the *Reformatorisch Dagblad*, Saturday, 5 January 2008/09.57.

10. Born in Clermont-Ferrand on 19 June 1623 and died in Paris on 19 August 1662.

11. Pascal, *Pensées* (no. 201): "Le silence éternel de ces espaces infinis m'effraie."

12. Keilson, *Liever Holland*, 178.

2:13). "Be silent before the Sovereign Lord, for the day of the Lord is near" (Zeph 1:7). "But the Lord is in his holy temple; let all the earth be silent before him" (Hab 2:20). The command to be silent in these texts is inseparable from the appearance of God, from any theophany.[13]

When John the seer saw that the last, seventh seal of the scroll had been broken, the whole of creation held its breath, and there was silence in heaven for about half an hour (Rev 8:1).[14] John saw the scroll in the right hand of him who is seated on the throne. The scroll had writing on both sides and was sealed with seven seals (Rev 5:1). The contents of the sealed scroll were secret.[15]

That there were seven seals to be seen on the strings with which the writing was bound shows a parallel with a well-known Roman custom, where writings were also sealed with seven seals. In this case, it is the charter of the one seated on the throne, the sealed testament of God, his last will for "the inheritance of the holy ones in the light" (Col 1:12; Hebr 9:15; 1 Pet 1:4), that contains the fulfilment of all promises of salvation.[16]

The Jews believed that, at the end of time, the world would return to the chaos of the beginning and to the silence that existed prior to the first day of creation (4 Ezra 7:30). At the end of time, there will be silence in heaven, just as there was prior to God's first creative word.[17] Before creation, the earth was formless and empty (*tohu wa bohu*); darkness was over the face of the deep, and the Spirit of God hovered over the waters (Gen 1:2): it was a formless and meaningless chaos.[18]

God's appearance is always preceded by silence and breathlessness: "Let all the earth be silent before him" (Hab 2:20). "Be silent before the Sovereign Lord, for the day of the Lord is near" (Zeph 1:7).

> Silence can best be represented by "Silence" or "Sssh!" "Silence" is a cry expressed during the liturgy in the temple. . . . Around the Eternal One and before him there is 'always' speechlessness

---

13. Sweeney, *The Twelve Prophets*, 591–92.

14. Zechariah 2:13: "Be still before the Lord, all mankind."

15. Daniel had to keep things secret and the book sealed until the end of time (Dan 12:4). "For you this whole vision is nothing but words sealed in a scroll. And if you give the scroll to someone who can read, and say, 'Read this, please,' they will answer, 'I can't; it is sealed'" (Isa 29:11).

16. Behm, 34.

17. When God decides to create something, he says: "Be!" and it is (Q 2:117; 3:47; 6:73; 16:40; 36:82; 40:68). The likeness of "Îsâ" (Jesus) to God is the same as the likeness of Adam whom God created from the dust of the earth, saying to him, "Be," and he was (Q 3:59; cf. 19:35).

18. See the notes in the NIV Study Bible.

> because he is a calling silence and an eternal silence.... The one seated on the throne is silent. And when it really comes down to it, the whole of creation, the heaven of the Heavens, is tongue-tied, each word sticking in its throat, and there is only silence.[19]

It is from God's silence that, according to Ignatius, the Logos, the word, God's speech arises.[20]

Moses Was Not a Public Speaker?!

It is telling that God's great spokesman, Moses, claims that he is not a good speaker.[21] When God told him he was sending him to Pharaoh in Egypt, Moses replied: "O Lord, I have never been eloquent, neither in the past nor since you have spoken to your servant. I am slow of speech and tongue" (Exod 4:10). Did Moses have difficulty expressing himself? Did he stutter? This shows not only that he hesitated about the huge task God had given him—to free the people of Israel from Egypt—but also that he had respect and awe for the One speaking to him.

> The LORD said to him, "Who gave man his mouth? Who makes him deaf or mute? Who gives him sight or makes him blind? Is it not I, the LORD? Now go; I will help you speak and will teach you what to say." But Moses said, "O Lord, please send someone else to do it." Then the LORD's anger burned against Moses and he said, "What about your brother, Aaron the Levite? I know he can speak well. He is already on his way to meet you, and his heart will be glad when he sees you. You shall speak to him and put words in his mouth; I will help both of you speak and will teach you what to do. He will speak to the people for you, and it will be as if he were your mouth and as if you were God to him."

The Qur'an also alludes to the speech impediment that Moses had: Pharaoh looked down on him and despised him because he could not speak clearly (Q 43:52).

But the fascinating point is that it is Moses, who does not feel qualified to speak, who is given the words from God, while it is his spokesman

---

19. According to Nieuwenhuis in his explanation of the book of Revelation, *Johannes de ziener,* 761–62.

20. IngMg VIII, 2, cited in: *B.W.* s.v. "Zwijgen"

21. Like Moses, the prophet Jeremiah, when he is called to be a prophet, claims that he is much too young. God then touches his mouth and says to him: "I have put my words in your mouth" (Jer 1:6–7, 9; cf. Isa 6:6–7; Ezek 3:1–3; 2 Sam 23:2; Isa 59:21).

Aaron who is linked to the sin of the "golden calf" (Exod 32; Q 7:150–51; 20:92–94).

This is poignantly expressed in Arnold Schönberg's opera *Moses und Aron*, culminating in the final cry: "O Word, thou Word which I lack (or 'which is failing me')." George Steiner makes the following penetrating observation: "Precisely because the golden-tongued Aron can discourse so eloquently on God and on man's fate, that same Aron allows the representational and symbolic lie of the Golden Calf and the loud riot of Israel's falsehood. To Moses the stutterer, no words are available with which to articulate the essential, the election to suffering that is history, and the real presence of God as it was signified to him in the tautology ["I AM WHO I AM"] out of the Burning Bush. The fire there is the only true speech. Human saying lies."[22]

God is a Hidden God

"A religion that does not claim that God is hidden is false," states Blaise Pascal.[23] Martin Luther spoke of the *deus absconditus*, the hidden God.[24] In contrast to this *deus absconditus* is the God who reveals himself. How are the two connected? That is a question the Jewish, Christian, and Islamic traditions all ask. The answer to the question of what God is hiding and revealing of himself means must be sought in the Scriptures themselves, particularly in a passage in the prophet Isaiah: "Truly you are a God who hides himself, O God and Savior of Israel" (Isa 45:15). As with every text, this one must be viewed in its context. In this case, the text concerns Cyrus the Great, king of Persia, founder of the Achaemenid Empire (559–529 B.C.). He had conquered large parts of the then-known world and allowed the Jewish exiles to return to Jerusalem in 538 B.C. and rebuild the temple. He is later praised by Isaiah as God's shepherd, as the one who fulfils God's will (Isa 44:28), his anointed one, a Messiah (Isa 45:1) and righteous one (Isa 41:2), the one whom God called from the east and whom God loves (Isa 48:14–15).[25]

This confession of God's hiddenness is completely bound up with the outcome of Cyrus' conquests. Israel and the nations simply cannot comprehend how God saves Israel from exile. Why does God raise up Cyrus, make his ways straight and have him rebuild the city of Jerusalem and return the

22. Steiner, *Real Presences*, 112.
23. Cf. Brueggemann, *Isaiah 40–66*, 82.
24. He elaborated on his ideas in his *De servo arbitrio* (1525).
25. *B.W.*, s.v. "Cyrus."

Jewish exiles (Isa 45:13)? When the nations belong to him, pass by him in chains, and bow before him, they will confess: "Surely God is with you, and there is no other; there is no other god" (Isa 45:14–15). "The amazement of the people about this kind of development of power by the prophet is only unfolded in the words: 'You are a God who remains hidden.'"[26]

Just like during Muhammad's time in Mecca, it is about "God" and the "idols." This is why it important to look at a passage in which Isaiah mocks the worship of images, saying how foolish it is to worship the idols of wood. Someone fells a couple of cedars, or chooses a pine or oak that he has allowed to grow in the forest with other tress, or a laurel he has planted and which grew because of the rain. He uses the trees for firewood, to keep warm or bake bread.

He could also carve the wood into an idol and bow down to it. With one half he feeds a fire on which he cooks meat, roasting it and then eating it. He warms himself by the fire and says: "This is nice and warm! I can see the fire!" He uses the rest of the tree to make a god, to which he kneels in prayer: "Save me, you are my god." The idolater does not realize the truth because he or she lacks the knowledge and insight to understand that with one half of the wood, they feed the fire on the glowing charcoal and bake bread and meat to eat and then make detestable images with what is left over, bowing before pieces of wood! What they are worshipping are ashes! Confused thinking has put them on the wrong path. They can no longer be saved because they do not ask: "Is not this thing in my right hand a lie?" (cf. Isa 44:6–20).

Isaiah exposes the folly of idolatry in a sharp satire. Those makers of idols are fools. They use neither their senses nor their heads. They are stupid and ignorant and have no sense of the absurdity of their actions. This foolish enterprise comes from a misled heart. Just as the Lord "made" Israel, so the idols made Babylon. These gods have no inherent power but were tailor-made, were manufactured. The "poet" pokes fun at the dragon about the way in which those images are made. A carpenter, the true creator of the gods, is a foolish figure, even a clownish one since he enjoys the fire while at the same time calling upon his creation to save him. How can a carpenter be so stupid as to expect both warmth and salvation from wood?[27]

God's Hiddenness and Revelation in the Qur'an

The Qur'an actually begins with the second and longest chapter, which is also called the "the small Qur'an." The first, opening chapter, *sûrat al-fâtiha*,

---

26. Beuken, *Jesaja deel II A*, 248.
27. Brueggemann, *Isaiah 40–66*, 82. Beuken, *Jesaja deel II A*, 208–17.

is a prayer. Thus, the Qur'an begins with the words: "That is the Book that is not to be doubted, right guidance for the god-fearing and those who believe in the Hidden One" (Q 2:1–3).[28] Nevertheless, the Hidden One (*ghayb*) is the object of the belief, just like the *word* that was revealed to the prophet (Q 2:4). That is why humans must hold on to the unknowable mystery.[29]

The word "hidden," which can also be translated as "unseen"[30] or "unknown,"[31] refers to both the absolute mystery and to what is inaccessible, the hidden things.[32] The word "hidden" is also a vehicle for the idea that there is an invisible world, entirely removed from the knowledge of humans, to which the future belongs, which no creature is able to penetrate and to which only God has the keys.

There are five situations that only God knows: "No one knows what will happen tomorrow, no one knows beforehand what is in the womb, no one knows what he is going to do tomorrow, no one knows where he will die, and finally, no one knows when the rain will come" (Q 31:34).[33]

What does it mean that humans are excluded "forever" from the secrets of the Hidden things? God in his mercy has the power to give certain fragments of these Hidden things to whomever he wishes. God is the one who knows what is Hidden. He does not disclose it to anyone, except to his messenger with whom he is well-pleased and whom he feels worthy to be initiated in that which is hidden (Q 72:26–27).[34] It is not possible for God to give ordinary believers insight into the Hidden things. He chooses the messenger he wants. This is why people are summoned to believe in God and his messengers (Q 3:179).

God is the only one who encompasses both worlds, the seen and the unseen; humans only have knowledge of the seen. God is the knower

---

28. "Das Übersinnliche; das Verborgene," translation by Paret, *Der Koran: Übersetzung*, "The Unseen" (Tarif Khalidi).

29. Thus *ghayb* in the Qur'an can at times be revelation, at times the unknown, as well as both. "That is the account of the tidings of the Unseen, that We reveal to thee" (Q 3:44, words spoken to Mary). "That is part of the story of what is Hidden (for ordinary mortals). We reveal it to you. You did not know it beforehand, nor did your people" (Q 11:49, the story of Noah; cf. also 11:49; 12:102).

30. Ambros, *A Concise Dictionary*, 205. Wehr, *A Dictionary*, s.v. "Ghayb": "hidden, concealed. invisible. That which is hidden, the invisible; that which is transcendent; the supernatural; divine secret."

31. Blachère, *Le Coran*, 731.

32. *Dictionnaire*, s.v. "Invisible," 425.

33. According to Bukhari on Q 31:34, cited by *Dictionnaire*, s.v. "Invisible," 426.

34. *Dictionnaire*, s.v. "invisible," 426. Translated by Paret, *Der Koran: Übersetzung*: "Has he (the unbeliever) become acquainted with the hidden or has he made a covenant with the Merciful One?" (Q 19:78).

par excellence of what is hidden (Q 5:109, 116; 9:78; 34:48). That which is unseen belongs to him alone (Q 10:20).[35] He is the knower of the things unseen, the guardian of absolute knowledge (Q 34:48; cf. 10:20).[36]

God (alone) has the keys[37] to access the Hidden things (Q 6:59; cf. 39:63; 42:12). Humans must therefore cling to the unknown mystery. The Qur'an does not communicate *everything* that is hidden to humans, but the entire Qur'an is a (partial) communication of it—thus the beautiful, poignant title of the large Qur'an commentary by Fahr al-Dîn al-Râzî († 1209 in Herat): *The Keys to the Unknown*.[38] In his "Testament" al Râzî writes: "I have gained experience in all methods of Islamic theology (*'ilm al-kalâm*) and have traveled along all the paths of philosophy (*falsafa*), but I have not found any satisfaction nor comfort that equals what I have found in reading the Qur'an."[39] The holy Scripture is its own interpreter.[40]

Ignaz Goldziher, the renowned Hungarian-Jewish Islamic scholar of the early twentieth century, delivered a lecture on Islamic theology, the *ilm al-kalâm*, in his *Vorlesungen über den Islam*. The first sentence reads: "Prophets are not theologians."[41] Christian theology—and, to a lesser degree, Islamic theology and, to an even lesser degree, Jewish theology, both of which do not usually speak of theology—claims to knows more about God than the prophets do.

When God asks Jesus in the Qur'an: "Jesus, son of Mary! Have you ever told the people: 'Adopt me and my mother as gods in addition to God,'" Jesus answers: "To you be the glory! I cannot say what I have no right to. If I did indeed say it, you would know. You only have knowledge of hidden things" (Q 5:116).

When it comes to explaining the Qur'anic texts, particularly with regard to texts about Jesus, which I believe can be explained in other ways than the usual, Muslims often neither confirm nor deny what I say but reply: "Allah knows, and he knows better." That seems to me to be a correct and respectful response.

One can actually speak about God in an authentic way only by addressing the One in prayer. How can the word of that Unseen God be understood other than with a prayer on one's lips? "Great God, You have broken

---

35. *Dictionnaire*, s.v. "invisible," 426. Cf. Paret's translation in *Der Koran: Übersetzung*.
36. *Dictionnaire*, s.v. "invisible."
37. *mafâtih*.
38. *E.I.* s.v. "al-Ghayb."
39. *E.I.* s.v. "Fakhr al-Dîn al-Râzî."
40. *Scriptura sacra sui ipsius interpres*.
41. Golziher, *Vorlesungen*, 71.

the silence with your own sweet voice. Make the path to you passable, let us understand you. Speak, Lord, your congregation listens" (Jan Wit).[42]

God's Name

The most important text in the Bible about the revelation of God's name can be found in the story of the revelation of God to Moses in the burning bush. There God reveals his name. After being called to act as the liberator of God's people from Egypt,

> Moses said to God, "Suppose I go to the Israelites and say to them, 'The God of your fathers has sent me to you,' and they ask me, 'What is his name? Then what shall I tell them?'" God said to Moses, "I AM WHO I AM. This is what you are to say to the Israelites: 'I AM has sent me to you.'" God also said to Moses, "Say to the Israelites, 'The LORD, the God of your fathers—the God of Abraham, the God of Isaac and the God of Jacob—has sent me to you.' This is my name forever, the name by which I am to be remembered from generation to generation" (Exod 3:13–15).

When explaining the Year of Jubilee—which is celebrated every fifty years and which, beginning with the Day of Atonement, gives the inhabitants of the country their freedom back—Willem Barnard writes that the idea of the Torah is that only YHWH can conjugate the verb "to have." The earth belongs to him and it returns to him each jubilee year—to YHWH, not to the "original possessors." Therefore, all people are "strangers," just like Abraham, who was a wandering migrant.[43] "My father was a stranger" is thus also found in the Hebrew liturgy (cf. Deut 26:5).[44]

The thoroughness and precision with which God makes his name known here is without parallel. God's name serves to confirm to his envoy the mission He has entrusted to him. Moses speaks in the name of and by order of the LORD (cf. Deut 18:19–20) or with the introductory formula that often appears with the prophets: "This is what the LORD says." That God will carry his people away from their troubles in Egypt is connected directly to this. God will grant the repressed people freedom from the resistance of Pharaoh who will not let the people leave if a mighty hand does not compel him (Exod

---

42. Hymn 317:1 from the hymnal *Zingen en bidden in huis en kerk*.

43. "My father was a wandering Aramean" (Deut 26:5). According to commentators, the expression is a collective reference to all three patriarchs (Num 30:15; Ps 105:12–13). Lundbom, *Deuteronomium*, 726.

44. Barnard, *Een winter*, 139. On the Year of Jubilee, see Barnard, *Een winter*, 4.

3:19). God is the one who liberates people from dependence on stranger foreign land or nation and wants to create a community (cf. Deut 4:34).[45]

Out of reverence and awe for God Jews never utter this name. This custom developed prior to the advent of the Christian Era, apparently becoming more popular in the Hellenistic period. A point of contact was found in the abbreviated form of "eternal" (Exod 3:15), which is explained as "hidden." When Jesus was on earth, the name was only used once a year on the Day of Atonement.[46]

"Water and Fire": "God Lives in the Thorn Bush"

Water and fire are linked in the Qur'an. There are two words for "sea" (*bahr* and *yamm*). The sea is powerful, and God swears by Mount Sinai, by the Torah, by Ka'ba, by the firmament and by the sea with its masses of water that will bring judgment (Q 52:1-7). The sea is a place of terror and darkness. "God has appointed for you the stars, that by them you might be guided in the shadows of land and sea" (Q 6:63, 97; 27:63). Water can be an instrument of punishment. One example of this is the flood that covered the city of Seba or Saba' when the Marib Dam burst (Q 34:16). The most dramatic example is the flood by which Noah's people, the Nûh, were punished (Q 54:11-12. Cf. 69:11). The sea in which Pharaoh and his army drowned is another example (Q 7:136; 20:78; 28:40; 51:40; 10:90; 44:24).

"God controls the waters, and he saved Noah who sailed safely in the ark on the waves like mountains" (Q 11:42) and "He saved Moses from Pharaoh by dividing the sea" (Q 2:50; 7:138; 20:77; 26:63).[47]

In the stories about Moses leading the children of Israel out of Egypt (Q 2:50; 7:136, 138; 8:54; 10:90; 17:103; 20:77-78; 26:63-66; 28:40; 44:24-25; 51:40), both words for "sea" are used: the one (*bahr*) for the successful crossing of the children of Israel, and the second (*yamm*) for the fatal crossing of Pharaoh's army. This indicates the ambiguous nature of the water: it gives life (*bahr*), but it is also like a deadly fire, a meaning that is found within the other word for sea (*yamm*). The flood the Qur'an speaks about can be regarded as a flood of hot water, of liquid fire. This idea can also be found in the Talmud and the Midrash.

This information is necessary for understanding what it means that Moses sees fire when God reveals himself to him. When Moses and his family are in the desert (Q 20:9-14; 27:7-9; 28:29-30) he sees a fire one night

---

45. Fischer and Markl, *Das Buch Exodus*, 55-56.
46. Ibid., 56.
47. *E.Q.*, s.v. "Water."

and at first thinks that it is a campfire. But when the bush begins to speak, he realizes that God is appearing to him in the form of that fire. "The burning bush is a complex figure where life-giving water and deadly fire are in balance." In other words: it appears to be a perfect metaphor for what gives life and death, a perfect metaphor for God.[48]

When Moses approaches the fire, a voice calls to him from the bush from the right side of the valley: "Moses, I am God, the Lord of all the worlds"(Q 28:30). "You are in the holy valley of Tuwâ. I myself have chosen you: therefore listen to what will be revealed here." Moses is then informed: "I am God; there is no god but I" (Q 20:10-14; 79:17). He is then called by God to go to Pharaoh in Egypt to save the people (Q 37:114-22).

Commentators believe that it is no coincidence that the Hebrew words for bush (shenê) and Sinai (Sînay) sound alike. The emblem of the God of Sinai was a tree in some shape or another. The blessing bestowed on the tribe of Joseph mentions YHWH "who dwelt in the burning bush" (Deut 33:16). The tree is an external manifestation of God's presence. YHWH is thus the "numen" of the tree. In Moses' encounter with the burning bush, the two emblems, tree and fire, clash, but neither overpowers the other. Both emblems reappear in the menorah, the lampstand, which is actually a stylized tree with branches, almond-shaped buds and flowers, and leaves. Moses was commissioned to make that lampstand, and it became one of the most important holy objects in the tabernacle (Exod 25:31-39). The seven lights were "the eyes of the Lord" (Zech 3:9), lighting the golden lampstand that stood between two olive trees whose fruit provided the oil for the lamps. Not only was it in the tabernacle during the journey through the desert but it was also placed in the temple Solomon built (1 Kings 7:49). "The temple in Jerusalem was lit by the fires of the burning bush." The lampstand from Herod's temple is still pictured on the Arch of Titus in Rome.[49]

The Parable of the Olive Tree

God is the light of the heavens and the earth. His light can be compared to a niche[50] (or window) containing a lantern. That lantern is in a glass and therefore resembles a shining star. It burns on the oil of a blessed olive tree that is neither of the east nor the west and gives the oil a sheen without the

---

48. *E.Q.*, s.v. "Fire."

49. Levenson, *Sinai and Zion*, 20-21; *KBS* on Exodus 25:31; Brosse, *Mythologie*, 60.

50. The word used, *mishkât*, is borrowed from Ethiopian. Jeffery, *The Foreign Vocabulary*, 266; Paret, *Der Koran: Kommentar*, 360. Cf. Speyer, *Die biblischen Erzählungen*, 62-66.

use of fire. Light above light. God leads whomever he wants to his light and instructs the people through parables. God is omniscient (Q 24:35).

It is assumed that during his travels through the desert, Muhammad saw the lights that the Christian ascetics used for their nightly spiritual rituals.[51] Together with two other disciples, Peter witnessed Jesus' transfiguration on the mountain and expresses this in one of his letters as follows: "And we have the word of the prophets made more certain, and you will do well to pay attention to it, as to a light shining in a dark place, until the day dawns and the morning star rises in your hearts" (2 Pet 1:19).

To ascend the holy olive tree originally meant to return to the "lap of Abraham," as we can see from a dream Muhammad had that is recorded in a tradition:

> I saw in this night two men, who came and took me by the hand to lead me to the holy earth. . . . They led me to a large garden. There was a huge tree and in the trunk of that tree was an old man and children. One man lit a fire close to the tree. They allowed me to climb the tree and led me to a place more wonderful than I have ever seen.

Thus, there was an old man and children. The prophet asked both of his guides about the meaning of what he had just seen. They replied:

> The old man you saw in the trunk of the tree is Abraham and the children are men. The one who lit the fire is the guardian of the fire. The first room you entered in that of ordinary believers. Higher up in the tree is a more beautiful room. That is where the martyrs live. The crown of the cosmic tree (here an olive tree that touches the heavens) holds the paradise of the chosen, and its highest region is reserved for the martyrs, the (blood) witnesses, who gave everything for God, even their lives.[52]

The prayer rugs used by Muslims are often decorated with images of a niche, a lantern, and a stylized tree fed with oil. The famous Persian commentator of the Qur'an, Zamaksharî (1075–1144), explains in his *The Revealer of the Truths of the Revelation* that the purest olive tree grows in Syria and that the rising and setting sun must shine on that tree. This is the reason for the emphasis on east and west.[53]

In his *Niche of Lights* Abû Hâmid al-Ghazâlî († 1111) compares the five elements of the images that are used in the "Verse of Light": the niche,

---

51. Speyer, *Die biblischen Erzählungen*, 431.
52. Brosse, *Mythologie*, 234.
53. *E.Q.*, s.v. "Tree," 361.

the glass, the lantern, the tree and the oil, using the concepts of imagination, intellect, language and prophecy.[54] For al-Ghazâlî, the symbolic language of the Qur'an was a subject of thorough reflection, a way for the believers to build a bridge between the physical world of human acts and the spiritual area of divine truth. For him, the "verse of light" is an example of such a bridge. With the metaphor "God is the light of the heavens and the earth," he distinguishes between three levels where the meaning of light is concerned. The first is the physical phenomenon where human eyes see the earth because of the light of the sun. The second is the mental level where the intellectual capacity is enlightened by the light of the truth that can be found in the Qur'an itself. Finally, there is the spiritual dimension, in which the gnostic intuition is enlightened by the rays of the divine presence. An adult believer is someone who has achieved each of these three levels of perception/knowledge.[55]

The third level is called the "love that surpasses all knowledge" by Paul in one of his letters (Eph 3:19). The Greek word *gnosis* is used here.

Two Names for God in the Psalter

To fully understand something of the subtlety of the silence of God and of his speaking, we should note how the various names for God are used in the psalms. As a prayer book, as a psalter, the book is crucial for the deeper understanding of and explanation given in both the New Testament and the Qur'an. Most quotations and references to the Old Testament made in the New Testament are to the psalms. The same could be said for the Qur'an. In the Qur'an, the psalms (*zabûr*, pl. *zubur*) are expressly mentioned next to the Tawra (cf. the Tanakh) and the Injîl (the New Testament).[56] Sometimes there are references to psalms that are connected with David (Dâwûd). But the term is also used in the plural and is then usually translated as "(the whole of the) Scriptures." In addition to the name YHWH, which is usually translated as "Lord," in the psalms, the word El or Elohim, which is translated as "God" in English can also be found. "The name YHWH is widely used in the Psalter,[57] but it is also hidden. There is a certain mysteriousness surrounding this name of God."[58]

---

54. *E.Q.*, s.v. "Simile."
55. Gairdner, al-Ghazzalî's *Miskat*, 79–121. Cf. *E.Q.*, s.v. "Metaphor."
56. Cf. Speyer, *Die biblischen Erzählungen*, 497–98.
57. The Elohistic Psalter.
58. Hossfeld and Zenger, *Psalmen 51–100*, 505.

That secrecy surrounding the name of God also becomes clear on the basis of Jacob's history. After wrestling with a "stranger" for a whole night, Jacob is given a new name: "Israel," "the one who struggles with God" (Israel). The evening before his meeting with his brother Esau, Jacob (Ya'qûb) becomes very frightened. Earlier, he had persuaded Esau to sell his birthright for a bowl of stew (Gen 25:29–34). Then, using a clever deception, he stole the blessing his father Isaac was to have given Esau (Gen 27:35). Because Esau was planning to kill him to get revenge, Jacob fled (Gen 27:41–46). Muslim literature ascribes the name Israel to Jacob either because he was noble in the eyes of God or because he travelled at night to escape the Esau's wrath.[59]

> That night Jacob got up and took his two wives, his two maidservants and his eleven sons and crossed the ford of the Jabbok. After he had sent them across the stream, he sent over all his possessions. So Jacob was left alone, and a man wrestled with him till daybreak. When the man saw that he could not overpower him, he touched the socket of Jacob's hip so that his hip was wrenched as he wrestled with the man. Then the man said, "Let me go, for it is daybreak." But Jacob replied, "I will not let you go unless you bless me." The man asked him, "What is your name?" "Jacob," he answered. Then the man said, "Your name will no longer be Jacob, but Israel, because you have struggled with God and with men and have overcome." Jacob said, "Please tell me your name." But he replied, "Why do you ask my name?" Then he blessed him there. So Jacob called the place Peniel, saying, "It is because I saw God face to face, and yet my life was spared" (Gen 32:23–31).[60]

It is, after all, dangerous to see the face of God (Exod 33:20).

In any case, this story concerns the name that Jacob is given: "Israel," "one who struggles with God," as well as the question about the name of God. "That battle with God concerns the proof of God's being God in and for Israel before the nations of the world."[61] Israel is God's advocate. "When Israel is threatened, the God of Israel is threatened; when his name disappears, He, the

---

59. *E.I.*, s.v. "*Ya' kûb.*"

60. Because Jacob's hip had been wrenched, Jews may no longer eat the tendon attached to the socket of the hip (Gen 32:33). According to the Qur'an, prior to the revelation in the Torah, the Israelites were allowed to eat all food except what Israel itself had forbidden (Q 3:93). The Qur'an opposes the food laws of the Jews that were not given by God but imposed as punishment (cf. Q 6:145–53; 16:114–18; 4:160; 10:59–60). See also Paret, *Der Koran: Kommentar*, on Q 3:93.

61. Hossfeld and Zenger, *Psalmen 51–100*, 505.

God of Israel, disappears."[62] This is therefore also the case in the "battle" that the people of Israel must at times wage with the silence of God. To exaggerate, in the psalms Israel calls upon God to do something for God's own survival. This occurs in, for example, Psalm 83, which begins: "O God, do not keep silent; be not quiet, O God, be not still" (Ps 83:1). By the end, however, this is expressed with more power: "Let them know that you, whose name is the Lord—that you alone are the Most High over all the earth" (Ps 83:18). And the difference between the beginning and the end lies (partially) in the use of the name of God, El/Elohim (God) or YHWH (Lord). As the "silent God," God is called Elohim or El and he is, so to speak, "a distant God." Israel, the man who struggled with God, forces the Lord (YHWH) to nevertheless give up "being distant." The Lord is begged to reveal himself in his name YHWH, with all that that name entails and means in order to prove that he is the God of both Israel and the world (Ps 83:18)!

Elijah's Confrontation with the Dumb Gods

Elijah (Ilyâs) was a great prophet (1 Kings 17:8–2 Kings 2:13). His name implies his task and sounds like a program for action: "YHWH is God." Only the Lord is God and therefore Baal is not, one must concede. YHWH is "the God of Israel" (1 Kings 17:1), "the Lord Almighty" (1 Kings 18:15),[63] "the God of Abraham, Isaac and Israel" (1 Kings 18:36). Elijah followed the tradition of Israel in the desert. This is apparent from the journey that he himself took through the desert on his way to Mount Horeb. On that mountain he experienced the visible manifestation of God, which immediately reminds us of God's self-revelation to Moses on Mount Sinai (Exod 19). His opponent was Ahab, the king of the northern kingdom of Israel, of which Samaria was the capital. Faith in God was barely able to gain a foothold in that city (1 Kings 16:32; 2 Kings 10:19-20). A political alliance existed between Israel and the Phoenicians. Ahab had married Jezebel, the daughter of the king of Tyrus, and, under her influence, the Tyrian religion of Baal penetrated Israel. The building of a temple to Baal and an altar in the capital city of Samaria were signs of this (1 Kings 16:31–33). The conflict between Israel's God and the god Baal was not simply between the two gods but

---

62. Ibid.

63. The powers or the hosts are all elements of heaven and earth that serve the purpose of the Lord. They are also called "the army of the stars" (Judg 5:20) or "Israel's armies" (1 Sam 17:45). See, for example, *KBS* on 1 Samuel 1:3, where the expression appears for the first time.

involved two competing social systems that embraced two alternative views of the world.[64]

The prophet Elijah comes into contact with Obadiah, the king's steward (1 Kings 18:1–16). Obadiah is also a "servant of God," and thus an "undercover agent" for faith in God.[65] He saved a hundred prophets of the LORD by hiding them, most likely in the caves of Mount Carmel and provided them with bread and water. During the drought, Obadiah arranged a meeting between the king and Elijah at Elijah's behest.

A dramatic confrontation between Elijah and the prophets of Baal on Mount Carmel follows (1 Kings 18).[66]

The contest between Elijah and the prophets of Baal reveals who arouses the attention of and a sympathetic ear from their God/gods. Elijah's God answers; the god Baal remains dumb. He hears nothing, gives no answer. The prophets of Baal receive no response from their god (1 Kings 18:26).

When the prophets of Baal call in vain, "Baal, answer us!" Elijah taunts them: "Shout louder! Surely he is a god! Perhaps he is deep in thought, or busy, or travelling. Maybe he is sleeping and must be awakened." So they shout louder and slash themselves with swords and spears, as was their custom [to add power to their prayers],[67] until their blood flows. Midday passes, and they continue their frantic prophesying until the time for the evening sacrifice. But there is no response, no one answers, no one pays attention (1 Kings 18:27–29).

When it is Elijah's turn to call on God the LORD, he says: "Answer me, LORD, answer me, so these people will know that you, LORD, are God, and that you are turning their hearts back again" (1 Kings 18:37).[68] When the time came to sacrifice, the prophet Elijah stepped forward and prayed:

> LORD, the God of Abraham, Isaac and Israel, let it be known today that you are God in Israel and that I am your servant and have done all these things at your command. Answer me, LORD, answer me, so these people will know that you, LORD, are God, and that you are turning their hearts back again." Then the fire of the LORD fell and consumed the sacrifice, the wood, the stones and the soil, and also licked up the water in the trench. When all

---

64. Brueggemann, *1 and 2 Kings*, 228–29.
65. Ibid., 221.
66. *B.W.*, s.v. "Obadja."
67. Cf. Jeremiah 16:6; 41:5; 47:5. This is forbidden in Leviticus 19:28, 21:5, and Deuteronomy 14:1. In the northern kingdom of Israel, similar religious practices were widespread from the ninth to the seventh centuries B.C. (Lundbom, *Deuteronomium*, 464).
68. Hossfeld and Zenger, *Psalmen 51–100*, 506.

the people saw this, they fell prostrate and cried, "The LORD—he is God! The LORD—he is God!" Then Elijah commanded them, "Seize the prophets of Baal. Don't let anyone get away!" They seized them, and Elijah had them brought down to the Kishon Valley and slaughtered them there (1 Kings 18:36-40).[69]

This is a "trial by ordeal." It is a procedure whereby the decision in a trial is left to God. Trials by ordeal take place in most cultures. In the Code of Hammurabi, trials by ordeal were arranged legally.[70] The eradication of the prophets of Baal must be viewed as God's right: "Whoever sacrifices to any god other than the LORD must be destroyed" (Exod 22:20).[71]

In the Qur'an, Elijah is a "just man" and is mentioned in the same breath as Zachariah and his son John the Baptist (Q 6:85). The Qur'an alludes to Elijah's actions against Israel's worship of Baal. Elijah was sent to his people to eradicate this worship. When he said to his people: "'Will you not fear God? Will you worship Baal and abandon the Best Creator imaginable? The one God your Lord and the Lord of your ancient forefathers?" he was called a liar. For that they will be judged,, except those who worship God sincerely." Elijah is finally described as one of the faithful servants of God (Q 37:123-32).

Inspired by the *haggada*, Muslim tradition links Elijah to the priestly line of Aaron (Hârûn) and to the character of Khidr[72] (Q 18) and Henoch (Idrîs), who are mentioned among the prophets (Q 21:85; cf. Gen 4:17-18) and described as true to their promise or faithful (Q 19:56). The immortality ascribed to both of them allows them to rescue those in desperate situations on land or at sea. They have thus acquired an important place in mysticism and folk religion.[73] After all, shouldn't a chair be reserved for Elijah in case he comes?

---

69. Cf. Deuteronomy 13:1-6. Prophets who attempted to divert the people from serving God were to be killed. The death penalty was applied because religious treason was dealt with as political treason. See Lundbom, *Deuteronomium*, 453, who cites Moshe Weinfeld here.

70. *B.W.*, s.v. "Godsoordeel."

71. *B.W.*, s.v. "Elia"; cf. Noegel and Wheeler, *The A to Z of Prophets*, s.v. "Elijah."

72. There is no biblical parallel, even though Khidr is compared to Elijah. He is called "the Green Man" (*khidr* means "green"). I present the narrative about him in the last chapter of my book *Islam in Stories*.

73. Cf. *E.I.*, s.v. "Ilyâs"; Ginzberg, *Legends of the Jews,* 195-235; Wessels, *Islam in Stories*, chapter X.

Elijah and the Judgments in the Qur'an

The events on Mount Carmel are dealt with in the Qur'an under the heading "Punishment Stories" (Q 37:71–148). Those about Elijah constitute only some of them (cf. Q 37:123–32).

The primary function of the stories about judgments is to warn about the punishment that will be imposed by God on the unbelieving inhabitants of Mecca if they do not repent and accept Muhammad's message (Q 41:13). After all, what happened to the unbelieving communities in the past could also happen to the Meccans in the present. These stories also encourage Muhammad himself to persevere in the face of disbelief. Everything that is told about the tidings the messengers bring is meant to encourage him (Q 11:120).[74]

The other punishment stories give just as many examples of cities and nations that had been destroyed by God because they rejected the messengers sent to them from within their own communities. This occurred in various times and at various places. Noah was the first in a series of messengers who came to warn others (Q 37:75–82).

These types of stories are not intended to entertain the listeners, to relate history, or even to educate. They are meant, above all, to warn, threaten, convince *and* reassure, so that people would act in such a way as to escape punishment![75]

Whatever holds for the psalms also holds for the interpretation of the New Testament *and* the Qur'an. When the Psalms (149:7–9a) sing about the process and goal of attaining God's order of justice in the world, they do not depict an irrational practice of retaliation and revenge but the application of just punishment for the injustices that have been done. All of this is done with the express goal of correction and transformation. The stories about punishment serve to educate the people. Thus, when the psalms present kings bound in fetters and nobles in shackles of iron (Ps 149:8), the intention is not to display them like a spectacle in a triumphant procession of defeated kings being brought to a place of execution. Rather, such texts point to the fact that not only Israel but all nations will be liberated from violent and exploitative regimes and that God will exercise his kingly rule.[76]

---

74. *E.Q.*, s.v. "Punishment Stories."
75. Welch, "Formulaic Features," 106–7.
76. Hossfeld and Zenger, *Psalms 3*, 652.

Elijah in Baalbek

More about Elijah can be found in later Muslim tradition. It is said that he was sent to the people after the death of Ezekiel[77] because the Israelites began to serve idols, including Baal who was worshipped by the people of Baalbek.[78] When the people of Baalbek tried to kill Elijah, he hid in a cave and was fed by a raven until he was finally able to return because another king had come to power.

That Elijah was fed by the raven (cf. 1 Kings 17:4, 6) speaks to God's generous and sympathetic care: "He provides food for the cattle and for the young ravens when they call" (Ps 147:9). Young ravens, viewed as helpless creatures because of their cries, were not admired nor very highly valued. They were seen as unclean animals (cf. Lev 11:15; Deut 14:14). That God provides for young ravens means that God takes special care of the least of his creatures. And if God does that for ravens, people can rely on his active protection all the more: "Who provides food for the raven when its young cry out to God and wander about for lack of food?" (Job 38:41). Young ravens and their cries to God are a metaphor for the poor who can trust in and call upon God.[79] Jesus uses the raven as a symbol for God's care.[80]

Elijah and the Gentle Whisper

After a very violent conclusion to the events on Mount Carmel, Elijah became a wanted man and had to flee for his life.

> He came to a broom bush, sat down under it and prayed that he might die. "I have had enough, LORD," he said. "Take my life; I am no better than my ancestors." Then he lay down under the bush and fell asleep. All at once an angel touched him and said, "Get up and eat." He looked around, and there by his head was some bread baked over hot coals, and a jar of water. He ate and drank and then lay down again. The angel of the LORD came back a second time and touched him and said, "Get up and eat, for the journey is too

---

77. Cf. Q 2:243: "'Have you not seen those who fled by the thousands in fear from their homes?' God said, 'Die.' Then he revived them." Muslim exegetes link this verse to Ezekiel 37:1–14, the passage about the valley with dry bones that come back to life. Cf. *E.Q.*, s.v. "Ezekiel."

78. Some hold that they worshipped Baal in the shape of a woman. In addition to prophets of Baal, Elijah also had to deal with prophets of Asherah, one of the heathen goddesses (1 Kings 18:19).

79. Hossfeld and Zenger, *Psalms*, 625.

80. *B.W.*, s.v. "Raaf."

much for you." So he got up and ate and drank. Strengthened by that food, he traveled forty days and forty nights until he reached Horeb, the mountain of God. There he went into a cave and spent the night. And the word of the LORD came to him: "What are you doing here, Elijah?" (1 Kings 19:4–9)

Then an encounter with God took place that is similar to the encounter Moses had with God.

God's revelation of himself to Moses began with thunder and lightning. "On the morning of the third day there was thunder and lightning, with a thick cloud over the mountain, and a very loud trumpet blast. Everyone in the camp trembled" (Exod 19:16). "Mount Sinai was covered with smoke, because the LORD descended on it in fire. The smoke billowed up from it like smoke from a furnace, and the whole mountain trembled violently." (Exod 19:18). The people *and* the listener/reader wait with bated breath and alertness for what is about to happen.[81]

The word of the LORD came to Elijah in the cave he had spent the night in:

> "What are you doing here, Elijah?" He replied, "I have been very zealous for the LORD God Almighty. The Israelites have rejected your covenant, torn down your altars, and put your prophets to death with the sword. I am the only one left, and now they are trying to kill me too." The Lord said, "Go out and stand on the mountain in the presence of the LORD, for the Lord is about to pass by." Then a great and powerful wind tore the mountains apart and shattered the rocks before the LORD, but the LORD was not in the wind. After the wind there was an earthquake, but the LORD was not in the earthquake. After the earthquake came a fire, but the LORD was not in the fire. And after the fire came a gentle whisper. (1 Kings 19:9–12)

Storms, earthquakes, and fire were all characteristic of theophanies, of God's appearances to humankind. That is also what happened when God appeared to Moses and the people. But apparently that was not the case with Elijah: "God was not in it."

What happened then is related by using an expression that is enigmatic and difficult to translate. It is often translated into English as "a still, small voice" (KJV, RSV); the NIV has "gentle whisper." Karel Deurloo, an Old Testament scholar at the University of Amsterdam, suggests it was not a voice or sound but a frightening, mysterious, loaded silence evoking a sense of the holy or the Holy One, a deep sense of awe. Kees Waaijman writes:

---

81. Fischer and Markl, *Das Buch Exodus,* 218.

The story forces the narrator and the hearer to make a choice. The "voice that pounds one into silence" opens up those two possibilities: the silence of death and the fear of death and the silence of repentance and hope. . . . The "desert" of death and loneliness" (1 Kings 19:4) becomes the desert of Israel's origins (1 Kings 19:8). The narrator shows in all possible ways that the silence has two sides: the deathly silence and the silence of expectation.[82]

Elijah does not have the experience on Mount Sinai Moses had. God does not reveal himself in a spectacle of storm, thunder, heavy clouds and fire as he did to Moses nor as the storm god Baal did. Elijah has to be alert to the almost imperceptible sign and no longer expect a dramatic intervention as had characterized Moses' career. And, apparently, neither did he have to expect that God will once again reveal himself in the way he just had in his encounter with the prophets of Baal on that other mountain, Mount Carmel. Moses' time was different from the time that followed. Israel never had another prophet like Moses whom the LORD knew face to face (Deut 34:10).[83]

Whatever may be meant by the expression "a gentle whisper," it demands Elijah's full attention. As Moses had once done (Exod 33:21-23), so he too stands at the entrance of a cave. As soon as Elijah experiences "this," he covers his face with his mantle. Moses did something similar:

> There the angel of the LORD appeared to him in flames of fire from within a bush. Moses saw that though the bush was on fire it did not burn up. So Moses thought, "I will go over and see this strange sight—why the bush does not burn up." When the LORD saw that he had gone over to look, God called to him from within the bush, "Moses! Moses!" And Moses said, "Here I am." "Do not come any closer," God said. "Take off your sandals, for the place where you are standing is holy ground." Then he said, "I am the God of your father, the God of Abraham, the God of Isaac and the God of Jacob." At this, Moses hid his face, because he was afraid to look at God. (Exod 3:2-6)

---

82. Waaijman, *De profeet Elia*, 73.

83. Levenson, *Sinai and Zion*, 89-90. Deuteronomy speaks of prophets up until that time; Moses says that YHWH would send another prophet like himself (Deut 18:15-18), and Jeremiah saw himself as a prophet like Moses. That Moses met with YHWH face to face is not to be understood in a visual sense but in an aural one and refers to speech between God and Moses (Deut 5:4; Exod 33:11; Num 12:8). Even Moses was not permitted to see God's face (Exod 33:20-23; cf. John 4:12); Lundbom, *Deuteronomium*, 948. Both Jesus and Muhammad are viewed as prophets like Moses.

It is striking that something similar happened to the prophet Muhammad twice when he received a revelation. He was addressed by God: "O God, wrapped in your robes" (Q 73:1; cf. 74:1), "keep vigil in the night" (Q 73:2).

Let us return to Elijah. Elijah goes outside and remains standing by the entrance to the cave. Then he hears a voice that asks: "What are you doing here, Elijah?" (1 Kings 19:13). Elijah exposes himself to the penetrating presence of YHWH and is prepared to be spoken to, to listen. God does not think of Elijah's suffering, the loneliness that he must have endured nor of his fear of Ahab and Jezebel from whom the prophet has fled. No, God is completely focused on the public mission he is giving Elijah at that moment. When God speaks, it is an order: "Go back!" In his revelation to Moses, God had also told Moses that he must return to Egypt, despite the fact that he had just fled from there after killing an Egyptian. Elijah also has to return to the conflicts he had fled from, and face all the risks that return entails. Once again, he has to accept the dangerous role of a prophet.[84]

"God (YHWH) or Baal?" is the question that lies at the center of all of Elijah's actions. The Lord speaks to the house of Israel: "Seek me and live" (Amos 5:4). God can be sought by going to the temple or consulting him through a priest or prophet. But the Lord can also be sought in the ethical sense by learning his will and orienting oneself toward it and acting according to it. That is what brings life.[85] One must seek the name of the Lord: he who needs help should seek the face of God (Ps 24:6).[86]

Felix Mendelssohn uses the words of Deuteronomy in his *Elijah* oratorio (1846): "But if from there you seek the Lord your God, you will find him if you seek him with all your heart and with all your soul" (Deut 4:29; cf. 2 Cor 15:4; Ps 27:8).[87] And he also cites a verse from Jeremiah: "You will seek me and find me when you seek me with all your heart" (Jer 29:13). In that same *Elijah* oratorio, Obadiah, King Ahab's steward, sings in the tenor solo:

> "If with all your hearts ye truly seek Me, ye shall ever surely find Me." Thus saith our God. Oh! that I knew where I might find Him, that I might even come before His presence!

And the chorus then answers:

> Thus saith our God, "Ye shall ever find me."
> Thus saith our God.[88]

---

84. Brueggemann, *1 and 2 Kings*, 235–37.
85. *KBS* on Amos 5:4.
86. *B.W.*, s.v. "Zoeken."
87. Ibid.
88. Part 1, no 4 Air, no 5 Chorus; cited by Lundbom, *Deuteronomium*, 250–51. Cf.

Elijah's Ascension

Some time after the events on Mount Carmel and in Baalbek, God appointed Elisha to be Elijah's successor. Elijah and Elisha (al-Yasaʿ) travelled and worked together for a while. At a certain moment, a chariot of fire and horses of fire appeared and separated them. Elijah went up to heaven in a whirlwind—"You who were taken up by a whirlwind of fire, in a chariot with horses of fire" (Sir 48:9). When Elijah disappeared in the whirlwind, Elisha was filled with his spirit: "in all his days he did not tremble before any ruler, and no one brought him into subjection" (Sir 48:12). When Elisha saw that his teacher had been taken up, he cried out: "My father! My father! The chariots and horsemen of Israel!" (2 Kings 2:11–12; cf. Sir 48:9, 12). Wahb b. Munabbih, who wrote a collection of Jewish tales about prophets (*Qisâs al-Anbiyâ*),[89] says that Elijah asked God to take him away, and in response to which God took him up to heaven on a steed.[90]

Elijah made quite an impression with his mysterious ascension (2 Kings 2:11; Sir 48:9, 12) and the predictions of his return (Mal 3:1, 23–24). The Jews certainly had expectations of his return during Jesus' time as well as in the centuries thereafter.[91]

Moses' Encounter with God in the Qur'an and Isaiah on Idolatry

It is striking that the manner in which the Qur'an presents Moses' experience of his encounter with God contains a clear reference to the contrast between God and the idols. When Moses and his family were on the road, he saw a fire on the side of Mount Tûr[92] (Mount Sinai). "He said to his household: 'Stay here; I see a fire. Perhaps I will tell you about it or bring a faggot from it so that you can warm yourselves'" (Q 28:29; cf. 20:10 and 27:7). This passage contains a clear allusion to the discussion on idolatry that is also found in Isaiah. Although Isaiah does not appear among the 25 prophets named in the Qur'an, he is often linked to the prophesies about

---

Jeremiah 29:14: "'I will be found by you,' declares the LORD, 'and will bring you back from captivity. I will gather you from all the nations and places where I have banished you,' declares the LORD, 'and will bring you back to the place from which I carried you into exile'" (Jer 29:14). The word "found" here means "prayed to." See also Jeremiah 10:21; 29:7; Isaiah 55:6; 65:1; Acts 17:27.

89. Newby, *A History*, 143, note 88.
90. *E.Q.*, s.v. "Elijah."
91. *KBS*, 1 Kings 17:1.
92. *E.I.*, s.v. "al-Tûr."

the coming of Jesus and Muhammad. According to Thaʿlabī's *Tales of the Prophets* (1035), Isaiah saw the announced destruction of Jerusalem as a prediction of the coming of the two prophets with good tidings: "Rejoice, o Jerusalem, presently he who is seated on a donkey will come to you and after him will come someone riding on a camel."[93]

There are various works in Islamic art that depict these two riders, the one riding a donkey and the other a camel. From behind a window, a watchman—or a prophet—is looking at the two approaching riders. The scene in such works is explained as depicting the coming of, respectively, Jesus (riding on a donkey) and Muhammad (riding on a camel).

The source for this Muslim interpretation is linked to a "poem" from the book of Isaiah that deals with the fall of Babylon:

> They set the tables,
>> they spread the rugs,
>> they eat, they drink!
>
> Get up, you officers,
>> oil the shields!
>
> This is what the Lord says to me:
> "Go, post a lookout
>> and have him report what he sees.
>
> When he sees chariots
>> with teams of horses,
>
> riders on donkeys
>> or riders on camels,
>
> let him be alert,
> fully alert."
>
> And the lookout shouted,
> "Day after day, my lord, I stand on the watchtower;
>> every night I stay at my post.
>
> Look, here comes a man in a chariot
> with a team of horses.
>
> And he gives back the answer:
>> 'Babylon has fallen, has fallen!
>
> All the images of its gods
>> lie shattered on the ground!'"
>
> (Isa 21:5–9)

93. *Dictionnaire*, s.v. "Isaïe"; Rubin, 37. I used a Muslim depiction of this scene on the front cover of my book, *Islam in Stories*.

This mysterious poem has apocalyptic features: it is a vision about an enemy that would finally destroy the city of Babylon. Historically, one could think of the Persian sovereign Cyrus (Hebrew: Kores) who will conquer the city. The oppressive Babylon, which has caused so many sighs and groans among the oppressed, would now come to an end.[94]

The fall of Babylon did indeed become a historical fact. After describing the city extensively, Herodotus also relates Babylon's capture by the Persian sovereign Cyrus the Great.[95] Later, another Persian sovereign, Darius, would conquer Babylon for the second time. After that conquest, Darius had the city dismantled and the gates lifted off their hinges, something that Cyrus had never done after his conquest. Moreover, three thousand prominent inhabitants were crucified. What was left of the population was allowed to stay in the city.[96]

Isaiah's poem begins with a scene of a self-satisfied Babylon living in luxury. The political and military leaders are sitting at table, eating and drinking at their ease. But then the scene suddenly changes, a very abrupt call to ready themselves for battle is heard. The alarm has been raised because of a troops invading the city. The scene jumps to an observation post, and from there riders on horses, donkeys, and camels can be seen—all possible means of transportation are used. The watchman is alert and at his post to report constantly, day and night, on the continuous flow of attackers. "And the lookout shouted, 'Day after day, my lord, I stand on the watchtower; every night I stay at my post. Look, here comes a man in a chariot with a team of horses'" (Isa 21:8–9a). At long last the final report is brought: "Babylon has fallen, has fallen!" (Isa 21:9b). While it initially seemed as if Babylon would exist forever, this great empire came to a sudden end. Babylon, which had ruled the world, was gone: "Announce and proclaim among the nations, lift up a banner and proclaim it; keep nothing back, but say, 'Babylon will be captured; Bel will be put to shame, Marduk filled with terror. Her images will be put to shame and her idols filled with terror'" (Jer 50:2).

The whole of the Ancient Near East had been subjected to the hegemony of Babylon and its gods. But the announcement in Isaiah tells us that it has come to a sudden end and, with it, the apparently so powerful Babylonian gods. The downfall of Babylon is that of its gods as well. They have been put to shame. Babylon, viewed as the "enemy from the north"

---

94. Brueggemann, *Isaiah 1–39*, 169–70. During a great banquet held by King Belshazzar, writing appeared on the wall, a kind of rebus that announced that the king of the Chaldeans would be killed. The meaning of the rebus was: "God has numbered the years of your reign and brought it to an end" (Dan 5:25).

95. Herodotus, *The Histories*, I, 188–91. This is the first account of the city's capture.

96. Herodotus, *The Histories*, III, 159.

for such a long time, has been defeated by another "enemy from the north." The defeat of Babylon would mean the end of exile for the Jews: the people who had been deported could return.[97] This military event is represented as and converted into a religious battle in which the Babylonian gods are defeated and humiliated by the greater power of God. The defeat of Babylon is a historical fact, but in the prophetic presentation it is about the power of God to destroy evil.[98]

Horses and Donkeys

To understand just what it is the watchman sees, it is important to know what is understood by horses and donkeys in the Scriptures.

The horse was the symbol of power, especially of the armed forces, and thus of the power of the king. Horses and chariots were part of Israel's military might since the time of Solomon and directly under the sovereign's authority.

It should be noted that Solomon had those "horses and chariots" imported from Egypt (1 Kings 10:28-29), the country the Israelites had left. And Pharaoh had pursued them with all of his horses, chariots, and charioteers—yes, his entire army. God purposely destroyed Egypt's horses and chariots at that time (Exod 14–15), but Solomon introduced horses and chariots into Israel's armed forces (1 Kings 5:6; 9:19; 10:26), giving Israel control over a great potential force. These resources were seen as political instruments that went against God's laws in broad circles of the population and, above all, by the prophets. In the Qur'an account of King Solomon, horses play a negative role because the king's admiration for them keeps him from prayer (cf. Q 38:32, 35 100:8; 89:20).[99]

Isaiah later calls out "Woe to you" to those who go to Egypt for help, rely on horses, trust in chariots, and in the great strength of their horsemen, even though the Egyptians are mere mortals and not gods, and their horses flesh and not spirit (Isa 31:1, 3). Naturally, at that time, the real threat of a political power was considered as well. But the metaphor for military power is also involved: horses and chariots. After all, they are nothing more than a means for self-deception; they can offer no security. Egypt is unable to save them because Egypt is human and not divine, flesh and not spirit. Unlike God, Egypt has no power or authority to produce something new. Its military power cannot create life. The prophet criticizes the ideology and

---

97. Brueggemann, *A Commentary*, 464–65.
98. Brueggemann, *Isaiah 1–39*, 171–72.
99. Cf. Wessels, *The Torah*, 140, 141.

idolatry of military power because that power can only lead to death.[100] The alternative is God—in contrast to what earthly sovereigns, He is the one who can truly help (Ps 146:3-4).

During the time of exile and during the post-exilic period, the attempt was made several times to free the Messianic ideal of kingship from symbols of power. When the visions of the prophets state that God would destroy all horses and chariots, they are only being consistent (Mic 5:9; Zech 9:10).[101]

Riding on a Young Donkey

Donkeys are the opposite of horses, the antithesis to the chariots and steeds of the kings. But David and Solomon rode mules. Solomon was also seated on a mule when he entered Jerusalem as king. He was placed on King David's mule and escorted to the well located at the foot of the southeastern hill of Jerusalem (1 Kings 1:38). Thus, donkeys and mules were also used by sovereigns. In the Song of Deborah, the leaders of Israel are described as riding on white donkeys. They sat on rich saddle blankets and rode along the road (Judg 5:10). Zechariah portrays the Messiah as a peace-loving ruler: righteous and victorious and lowly and riding on a donkey (Zech 9:9-10). This Messianic vision is later fulfilled in Jesus' entry into Jerusalem (John 12:15). But the crowd present at that entry has a completely different view of Jesus' entry: they expect something like the one that had occurred earlier in the spring of 141 B.C. Simon the Maccabee entered the liberated city of Jerusalem together with the Judeans: "this terrible threat to the security of Israel had come to an end. Simon and his men entered the fort singing hymns of praise and thanksgiving, while carrying palm branches and playing harps, cymbals, and lyres" (1 Macc 13:51). In that time the palm branch symbolized victory. "But now, carrying green palm branches and sticks decorated with ivy, they paraded around, singing grateful praises to him who had brought about the purification of his own Temple" (2 Macc 10:7).[102]

In the perilous times Jesus lived in, under violent Roman oppression, this waving with palm branches bore witness to nationalistic feelings and the hopes for a violent act of liberation against the occupying Roman power. The people were hoping for a repeat of the Maccabean liberation from the Greek yoke. There were a number of new Jewish uprisings in the first and second centuries after Christ. The demonstration at Jesus' entry was also

---

100. Brueggemann, *Isaiah 1-39*, 249-50.
101. Hossfeld and Zenger, *Die Psalmen*, 138-39.
102. Both quotes are from the Good News Translation.

unmistakably a political demonstration: the people wanted to make this a triumphant entry and make Jesus a sort of "Jesus the Maccabee."[103]

But Jesus had purposely and determinedly chosen a donkey as his mount. Translated literally, the word means "a young donkey," or colt, and therefore—literally—he could not have risen above the crowd. Jesus thus toned down the prevailing unrealistic national expectations and wanted to show that he has in mind a different kind of kingship than the crowd dreamed of.

The evangelist John therefore cites the opening words of the quote from the prophet Zechariah but changes it somewhat. Rather than the words: "See, your king comes to you, righteous and victorious, lowly and riding on a donkey, on a colt, the foal of a donkey" (Zech 9:9), he writes: "Do not be afraid, Daughter of Zion; see, your king is coming, seated on a donkey's colt" (John 12:15).[104] No one need be frightened of this king. On the contrary! The young donkey symbolizes his love for peace. Jewish tradition emphasizes the peaceful nature of the entry of the king (1 Kings 1:33) and therefore also that of the Messiah. This is the only reason why Jesus enters the capital on a young donkey (Matt 21:2–7).[105] The nature of the new kingship that is inaugurated here is completely different, going contrary to everything rulers and warlords desire.[106]

Visitors Come to Ebenezer Scrooge

In the last part of this chapter, we will consider another line from the Sinterklaas song mentioned earlier: "Will you please make a stop at our door," i.e., a request for Saint Nicholas to pay them a visit.

A dramatic and illustrative example of a nightly visit is described by Charles Dickens in his famous *A Christmas Carol*. The miser Ebenezer Scrooge is visited on a dark evening by the spirit of his former business partner Jacob Marley. Marley warns Scrooge that he has to change his attitude toward life drastically and tells him he will be visited that same night by three other spirits. Scrooge does not know what is happening to him and does not believe Marley until the Spirit of Christmas Past appears before him. This spirit shows him his past as a lonely youth. He is then visited by the Spirit of Christmas Present, who shows him how poor people could also

---

103. Nieuwenhuis, *Johannes de ziener*, 238.

104. Cf. Zeph 3:16: "On that day they will say to Jerusalem, 'Do not fear, Zion; do not let your hands hang limp.'"

105. *B.W.*, s.v. "Ezel."

106. Nieuwenhuis, *Johannes de ziener*, 240.

be happy by being kind to others. To make this point, he takes him to the Christmas dinner his nephew Fred is hosting and the dinner the poor family of his employee Bob Cratchit enjoy. Scrooge's final visitor is the Spirit of Christmas Yet to Come, who takes him into the future, after he himself has already died. He discovers that no one mourns his death and that Tiny Tim, Bob Cratchit's handicapped child, has passed away.

Once he awakens in his bedroom, Scrooge realizes that he has to make a radical change in his life. He buys a turkey and presents and gives money to the poor. He visits his nephew Fred and offers him a position as a business partner. When Bob comes to work a little late the next morning, Scrooge feigns irritation and then surprises him by giving him a raise. He also becomes a second father to Tiny Tim, providing him with proper medical care.

What does "Visit" Mean in the Bible?

In the Bible we read that God also "visits" people/the people. The various phases in history are marked by the "visits" by God. The word "visit"[107] can mean both "visiting" in the social sense and "visitation." It can refer to God's mercy as well as his punishment. To put it in the simple words of the Sinterklaas song: "I've rods for the naughty; and sweets for the good."[108]

"Visitation" in biblical translations is often understood as "coming to a person's aid." God shows his mercy to the individual: the LORD looked after Hagar, the mother of Ishmael (Gen 16:13) *and* after Sarah, the mother of Isaac (Gen 21:1). When Joseph, the son of the patriarch Jacob, feels his end nearing, he says to his brothers: "I am about to die. But God will surely come to your aid [visit you] and take you up out of this land to the land he promised on oath to Abraham, Isaac and Jacob" (Gen 50:24). Joseph has his brothers, the "sons of Israel" (=Jacob), swear an oath just before he dies, saying: "God will surely come to your aid [visit you], and then you must carry my bones up from this place" (Gen 50:25).

When he is dying, Joseph realizes that the path of his people will correspond with the path that God has travelled with him: visited by God in a dream, in God's way and in God's own time. That visit is Israel's source of hope. A history that is not "visited" is not history, but Joseph knows that Israel's history will be visited in powerful and irresistible ways. The story of

---

107. Hebr. *quddâ*; Gr. *episkepsomai*.

108. From the Sinterklaas song "Zie ginds komt de stoomboot"; translation by Ruben 't Lam, Dutch Saint Nicholas songs translated into English; http://www.stnicholascenter.org/pages/zie-ginds-komt-de-stoomboot/.

Joseph ends in Egypt, anticipating the "visit from God." The storyteller is certain that the visit will take place.

"The visit from God created the possibility of a new beginning." Joseph, the viceroy of Egypt, dies but hopes for a new beginning, "a new Genesis."[109]

And God watched over the children of Israel in Egypt, visiting them: "I have watched over you and have seen what has been done to you in Egypt" (Exod 3:16). When Moses returns to Egypt to free his people after being called by God in the burning bush, together with his brother Aaron, he calls the elders of Israel together. Aaron reports on the words that the Lord spoke to Moses. "He also performed the signs before the people, and they believed. And when they heard that the Lord was concerned about them [visited them] and had seen their misery, they bowed down and worshipped" (Exod 4:30–31).

The same expression is used again during the time of exile: "This is what the Lord says: 'When seventy years are completed for Babylon, I will come to [visit] you and fulfil my good promise to bring you back to this place'" (Jer 29:10).

The prophet Zephaniah, an older contemporary of the prophet Jeremiah, anticipates the salvation of the Israelites in the future: God will "care" for (visit) them and restore them to their earlier state (Zeph 2:7).

Centuries later, the father of John the Baptist praises God in a hymn that begins: "Praise be to the Lord, the God of Israel, because he has come to [visited] his people and redeemed them" (Luke 1:68); and it ends: "because of the tender mercy of our God, by which the rising sun will come to [visit] us from heaven to shine on those living in darkness and in the shadow of death, to guide our feet into the path of peace" (Luke 1:78–79).

But visitation can also mean "punishment." Isaiah tells us so in the following poem:

> Woe to those who make unjust laws,
> > to those who issue oppressive decrees,
> to deprive the poor of their rights
> > and withhold justice from the oppressed of my people,
> making widows their prey
> > and robbing the fatherless.
> What will you do on the day of reckoning [of visitation],
> > when disaster comes from afar?
> To whom will you run for help?
> > Where will you leave your riches?
>
> (Isa 10:1–3)

---

109. According to Brueggemann, *Genesis*, 379.

The prophet understands his time as one in which making laws is the privilege of the powerful—specifically, laws that are to their advantage. But the day of visitation, the day of punishment, will come, for such actions will not remain unnoticed, unavenged, and without retribution. There will be a devastating storm (*shoah*) from which no one can find any safety, refuge, or shelter. Even the rich and the powerful will be forced to run and hide, abandoning their riches!

The Ten Commandments already declared that children would be punished (visited) for the sins of the parents to the third and fourth generation (Exod 20:5). This is a reflection of the view that father acts on behalf of his family; his sin is therefore also the sin of the entire family—to the third and fourth generation.

God shows His goodness, however, to "a thousand generations" (Exod 20:6; cf. the parallel text in Deut 7:9). This declares that God's mercy far exceeds his punitive justice or his visitation. His punishment is also directed at the sins of the heathen nations.[110]

Visits in the Qur'an

The Qur'an relates a parable about how God tests people. The owners of a garden swore they would pick the fruit of the garden in the early morning and did not add the qualification that that would only happen "Allah willing" (*in sha' Allâh*) (cf. James 4:15–16[111]).

> Then the Lord visited them while they were sleeping. And in the morning they discovered that everything in the whole garden had already been picked. They called to one another: "Go to your fields early if you want to harvest anything!" So they went, whispering to one another, "No needy person will enter your garden today." And they went early, determined to prevent any poor person from entering. But when they saw it, they said, "Surely we've lost our way." Or, rather: "We've been robbed!"

---

110. *KBS* on Exodus 20:5. Cf. *KBS* on Exodus 34:7: "He punishes the children and their children for the sin of the parents to the third and fourth generation." Cf. Deuteronomy 5:9. *KBS*, on Deuteronomy 7:9–10, says that the sinner will be punished personally. "Know therefore that the Lord your God is God; he is the faithful God, keeping his covenant of love to a thousand generations of those who love him and keep his commandments. But those who hate him he will repay to their face by destruction; he will not be slow to repay to their face those who hate him" (Deut 7:9–10). *B.W.*, s.v. "bezoeking"; Kittel, II *Th.W.*, ii, 595–604. Cf. Schuman, *Gelijk om gelijk*.

111. "Instead, you ought to say, 'If it is the Lord's will, we will live and do this or that.' As it is, you boast in your arrogant schemes. All such boasting is evil."

The most thoughtful of them said, "Didn't I tell you, 'Why don't you praise God?'" They said, "Glory be to God, our Lord; truly we have done evil." And they turned to one another, blaming each other. They said, "Woe to us! Truly, we have been insolent. Maybe God will give us something better than the garden. We humbly turn to our Lord." (Q 68:17–32)

The Arabic word that is translated as "visit" makes one think of a "spiritual appearance" of sorts, like the spirit of Marley that visited Scrooge. The word can be explained as a kind of visitation by a supernatural being.[112] Some theologians insist that it was a form of whispering or a low voice that was heard and incited people to act. Others believe that it was Satan who visits people in the form of emotions such as anger or jealousy. This parable of the "visit" by the Lord (Q 68:19) was originally aimed at the unbelieving inhabitants of Mecca, but it still holds an important message for each listener and reader today.[113]

"It's all a parable with a more than earthly mystery"

The title of this section is borrowed (in translation) from a hymn by Jan Wit[114] that links up with Paul's words in 1 Timothy 3:16: "The mystery from which true godliness springs is great." That expression is derived from a word that refers to closing or shutting one's mouth, lips, thus "silence." A *mysterion* is something one must be silent about after one has been initiated into it.[115]

"Great is the mystery of faith" is a phrase that is used in the liturgy of the church, but it could also be used for various faiths: the mystery of Israel,[116] the mystery of Ishmael,[117] or the mystery of the faith of countless people, no matter which faith they have (or do not have).
If we attempt to understand what the Bible and the Qur'an say about "God," would silence not be a sign of deeper piety than talking about God? Does it not involve a "hidden mystery," (initially) requiring silence, awe, respect and fear? Is it not still a hiddenness, a mystery, whose veil can be removed so that a revelation (apocalypse) can take place?

---

112. Paret, *Der Koran: Kommentar*, on Q 7:201. For the terms *tâifî* and *tâfa*, see Paret, *Der Koran: Kommentar*, on Q 68:19–20.
113. *E.Q.*, s.v. "Visiting."
114. Cf. Hymn 978:3 from the *Liedboek: Zingen en bidden in huis en kerk*.
115. Zenger, *Stuttgarter Psalter*, 156.
116. Gilet, *Communion*, 211.
117. Cf. Hayek, *Le Mystère*.

II

Abraham Visited by Three Strangers

One would want to know more since all life, all thought and action of Louis Massignon was changed by this visitation by the Stranger, by the conversion that followed and by the memory of the sacred Muslim hospitality to what he thinks he owed his life.[1]

Introduction

What do we understand by the term "stranger" and how should we deal with the person we consider a stranger? Who is that stranger? Abraham, the father of all believers—in whom Jews, Christians, *and* Muslims have their spiritual if not physical origin—is an example par excellence, looking at the hospitality he gave to the three strangers in his tent. Following in his footsteps was his nephew Lot, who received these same strangers in Sodom, where he was living, at great risk to himself and his family. In the East, hospitality has been of old a sacred thing because some, without knowing it, have welcomed *angels* (Hebr 13:2) or even God himself.

The Israelites have always remained conscious of the fact that they are descended from nomads and have never been ashamed of that. A distinction was made between donkey nomads and camel nomads, with the latter being considered more aggressive.[2] They often forgot their origins as soon as they found some place to settle. This was true for the Canaanites, Assyrians, and Phoenicians, nomads who left few traces behind. The latter ceased to use the names typically found among nomads, such as "sons of."

---

1. Massignon, *L'hospitalité Sacrée*, 42.
2. Attema, *Arabië*, 50.

This custom, however, was continued among the Israelites: *bene Israel, bene Ja'akob*, or *Banû Isra'îl* in Arabic.³

The patriarchs Abraham, Isaac, and Jacob were true nomads with small livestock, travelling around limited areas with their herds. Typical of all nomads is that they are constantly on guard against confrontations with other groups that may dispute their grazing areas or attack them outright. Naturally, they themselves also tended to raid in order to safeguard their existence. We can think of Ishmael here, about whom it was said: "He will be a wild donkey of a man; his hand will be against everyone and everyone's hand against him, and he will live in hostility toward all his brothers" (Gen 16:12).⁴ Ishmael's descendants were nomads who were compared to wild donkeys because of their independence and their nomadic existence.⁵

One day, Abram (Abraham) the Hebrew received the message that his "brother" Lot had been captured. Abram summoned all the experienced men (318 of them) in his household to arm themselves, and he pursued his enemies up to the city of Dan in the north. Together with his servants, he attacked them by night from all sides, defeated them and pursued them north of Damascus. He recaptured all of his goods, brought back Lot and his possessions as well as the women and military personnel (Gen 14:14–16). Esau, Jacob's brother, attacked Jacob one time with four hundred armed men (Gen 32:6).⁶

The name "the God of Abraham, the God of Isaac, the God of Jacob" also reminds us of how nomads usually spoke of their gods.

Nomads have a great respect for hospitality, which is invaluable for those living in a steppe or desert area. Without it, travelling, migrating and trading would be practically impossible. Nomads receive their guests with great ceremony. "The law of hospitality is so prominent that, more than anything else, it gives desert people the awareness that they need to follow nobler laws to follow than people in permanent settlements, where people often seek hospitality in vain. Everywhere in the desert, receiving and being generous to strangers is an unquestioned practice."⁷ The hospitality shown

---

3. Ibid., 51.

4. Dumah and Tema are listed among his descendants, together with their ten brothers: twelve sovereigns of twelve tribes (Gen 25:12–18).

5. Cf. *NIV*. See also Job 39:5–8: "Who let the wild donkey go free? Who untied its ropes? I gave it the wasteland as its home, the salt flats as its habitat. It laughs at the commotion in the town; it does not hear a driver's shout. It ranges the hills for its pasture and searches for any green thing." Cf. *KBS* on Genesis 16:12: "A wild donkey will not allow itself to be tamed."

6. Attema, *Arabië*, 51.

7. Attema, *Arabië*, 56–57.

by the poor is the most striking. The poorest people will slaughter their last sheep for their guest and not allow him to see anything of their own poverty and troubles. They expect no gratitude for the hospitality offered and wish to prove their generosity to their guest and make his stay a pleasant one. They are prepared to give up everything they possess. The question as to whether we could speak of a *nomadic ideal* among Israel's prophets is answered as follows: "If there is anything in the prophets that recalls the nomadic period, it is the idea of being under way, being directed toward the future, but then with the condition of 'being *comforted* on the way' because the promises of YHWH, which are irrevocable, shine on the dark present."[8]

Gods as Strangers in Classical Literature

Stories about gods who visit people as strangers can be found all over the world. The visit by a stranger is of vital importance and decisive for the one who is visited. After all, the stranger comes from another (part of the) world and brings a message from there. That is the starting point of a series of events initiated by someone from afar. The New Testament alludes to an example from classical antiquity. When the apostle Paul and Barnabas healed people in Lystra, south of Iconium (today's Konya in Turkey, where the very illustrious Jalâl al-Dîn Rûmî is buried), they were viewed as gods: "The gods have come down to us in human form! Barnabas they called Zeus, and Paul they called Hermes because he was the chief speaker" (Acts 14:11–12; cf. 28:1–6).[9] Two examples from classical literature are Homer's *Odyssey* and Ovid's *Metamorphoses*.

Odysseus as a Stranger in his Own House

During Odysseus' long absence during and after the Trojan War—thus *before* he returns home to his wife Penelope and his son Telemachus—his palace is filled with "suitors." One of Penelope's suitors, Antinous, conceives of a plan to kill Telemachus. But the plan fails. When Odysseus then appears incognito in the palace, as a beggar, Antinous speaks to him:

> "Sit and eat in peace, sir," Antinous retorted, "or take yourself elsewhere. Otherwise your freedom of speech will end in our

---

8. Ibid., 61.

9. Westermann, *Genesis 12–36*, 276–77; Haenchen, *Die Apostelgeschichte*, 367–68; Stählin, *Die Apostelgeschichte*, 191.

young men dragging you out of the place by the leg or arm and flaying you from head to foot.

But the rest of them felt the utmost indignation, and the general sense was expressed by one young gallant who said: "Antinous, you did wrong to strike the wretched vagabond. You're a doomed man if he turns out to be some god from heaven. And the gods do disguise themselves as strangers from abroad, and wander our towns in every kind of shape to see whether people are behaving themselves or getting out of hand."[10]

Philemon and Baucis Visited by Two Strangers

One day, the pious and aged Phrygian Philemon and his wife Baucis receive a visit from two strangers, two travelers. They do not know that it is the god Zeus or Jupiter and his messenger Mercury or Hermes. The name Zeus (Xenios), the patron of hospitality, proves that "hospitality" is protected by God and any violation of it is regarded as a crime (cf. Gen 19:5–14.; Judg 19:16–30).[11]

While rich and prominent people shut their doors to them, both of these old people, despite their poverty, offer hospitality. They receive the guests with open arms and provide them with a delicious meal. When the pitcher of wine does not empty, it becomes apparent that there is something special about these guests. To pamper their guests, they decide to kill their only goose. Baucis chases it, but the goose keeps eluding her. When the goose sits on the lap of the supreme deity, the visitors reveal their identities as Zeus and Hermes. This old couple has offered hospitality to the gods while the rest of the village turned them away. Zeus and Hermes ask whether Philemon and Baucis have a wish that the gods can fulfil as thanks for the hospitality they enjoyed. Philemon and Baucis say that they desire nothing other than to devote their lives to the two gods, upon which their small hut suddenly changes into a large temple. They also both passionately desire to live together and express the wish that they both die at the same time. Philemon and Baucis thus stand in front of the temple one day, changed into an oak tree and a linden tree. And there they stood for many years, their trunks entwined.[12]

Ovid tells the story in a similar way in his *Metamorphoses*:

---

10. Homer, *The Odyssey*, book XVII, 477–78 (p. 271).
11. *RGG*, s.v. "Gastfreundschaft" (J. de Vries).
12. Ovid, *Metamorphoses*, book 8.

Jupiter visited this place, disguised as a mortal, and Mercury, the god who carries the magic wand, laid aside his wings and accompanied his father. The two gods went to a thousand homes, looking for somewhere to rest, and found a thousand homes bolted and barred against them. However, one house took them in: it was, indeed, a humble dwelling roofed with thatch and reeds from the marsh, but a good-hearted old woman, Baucis by name, and her husband Philemon, who was the same age as his wife, had been married in that cottage in their youth, and had grown grey in it together. By confessing their poverty and accepting it contentedly, they had eased the hardship of their lot" (VIII, 626–34).

As the dinner went on, the old man and woman saw that the flagon as often as it was emptied, refilled itself of its own accord, and Baucis and Philemon were awed and afraid. Timidly stretching out their hands in prayer, they begged the gods' indulgence for a poor meal, without any elaborate preparations. They had a single goose, which acted as guardian of their little croft: in honor of their divine visitors, they were making ready to kill the bird, but with the help of its swift wings it eluded its owner for a long time, and tired them out, for age made them slow. At last it seemed to take refuge with the gods themselves, who declared that it should not be killed. "We are gods," they said, "and this wicked neighborhood is going to be punished as it richly deserves; but you will be allowed to escape this disaster. All you have to do is leave your home, and climb up the steep mountainside with us." The two old people both did as they were told and, leaning on their sticks, struggled up the long slope.

When they were a bowshot distant from the top, they looked round and saw all the rest of their country drowned in marshy waters, only their own home left standing. As they gazed in astonishment, and wept for the fate of their people, their old cottage, which had been small, even for two, was changed into a temple. (VIII, 679–700)

Then Saturn's son spoke in majestic tones: "Tell me, my good old man, and you, who are a worthy wife for your good husband, what would you like from me?" Philemon and Baucis consulted together for a little, and then the old man told the gods what they both wished. "We ask to be your priests, to serve your shrine; and since we have lived in happy companionship all our lives, we pray that death carry us off together at the same instant, so that I may never see my wife's funeral, and she may never have to bury me." Their prayer was granted. They looked after the temple as long as they lived.

Then, one day, bowed down with their weight of years, they were standing before the sacred steps, talking of all that had happened there, when Baucis saw Philemon beginning to put forth leaves, and old Philemon saw Baucis growing leafy too. When the tree-tops were already growing over their two faces, they exchanged their last words while they could, and cried simultaneously: "Good-bye, my dear one!" As they spoke, the bark grew over and concealed their lips. The Bithynian peasant still points out the trees growing there side by side, trees that were once two bodies. This tale was told me by responsible old men, who had nothing to gain by deceiving me. Indeed, I myself have seen the wreaths hanging on the branches, and have hung up fresh ones, saying: "Whom the gods love are gods themselves, and those who have worshipped should be worshipped too." (VIII, 703–24)[13]

In the Middle Ages, Ovid's story was often told as a counterpart to the story of Abraham and Lot. The theme is described in later literature (in the satiric poems of De la Fontaine) and depicted in operas by Hayden (*Pfeffel*, 1773) and Gounod (*Barbier and Carré*, 1860). Rembrandt painted the welcoming of the gods in the humble hut in a composition that resembles the story of Jesus and the travelers on the road to Emmaus. While they are on their way to Emmaus after Jesus' crucifixion, they are suddenly joined by a stranger who walks with them without their recognizing him. When Jesus asks them what they are so talking about so intensely, one of them replies: "Are you the only stranger in Jerusalem?" (Luke 24:13–18).[14]

The Stranger in the Torah

An important word used in the Old Testament for stranger is the Hebrew word *ger*, of which the oral Jewish tradition mentions two types. The first is the *ger tzedek*, those who have joined the people of Israel. Ruth, the Moabitess, is the classic example of this type. She says to her mother-in-law Naomi: "Your people will be my people and your God my God" (Ruth 1:16). The second type is the *ger toshav*, a resident stranger who has chosen to live in the country without converting but is prepared instead to adhere to the Noachian commandments written for the whole of humankind. The

13. Cf. Ovid, *Metamorphoses*, 610–13 (pp. 195–98).
14. Moorman and Uitterhoeve, *Van Achilles tot Zeus*, 219.

ger toshav law represents the biblical form of the "rights of minorities."[15] The seven requirements of the Noachian commandments were established by the synagogue that was built after the exile. They are: the dispensation of justice, the commandments concerning idolatry, blasphemy, injustice, murder, robbery, and eating the meat of an animal while it is still alive. In contrast to the law given on Mount Sinai, these laws obtain for all peoples and must serve as a kind of natural law that is the foundation for the responsibility of these people in the sight of God.[16]

"Do not oppress a foreigner; you yourselves know how it feels to be foreigners, because you were foreigners in Egypt" (Exod 23:9). The Bible is very strict about protecting the stranger against injustice (Deut 24:17; 27:19). Warnings against doing evil to a stranger occur in 16 or 46 places in the Torah.[17]

The primary experience of social need by the children of Israel is that they themselves were oppressed in a strange land (Egypt). That experience alone is sufficient to induce them to never oppress a stranger, allowing for empathy with the stranger's "soul" (Exod 23:9), to understand how the stranger feels. The soul[18] actually refers to the "throat," *the* body part of life. One breathes, eats, drinks, and speaks with the throat, which is why "soul" can also be translated as "life." When one can no longer do all of this—breathe, eat, and drink—he or she dies. The "soul" is the organ of the hunger and passion for life, and if this organ is hindered or obstructed in any way, the person or animal dies.[19] Having that basic experience is the basis for every true social conviction. This is why "the foreigner who lives in your land" must not be treated badly. He has the same rights as one born an Israelite, as a native, as an indigenous—to use a more modern term—person. Yes, we must love the stranger as we love ourselves: "When a foreigner resides among you in your land, do not mistreat them. The foreigner residing among you must be treated as your native-born. Love them as yourself, for you were foreigners in Egypt. I am the Lord your God" (Lev 19:33–34).[20] In the Naarden Bible by Pieter Oussoren, this reads (translated from Dutch): "And suppose there is a foreigner in your country: you shall not make his life miserable. Just as your descendants are, so shall the stranger be in your

---

15. Sacks, *Covenant and Conversation*, 179–80.

16. B.W., s.v. "Noachitische geboden/Noachian commandments." The Apostolic Decree or the "Apostolic Council" (Acts 15:20, 29) contains similar requirements.

17. Sacks, *Covenant and Conversation*, 181.

18. *Nephesh* (Hebr.), *nafs* (Ar.): "soul," especially a living person. *Nafs* has the same meaning, E.I., s.v. "nafs." Cf. *tanaffasa*: "breathing." Ambros.

19. Zenger, *Stuttgarter Psalter*, 270, 576.

20. Fischer, *Das Buch Exodus*, 257. Cf. Deuteronomy 10:19.

country: you shall love him as you love yourself, for you were strangers in the land of Egypt; I, the One God, am your God!" (Lev 19:33–34). Indeed, even the Egyptians and Edomites were not to be abhorred or detested, for the children of Israel were themselves strangers in their country (Deut 23:7). The Egyptians were given preferential treatment because they were Israel's hosts when Joseph went to Egypt (Rashi).[21]

Naturally, it is very understandable, according to Rabbi Jonathan Sacks, that the Israelites would carry their feelings of revenge and hatred out of Egypt. In their defense, it could be said that they even have a right to it. But this short command to treat the Egyptians hospitably bears witness to a deep insight. Any people that fosters revenge and continues to hate cannot be truly free. If they carried with them the burden of hatred and the desire for revenge, Moses may have taken the people out of Egypt, but he would not have taken "Egypt out of the children of Israel." There is a fundamental difference between living with the past and living in the past. Do not oppress the stranger, the Torah commands, because you know what it is like to be a stranger. Do not do to another what you yourself have suffered, do not impose that on him. The memory of what it was like to be a stranger is a moral lesson. Thinking back to the past is done so as not to repeat it: "Remember not to hate."[22]

The Traveler as the Preeminent Stranger (the Qur'an)

An expression that comes close to "stranger" in the Qur'an is the "son of the way" (*ibn al-sabīl*). People are called to treat parents and relatives, the orphans and the poor, neighbors far and near and the *son of the way* well (Q 4:36; cf. 17:26; 30:38).[23] The most inclusive definition of "the fear of the Lord" is: "Piety does not consist in turning your face to the east or to the west. True piety consists much more in believing in God, the final judgment, the angels, the Scripture, and the prophets, and giving one's money and goods, despite one's love for them, to one's family and the orphans, the destitute and the son of the way. Piety is shown by those who are patient in times of violence and whenever they have entered into a commitment, and who only are honest and God-fearing" (Q 2:177).[24] Jews and Muslims most certainly know the direction in which to pray toward Jerusalem and Mecca,

---

21. Lundbom, *Deuteronomium*, 650.
22. Sacks, *Covenant and Conversation*, 93.
23. Cf. Q 2:177; 8:41; 59:7; 2:215; 30:38; 24:22; 4:8; 16:90; 90:13–16; 78:8; 89:17–19; 69:34; 107:2–3; 74:44.
24. Cf. Paret's translation in *Der Koran: Übersetzung* and E.Q. s.v. "Piety."

but those directions were also somewhat arbitrary. After all, east and west belong to God. The decisive factor is whether we are on the path of God (Q 2:142). True piety is not simply a formality but the fulfilment of what God has commanded, the *performance* of the commandments, as Jesus states in the Sermon on the Mount: "Not everyone who says to me, 'Lord, Lord,' will enter the kingdom of heaven, but only the one who does the will of my Father who is in heaven" (Matt 7:21). And the commandments are particularly emphasized in the Qur'an (Q 2:177).

Particular attention must be paid to the second part "the way *of God*" in the phrase "son *of the way*." Believers, the God-fearing people who follow Muhammad's preaching, struggle along "on the road of God." Putting everything on the line for it could lead to our mistreatment because our adversaries attempt to lure us from that way of God or to stray from it through persuasion, pressure, or even violence. Seen in this light, the "son of the way" is therefore someone who follows the way of God, come what may. One can think of the followers of the prophet Muhammad from the poorer strata of the population of Mecca and who, upon their conversion to Islam, became completely destitute and without means of supporting themselves (cf. Q 24:22) and thus needed special care. They were usually forced to go away and had to do without the support of their family and tribe.[25]

When Muhammad, who had been driven out of Mecca himself, fled to Medina with his friend and companion Abû Bakr, they were forced to seek refuge in a cave for a while to hide from his Meccan adversaries who were pursuing them. Muhammad then said to his companion: "'Do not be anxious; God is with us.' Then God sent down His peace[26] and strengthened him with legions they did not see" (Q 9:40). The verse that follows relates a call issued to all believers to turn out, lightly or heavily armed, and to *dedicate themselves to the way of God* with all their possessions and their selves (Q 9:41).[27]

Hospitality in the Bible and the Qur'an

One condition for dealing with strangers is hospitality. Abraham and Lot are both examples of this. Hospitality entails offering shelter, washing the strangers' feet and feeding them. In arguing against his friends, Job says that they can testify that no stranger ever had to sleep outside and his door was

---

25. Paret, *Der Koran: Kommentar*, on Q 2:177, 38. E.Q., s.v. "Strangers and Foreigners." Cf. E.Q., s.v. "Justice and Injustice."

26. *sakîna*. Cf. *Schechina* in Hebrew.

27. *wa-jâhidû fî sabîli llâhi*.

always open to travelers (Job 31:31–32). Hospitality also entails that guests can count on protection and the right of asylum. It was viewed as a great virtue to insist on that in one's invitation, as Lot did. He did his utmost to have the strangers stay with him (Gen 19:3).

Offering no hospitality was a major offense (Judg 19:15). An example of this is given in the city of Gibeah, in the book of Judges. King Saul had come from that city and resided there as king (1 Sam 15:34; 22:6). Before Israel had kings, the refrain "each did what was good in their own eyes" (Judg 2:11; 3:7, 12) was often heard during the time of the judges. This happened in Gibeah. The hospitality that one of the inhabitants had offered was abused rather crudely: "While they were enjoying themselves, some of the wicked men of the city surrounded the house. Pounding on the door, they shouted to the old man who owned the house, 'Bring out the man who came to your house so we can have sex [know] with him.' The owner of the house went outside and said to them, 'No, my friends, don't be so vile. Since this man is my guest, don't do this outrageous thing'" (Judg 19:22–23). The host is prepared to go very far to prove his hospitality: "Look, here is my virgin daughter, and his concubine. I will bring them out to you now, and you can use them and do to them whatever you wish. But as for this man, don't do such an outrageous thing" (Judg 19:24). Refusing hospitality was viewed as an even greater sin.[28] Apparently, nothing would be spared in protecting and providing for a guest, even if that meant allowing one's own daughters to be abused. This becomes shockingly clear in the story of Lot as well, who was also prepared to allow his daughters to be abused to protect the strangers who were threatened (Gen 19:8). A desert adage says: "The guest shall be more valuable than your father."[29]

When Jesus was invited to dine with one of the leaders of the Pharisees, he noticed how those invited sought out the seats of honor. Then he told his host the following parable: "When you give a luncheon or dinner, do not invite your friends, your brothers or sisters, your relatives, or your rich neighbors; if you do, they may invite you back and so you will be repaid. But when you give a banquet, invite the poor, the crippled, the lame, the blind, and you will be blessed. Although they cannot repay you, you will be repaid at the resurrection of the righteous" (Luke 14:12–14).

Paul encouraged the church in Rome very urgently and pointedly to practice hospitality (Rom 12:13). Instead of waiting until strangers ask for help, one must take the initiative oneself and apply oneself to their needs. His letter shows how the Greek-Roman and Jewish ethic of hospitality is

---

28. *KBS* on Judges 19:23.
29. Attema, *Arabië*, 57.

given new life. No reward is expected from the guests and there are no requirements of good behavior. It does not matter whether the hospitality involves Jew, heathen, Greek or barbarian. There is no ulterior motive for providing hospitality to strangers. Given the importance of the ideal, the right to hospitality (*ius hospitii*), *and* the connection with piety (*pietas*) in the Roman cultural environment, Paul could count on the acceptance of this being an implication of love. The emphasis on this habit of hospitality was an important factor in the success of the community in the Roman environment! For a large number of Jewish Christians and other leaders who had returned to Rome after the edict of Caesar Claudius had been lifted—an edict that had provoked conflicts and animosity—there was a concrete need for this type of hospitality that characterized the Jesus movement and early Christianity.[30]

This is why Paul writes that the leader of a community (*ecclesia*) is expected to be hospitable (1 Tim 3:2; cf. 5:10), and he insists that hospitality is not to be neglected.[31] Thus some have unknowingly hosted angels. For the "some" here we can think of Abraham and Sarah (Gen 18:2–15), Lot (Gen 19:1–4), Menoah, the "father of Samson" (Judg 6:11–18; 13:3–22) and Tobias (Tob 12:1–20).[32]

God as the Host

In the famous twenty-third Psalm, "The LORD is my shepherd," the psalmist compares God with a host—and one who never ceases being a host (Ps 23:6). Then he is truly granted the opportunity to live and acquire new strength: to eat, drink, *and* to rest, by resting in green pastures and being led to quiet waters (Ps 23:2–3). The one praying is the lucky guest in the safe house of a Host who turns to him in person.

The connection between the image of shepherd and host can also be found in the description of the journey of the children of Israel through the desert. The question is asked: "Can God really spread a table in the wilderness? True, he struck the rock, and water gushed out, streams flowed abundantly, but can he also give us bread? Can he supply meat for his people?" (Ps 78:19–20). He rained down manna for the people to eat, he gave them the grain of heaven (Ps 78:24; cf. Exod 16, Num 11:6–9). "He brought his people out like a flock,/ like sheep through the wilderness./ He guided them safely, and they were unafraid;/ but the sea engulfed their enemies./ Thus he

---

30. According to Jewett, *Romans*, 765, who cites a series of studies.
31. B.W. s.v., "Hospitality." *Bijbelse Encyclopaedie*, s.v. "Gast."
32. Attridge, *The Epistle*, 386.

brought them to the border of his holy land,/ to the hill country his right hand had taken (Ps 78:52–54).

The meal that the host provides for the psalmist is a feast. Upon being received, he was first—as a mark of honor—anointed with oil in front of his enemies who threatened him and from whom the host offered him protection. We could also think of a feast following a rescue from the psalmist's enemies. Then he is truly granted sanctuary at that moment! The luxury of the meal is obvious not only from the anointing but also from the cup overflowing with wine.

Those who partook in the Exodus from Egypt expressed their doubt as to whether God could spread a table in the wilderness, could give bread and supply meat (Ps 78:19–20). The psalmist, however, experiences God as being able to provide him with the classic gifts of the promised land: bread, wine, *and* oil (Jer 31:12; Hos 2:7). He sees God as the one who can prepare all of creation: "He makes grass grow for the cattle, plants for people to cultivate—bringing forth food from the earth: wine that gladdens human hearts, oil to make their faces shine, and bread that sustains their hearts" (Ps 104:14–15).[33]

Even before the arrival of Islam, Arab society was familiar with extensive generosity and hospitality. The harshness of the environment of the desert and the serious danger of physical harm that threatened travelers without the protection of one's own tribe was mitigated by the custom of the three obligatory days of hospitality.

The Qur'an regards miserliness, hoarding, and neglecting the needs of the poor as the greatest moral shortcomings. Those who do not feed the poor will be condemned at the last judgment (Q 69:34; cf. 74:44; 89:18). There are repeated calls to be generous and to give alms (Q 2:215, 274, 280; 13:22; 22:35; 35:29; 57:7; 58:12; 76:8; 90:14–16), preferably in secret (Q 2:271; 4:38). In the Medinese period, the focus on giving alms (*zakât*) guaranteed that the poor and *travelers* would be cared for: charity had to be shown to the poor, to those hindered in their journey along the way of God (Q 2:273; cf. 2:215; 9:60).[34]

Rembrandt and the Three Strangers

Rembrandt produced various paintings of the three strangers who came to visit Abraham. It is fascinating that Rembrandt allowed himself to be influenced by various cultures, both Jewish and Islamic, in his work. That

33. Hossfeld and Zenger, *Die Psalmen*, 155–56.
34. *sabîl Allâh. E.Q.*, s.v. "Hospitality and Courtesy."

Rembrandt used models from his own Jewish surroundings for his biblical paintings and borrowed inspiration from people of the "Jewish quarter" in Amsterdam is well known.[35] He was inspired by the proximity of "the people of the book." "The eager contemplation of the small piece of Eastern reality of Amsterdam's Jewish quarter gave his expansive and lush imagination ample material for an eastern biblical world that no artist before him had displayed."[36] He maintained good relationships with prominent figures in the Sephardic Jewish community, such as Mennasse ben Israel, the Jewish doctor Ephraim Bueno, and Alphonso Lopez. The latter was a collector of Indian and Eastern art, which also interested Rembrandt greatly.[37] Rembrandt etched the portrait of his Jewish neighbor, the humanistically inclined scholar Mennasse ben Israel who, together with Spinoza, was one of the most famous figures of the Jewish community in Amsterdam at that time.

Menasse was born to Marrano parents—Jews in Spain who had been forced to convert to Roman Catholicism—who had moved to Amsterdam. After his schooling, he became a rabbi in the Portuguese Israeli community when he was only eighteen. He was also the first printer of Hebrew books in Amsterdam. Menasse enjoyed a certain prestige in Christian circles and was a source of information on theological questions for Christians. He was friends with Hugo the Great and two illustrious Remonstrant exiles: Gerardus Johannes Vossius, rector of and professor of history at the recently established Athenaeum Illustre in Amsterdam—an alternative to the University of Leiden—and Casparus Barlaeus, scholar, preacher, and professor of logic.

Menasse asked Rembrandt to make some illustrations for his cabbalist work *Piedra Gloriosa o de la estatua de Nebuchadnesar* (*The Glorious Stone*,[38] or *On the Statue of Nebuchadnezzar*), written in Spanish in 1655. The book explained Nebuchadnezzar's dream, in which he saw a huge statue that was shattered while he watched by a stone that had come loose without the help of any human hand (Dan 2:31–35). According to Menasse, this stone was the same as the one Jacob used for a pillow when he dreamt of a ladder that connected heaven and earth (Gen 28). This "glorious stone" is the Messiah, at whose coming the kingdom of Israel would be established. Rembrandt worked closely with the rabbi while he was making the illustrations. It is said that Rembrandt's etchings for this book were later replaced

---

35. Cf. Landsberger, cited by Visser 't Hooft, *Rembrandts weg*, 92.
36. Romein, *Erflaters*, 336.
37. Schama, *De ogen*, 432.
38. Cf. the designation of "rocks" for Christ (the Messiah).

by less imaginative illustrations by the Jewish artist, Salom Italia. According to Simon Schama, the fact that Menassse sent the Rembrandt edition of the book to the Leiden theologian Vossius, to whom he dedicated the book, shows that he had not rejected the strange and ghostly figures his friend had made.[39]

In the seventeenth century, the Mughal miniatures became famous in the Netherlands. Collectors used these drawings as part of their all-encompassing "world documentation." Nicolaas Witsen (1641–1717), regent, diplomat, and often mayor of Amsterdam, had an album full of them. The library of the stadtholder William III contained pictures of these Indian sovereigns. The inventory of Rembrandt's possessions in 1656 included an album with more than twenty of these miniatures. These pictures served as an example for Rembrandt and were an inspiration for his own art.[40]

An example of that Mughal influence can be seen in his *Abraham Serving the Three Angels* (1656). In addition to the general composition, there are some details that he borrows from the Mughal miniatures, including the imposing *white beard* of the figure of God, the *goblet* Abraham holds in his right hand, and the *dish* in the foreground of the painting.[41] The three angels are sitting in a lotus position or cross-legged on the ground. Abraham is at a much lower level and serves his guests. Two of the three men have wings. The figure on the left with his fist pointing to the ground just barely allows a glimpse of his folded wings. There is bread in the bowl. At the top left, Sarah, Abraham's wife, is listening. In the top center, a boy is aiming his bow and arrow at Ishmael. Ishmael is reported to have lived in the desert when he grew up and became a proficient archer (Gen 21:20).[42] "God" sits in the center, without wings and with the traditional appearance of an old man with a beard. With his one hand he raises a goblet and with his other he makes an inviting gesture toward the bowl with bread between himself and Abraham.[43]

---

39. Schama, *De ogen*, 609–10. See the picture in Schama's book. Rabbi Edward van Volen questions the commission Menasse supposedly gave Rembrandt. It is said that the four etchings are included in only three copies. These publications are located in the university library in Leiden. I follow Schama's explanation here.

40. Cf. Akveld and Jacobs, *Nationaal Jubileumboek*, 179.

41. Cf. Bikker and Weber, *Late Rembrandt*, 96–97.

42. Spijkerboer, *Rembrandts engel*, 20.

43. Or is he pointing to Abraham? Cf. Tümpel, *Rembrandt*, 34–35.

Abraham with the Three Angels (Marc Chagall)

At the center of Marc Chagall's *Abraham and the Three Angels* are stripes and lines that indicate a tent. The visit takes place at the hottest time of the day. Three men appear in the Mamre forest at Hebron, where Abraham and Sarah have set up their tent (Gen 18:1–15). Their sudden arrival shows that the visit is unexpected. The three remain standing before Abraham, which is an eastern way of "knocking."[44]

Sarah is on the very left. Under her feet is a paradise tree or a life tree, and under it a basket overflowing with exotic fruits, a symbol of fertility. Abraham is dressed in a caftan-like blue garment, matching the color of the garment of the angel on the right. The gold on his wings and the gold halo around his head obviously places this angel as the speaker in the foreground. The figure of Abraham has a white aureole around it. At the top of the painting is an open door and the small red camel rider marks the beginning of Abraham's journey, his Exodus from Mesopotamia (Gen 12:1).

Three angels are in the center of the painting, seated at a richly covered table. The angel in the middle and the one on the left have turned their faces so that they are looking at the viewer, thus including them in the event. The angels bring an incredible message: Abraham and Sarah—despite their age—will have a son. At the top right, in a circular area, the history of Abraham's intercession for Sodom is depicted (Gen 18:16–33). Abraham is clothed in a green garment between the three angels, the two behind him supporting him with their hands. The foremost angel, with three wings and his right hand over his heart, looks at Abraham with great concern. He stands next to the house of Sodom, and the orange light above the houses represents the fire that will destroy the city. On the right side of the painting is a lamb, possibly a reference to the suffering Servant of God who "will be led like a lamb to the slaughter" (Isa 53:7). Under the lamb is another angel, pointing to images of hope positioned on the right side of the painting: the tree of paradise and the bird of paradise. The houses of Chagall's hometown Vitebsk are included in the hopeful image on the lower right.[45]

Leaving Ur (Babel), leaving Vitebsk, leaving Paris—Chagall has put all of this into the same picture. When he was in America, not only Paris but his hometown as well was occupied by the Nazis.

One of the reasons for Chagall's fascination with Abraham and the angels was Andrei Rublev's icon of the Holy Trinity.[46]

---

44. Westermann, *Genesis 3*, 277.
45. *Bijbel met werken van Marc Chagall*, quotes 7, 8.
46. Wullschlager, *Chagall*, 351.

Abraham Shows Hospitality

The opening scene of the visit by the three strangers to Abraham in the Bible begins with the appearance of the LORD: "The LORD appeared to Abraham near the great trees of Mamre while he was sitting at the entrance to his tent in the heat of the day" (Gen 18:1).[47] An angel of the LORD travelled at the head of the Israelite procession during their journey through the desert (Exod 33:2) as the external manifestation in which the LORD revealed himself to the people, barely distinguishable from the LORD himself. The glory of the LORD was also revealed to the prophet Ezekiel in the form of a human (Ezek 1:26). The angel of YHWH could be a disguise for the LORD (Isa 6:1).[48] In the story of Abraham and the three strangers, the angel of the LORD is singular, the other two angels are his companions. They are sent on to Lot on their own mission.[49] After the three have brought the news to Sarah and Abraham, Abraham went for a walk with his guests. "Then the LORD said [again, the storyteller reveals that this is God], 'Shall I hide from Abraham what I am about to do?'" (Gen 18:17). "Then the LORD said, 'The outcry against Sodom and Gomorrah is so great and their sin so grievous that I will go down and see if what they have done is as bad as the outcry that has reached me. If not, I will know'" (Gen 18:20–21). "The men turned away [apparently two of the three] and went toward Sodom, but Abraham remained standing before the LORD [one of the three]" (Gen 18:23). "When the LORD had finished speaking with Abraham, he left, and Abraham returned home" (Gen 18:33).

The visit of the two angels to Lot is discussed next. They arrive in Sodom in the evening (Gen 19:1). The story of the strangers who visit Abraham and Lot therefore has two parts. They have two tasks to fulfil: the first is the announcement of a new beginning, the promise of the birth of a son that runs as a leitmotif throughout the entire Abraham cycle.[50] Second, they also have to announce the destruction of Sodom and Gomorrah: the cries of those who were being treated unjustly there had reached heaven.[51]

These tasks are also found in the Qur'an: the *first reason* for the visit of the guests is the announcement of the birth of a son, glad tidings (*bushrâ*) (Q 11:69; 29:31), the *second* is the announcement of the destruction of the cities because their inhabitants are committing injustices (Q 29:31–32).

47. Brueggemann, *Genesis*, 157.
48. *KBS* on Genesis 16:7.
49. *B.W.*, s.v. "Engel."
50. Westermann, *Genesis 12–36*, 279–80.
51. Ibid., 290.

It is made clear right from the beginning of the meeting between Abraham and the three strangers in the Bible who it is who is visiting Abraham and Sarah and who they are showing hospitality to. But in the Qur'an it is not initially clear to Abraham himself. In the Qur'an, the story begins as follows: "Have you [Muhammad] received the story of the honored guests of Abraham? When they came to him, saying 'Peace!' he said 'Peace! I don't know you'" (Q 51:24–25).

Abraham places a fatted calf before his guests but fears these strangers because they show no interest in the food, do not eat (Q 11:69–70). In certain early Jewish exegetes, the messengers do not eat because angels do not eat nor do they have any other physical functions. Abraham sees this refusal as hostility, and this frightens him. He fears for his safety.[52] Abraham says: "We are afraid of you" (Q 15:53; cf. 11:69).

The "honored guests"[53] are received hospitably by Abraham (Q 51:24; cf. 15:51–52; 29:31–32; 51:24–25).[54] As we saw earlier, hospitality had top priority among nomadic peoples. And Abraham is portrayed here as a host *par excellence*.[55]

Abraham greets his guests very respectfully: something unexpected and very important is about to happen. The hospitable reception is rewarded with a gift: the birth of a child.[56] But this announcement causes disbelief because both are old, to which the Lord says to Abraham: "Why did Sarah laugh and say, 'Will I really have a child, now that I am old?'" (Gen 18:13). Or, in the words of the Qur'an: "Woe is me! Shall I bear a child, being the old woman I am and my husband there a greybeard?" (Q 11:71–72).[57] The messengers said: "Don't be afraid; we bring you good tidings of a very clever boy" (Q 15:51–53; cf. 11:69). And then comes God's overwhelming question: "Is anything too hard for the Lord?" (Gen 18:14). For the first time it becomes apparent that the stranger is a messenger from God.[58] It is striking that, in the Qur'an, the announcement of glad tidings (*bushrâ*) concerns not only the birth of Isaac but also, after Isaac, Jacob (Q 11:71; cf. 6:84; 21:72; 29:27; 57:26); God made both of them prophets (Q 19:49)!

---

52. Paret, *Der Koran: Kommentar*, on Q 11:70.

53. *dayf ibrâhîm al-mukramîna*.

54. *E.Q.*, s.v. "Strangers and Foreigners."

55. *Dayf* = guest. The root of the word means "to turn aside and stop to visit someone." This is where its meaning as "guest" comes from. *E.I.*, s.v. "Dayf."

56. Westermann, *Genesis 12–36*, 274.

57. *E.Q.*, s.v. "Abraham," 6. TTB Hagigah 16a; *Targum Yerusshalmi* Gen 18:8; Genesis Rabba 48:14.

58. Westermann, *Genesis 12–36*, 279, 282.

Lot's Story

Lot was the son of Abraham's brother (Gen 11:27, 31) and accompanied Abraham when the latter left Harran (Gen 12:4–5). After living in Egypt with Sarah, Abraham took all his possessions and entered the Negev, and Lot went with him (Gen 13:1). But because their combined possessions were so large, Abraham though it better for them to separate. So Lot looked around and saw how rich the land along the Jordan was in water. Before the Lord destroyed Sodom and Gomorrah, this area—right up to Zoar—was the garden of the Lord, just as abundant in water as Egypt was. This was why Lot chose the land along the Jordan and travelled east, and the two "brothers" parted company (Gen 13:11).

Abraham stayed in Canaan, living like a nomad and shepherd on the bare steppe. Lot, however, possessed fruitful ground and sought a place to live in the cities close to the Jordan. He set up his tent close to Sodom and became a resident of the city, thereby exposing himself to the dangers and threats of the city.[59] The inhabitants of Sodom committed much evil and sinned against the Lord (Gen 13:10–13).

Lot is seen as the ancestor of the Moabites and the Ammonites. After the destruction of Sodom and Gomorrah, Lot lived in a cave with both of his daughters because he did not dare stay in Zoar, where he had originally fled. Both daughters got their father drunk and slept with him, becoming pregnant with Moab ("from father") and Ammon ("son of my father's people") (Gen 19:30–37). This story is meant to express the contempt for both people.[60] The lands of Moab and Ammon are promised to Lot (Deut 2:9, 19).[61]

The Moabites and Ammonites were regarded as Israel's enemies. During the Exodus, the Ammonites did not offer the children of Israel any hospitality, which they should have. This led to their condemnation: "For they did not come to meet you with bread and water on your way when you came out of Egypt, and they hired Balaam son of Beor from Pethor in Aram Naharaim to pronounce a curse on you" (Deut 23:5). And yet the Israelites were forbidden to attack the Ammonites or start a war with them because none of their land would be given to them since God had given it to the sons of Lot (Deut 2:19).[62] All of this was because Lot had shown hospitality to the angels for one night in his house in Sodom.[63]

---

59. Ibid., 309.
60. *KBS* on Genesis 19:30.
61. Amman is the capital of today's Jordan.
62. Lundbom, *Deuteronomium*, 200. Cf. the chapter "The Desert and the City" below.
63. Ginzberg, *Legends of the Jews*, 759, note 712.

It is striking that Ruth, a Moabitess, became the great-grandmother of David. She gave birth to Obed, the grandfather of David (Ruth 4:13–17), who is also the ancestor of Jesus (Matt 1:5).

Lot's Hospitality

Let us take a closer look at Lot's hospitality to the two angels of God. These angels arrived in Sodom in the evening, when Lot was at the city gate. The streets of ancient cities were very narrow, and only in front of the gate was there a square, the busiest area in the city, where goods were sold (2 Kings 7:1; Prov 31:31). The city gate (the square enclosed by the gate buildings) is where public life took place, including the administration of justice.[64] This is where a prophet would try to find listeners (Jer 17:19), where a teacher of wisdom would gather a circle of students around himself (Prov 1:21; 8:3), where elders would discuss local matters (Prov 31:23; Lam 5:14) or pronounce a legal judgment (Deut 21:19; 22:15; 25:7; Isa 29:21; Amos 5:10–15; Zech 8:16).[65] Legal matters were usually decided in the morning when people passed through the gate and could easily be called upon as witnesses (Jer 21:12).[66]

Although the three strangers came to Abraham in the middle of the day, the visit to Sodom took place in the evening. Thus, the scene was the city where Lot lived. And the city gate was also the place where a stranger could wait (Ruth 4:1; 2 Sam 18:24; 2 Kings 7:1) to see if someone would receive him.[67]

Lot was raised in Abraham's household and had therefore learned the custom of offering hospitality. As soon as he saw the angels, he invited them to stay in his house for the night. He assumed they were travelers. Because Sodom applied the death penalty to those who received strangers, Lot only dared to invite them under cover of darkness. Jewish tradition notes regarding this story that it was not the first time that the inhabitants of Sodom wanted to commit monstrous crimes. Shortly before, they had issued a law that all strangers were to be treated in a horrible manner. On that precise day that the angels arrived, Lot had been appointed judge and had tried to dissuade his fellow residents from this course of action: "My brothers, the generation of the flood was exterminated as a result of sins like those you want to commit." He was prepared to expose himself and his family to

---

64. *KBS* on Psalm 9:14.
65. *B.W.*, s.v. "Poort."
66. Lundbom, *Deuteronomium*, 606, on Deuteronomy 21:19.
67. Westermann, *Genesis 12–36*, 300–301.

danger rather than leave his guests to their fate. At least, that is the version told in Jewish legends.[68]

Lot asked the strangers to stay at his house, the house "of your servant," and to spend the night there so that they could continue their journey the following morning. Nonetheless, the two strangers wanted to stay outdoors for the night. But Lot insisted so vehemently (cf. Judg 19) that they finally agreed. When they arrived at his house, he made a meal with the unleavened bread that he had baked and they ate it (Gen 19:3).

Although the city itself could already have been a shelter for the travelers, a house offered even more protection. And just like Abraham, Lot provided hospitality, in contrast to the inhospitality that so characterized his fellow residents. He offered his guests protection under the shadow of his roof, gave them security.

But the strangers had not yet begun to relax in his house when the men of the city, gathered around Lot's house: young and old, the entire population. They called to Lot, saying: "Where are the men who came to you tonight? Bring them out to us so that we can have sex with them" (Gen 19:4-5). The idea behind hospitality was that one had to do anything for a guest. So Lot said, "No, my friends. Don't do this wicked thing. Look, I have two daughters who have never slept with a man. Let me bring them out to you, and you can do what you like with them. But don't do anything to these men, for they have come under the protection of my roof (Gen 19:8). Lot stood outside the door, thereby exposing himself to the attackers, without any protection: he closed the door behind him to offer his guests protection.[69] But the Sodomites tried to push Lot aside and break open the door. They replied: "This fellow came here as a *foreigner*, and now he wants to play the judge!" (Gen 19:9). The book of the covenant later says, that the stranger may not be mistreated (and may not be oppressed): "Do not mistreat or oppress a foreigner, for you were foreigners in Egypt" (Exod 22:20). According to Jewish exegesis, this means *verbal abuse*, where the stranger is reminded of his or her origins. This reveals a great *sensitivity to the language* as the creator or destroyer of social connections, someone's self-image or self-respect. A stranger is, after all, particularly sensitive to his or her status within society. He or she is an outsider and does not share memories, history, or a relationship with the indigenous population. And still he or she wants to belong. This is why the Torah calls for the consciousness of the vulnerability of strangers: be careful with them, do not hurt them, and do not constantly remind them that they are not "one of us."[70]

---

68. Ginzberg, *Legends of the Jews*, Volume I, 212, 214, note 176.
69. Westermann, *Genesis 12–36*, 301.
70. Sacks, *Covenant and Conversation*, 180–81.

Lot's strange guests ward off the immediate danger. They pull Lot back into the house and close the door behind him. They strike the people outside with blindness (Gen 19:9–11). It is that inhospitality that is the true cause of the destruction of Sodom and Gomorrah (Ezek 16:49).

Lot's Hospitality According to the Qur'an

In the Qur'an, Abraham's visitors are called messengers.[71] They were on their way to Sodom, where Lot lived (Q 11:69–74; 51:24–30; cf. 29:31). When Abraham's initial fear of his guests had subsided and the glad tidings had been delivered, he began to debate with God about "the people of Lot" (the name for the inhabitants of Sodom and Gomorrah in the Qur'an) with the hopes of averting their punishment (Q 11:74; cf. Gen 18:16–33).

When the messengers arrived at Lot's, he became concerned about them and did not know what to do with them. Lot was even prepared to sacrifice his daughters to his fellow citizens because of the requirements of hospitality: "He [Lot] said: 'Here are my daughters [take them], if you intend to do anything'" (Q 15:71). "And he said, 'This is a hard day.' And his people came running to him, people who had just been committing evil acts. He said, 'You there. Here are my daughters; they are purer for you than my guests. So fear God, and do not shame me to my guests. Is there not one just person among you?' They said, 'You know we have no right to your daughters, and you know very well what we want'" (Q 11:77–79; cf. 15:68).

The people in Sodom had set their heart on Lot's guests, and they wanted him to deliver them to them (Q 54:37). His fellow residents gave Lot to understand that they had forbidden him to get involved with outsiders (Q 15:68–70). In these stories, both Abraham and Lot feared that their guests would be dishonored and mistreated (Q 11:78; 54:37)—this is an echo of the Qur'an's warning to treat visitors and strangers well.[72]

Sodom's Destruction Because of Its Lack of Hospitality

The Qur'an places a number of its *own accents* in Lot's story. But the similarities or differences between the biblical story and the Qur'anic story and the reasons for this are not what we should be looking at. Our concern should be to figure out its contribution to the message of the Qur'an. This applies within the canon of the Bible as well. After all, the story of Sodom

---

71. *Rusul* in Q 11:69 and *mursalûn* in Q 51:31.
72. *E.Q.*, s.v. "Strangers and Foreigners."

and Gomorrah is used again and again by the prophets—to refer to Jerusalem, for instance (Isa 1:9; Ezek 16:46)—and is given its own twist each time.

What accents are found in the Qur'an?

(a) The cities are not mentioned by name.

(b) Lot is called a prophet.

(c) He emigrates (*hijra*, Exodus) together with Abraham from Mesopotamia, Egypt, *and* Sodom.

(d) The role of the night as opposed to the morning.

(e) It also discusses the reason for and the nature of the sin that leads to the destruction of the cities. And these cities are symbolic of so many other cities that were destroyed because they did not want to listen to the message of their prophets. The prophet Muhammad will refer to that constantly.[73]

(a)

Not mentioning the names of the cities makes it easier to indicate what *could* happen to cities in general. The cities are always referred to as "the Overthrown Cities" that were destroyed by God because of the sins of their inhabitants (Q 9:70; 53:53; 69:9). The city of Nineveh is also described in this way: it would be "overthrown" after a period of forty days (Jon 3:4).[74] The Bible always speaks of the *cities* of Sodom and Gomorrah whereas the Qur'an speaks of *the people of Lot*.[75]

(b)

Lot is placed in the row of successive prophets, such as Noah, the Arab prophets Hûd (the people of the 'Âdites), Sâlih (the people of Thamûd) and Shu'ayb or Jethro (the people of the Midianites) (Q 21:71). He is included among those who are sent (Q 37:133).[76]

Each one of the careers of the prophets is viewed as a prefiguring of Muhammad. He was also involved in a conflict with his fellow Meccan citizens, to whom he was to address his message. Muhammad was declared a liar by his people, as Noah, Hûd, Thamûd, Shu'ayb (Q 22:43) *and* Lot (Q 26:160; cf. 38:14; 50:14; 54:33) were by theirs.

(c)

---

73. Cf. also the chapter "The Desert and the City" below.
74. Firestone, *Journeys*, 53, 199, note 4.
75. *qawm Lût*.
76. *mursalîn*.

Lot believed in Abraham and his message and said: "I will go to my Lord" (Q 29:27),[77] which is to say: "withdraw," "emigrate," "complete the Exodus." Thus, together with Abraham, Lot completed the *hijra* or Exodus from Mesopotamia, on the way to the land that God would indicate.[78] Lot's move away from Abraham to Sodom and Gomorrah (Gen 13:8–12) is understood by the Qur'an as a move motivated by faith: someone who, as an emigrant (*muhâjir*), completes the *hijra* (the Exodus).[79] Some Muslim exegetes understand his journey to the promised land—the land that God had blessed and that is always referred to in the Qur'an as "the holy land" (Q 29:26)—as a journey to Mecca. But according to Tabarî, after his Exodus from Egypt with Abraham, Lot settled in "Jordan," and God sent him to the people of Sodom.[80]

(d)

When the guests or ambassadors of God arrived at Lot's in Sodom, he was ordered to leave with his household *at night*, and no one was to turn around (Q 11:81). According to the description in Genesis, Lot's departure took place at the break of dawn—which explains the urgency of the angels to leave as quickly as possible (Gen 19:15). According to the Qur'an, however, he left the city in the *dark of night*.

Jewish sources compare leaving Sodom at night with the Exodus from Egypt at night (cf. Exod 12:29, 31). "Because the Lord kept vigil that night to bring them out of Egypt, on this night all the Israelites are to keep vigil to honor the Lord for the generations to come" (Exod 12:42). In Hebrew, "keep vigil" sounds like *keeping watch, guarding* as in *preserving*. "Indeed, he who watches over Israel will neither slumber nor sleep" (Ps 121:4). The people have to keep that custom alive. This day is to be commemorated, a festival to be celebrated from generation to generation (Exod 12:14, 17).[81] The key words "watches over" appear six times in the pilgrimage song "The Lord is my keeper" (Ps 121). The Lord "your keeper" is mentioned three times (Ps 121:3, 4 and 5) and the verbal form "keep" is used three times (Ps 121:7–8).

When we are told that God rested after six days of creation (Gen 2:3; Exod 20:11), this does not mean that God is a *deus otiosus*—a weary God who turns away from the created world (Exod 20:11; 31:17). That the Lord who made heaven and earth comes to help (Ps 121:2) expresses the fact that

---

77. Cf. "Whoever travels on the way of God will find many refuges and plenty in the world" (Q 4:100).
78. Cf. Wessels, *The Torah*, chapter IV.
79. Speyer, *Die biblischen Erzählungen*, 146.
80. Noegel and Wheeler, *The A to Z of Prophets*, s.v. "Lot."
81. Fischer and Markl, *Das Buch Exodus*, 142.

he continues his *creative activity* (*creatio continua*). This is emphasized by the statement that he neither slumbers nor sleeps (Q 2:255). God does not abandon his creation but continues to be actively involved, especially as the Keeper who makes sure that Israel's dangerous road through history does not lead to a catastrophe.[82]

"He will not let your foot be moved; he who keeps you will not slumber. He who keeps Israel will neither slumber nor sleep" (Ps 121:3–4). This idea or expression of the "Keeper of Israel" evokes the memory of the great traditions about the origins of Israel. After all, the LORD was not only Jacob's keeper during his dangerous flight from the land of promise (Gen 28:15, 20), but he was also the keeper of the people of Israel on their journey from Egypt, through the wilderness and the hostile world (Babylon), to the promised land (Josh 24:17).

It is at night that decisions are made. When Abraham fell into a deep sleep at sundown and an intense fear and darkness overcame him, the LORD said to him: "Know for certain that for four hundred years your descendants will be strangers in a country not their own and that they will be enslaved and mistreated there. But I will punish the nation they serve as slaves, and afterward they will come out with great possessions" (Gen 15:12–13). Then God made a covenant with him. "When the sun had set and darkness had fallen, a smoking firepot with a blazing torch appeared and passed between the pieces [of sacrificial meat]" (Gen 15:17–18). God appeared to Jacob in Bethel during the *night*. After wakening, Jacob said: "How awesome is this place! This is none other than the house of God; this is the gate of heaven" (Gen 28:17).

The time of the decisive interference by God that ultimately leads to the Exodus under the leadership of Moses took place in the *night* in which the LORD killed all the firstborn in Egypt, and the Pharaoh and all Egyptians got up because there was no house without someone who had died (Exod 12:29–30).

(e)

The Qur'an often repeats the fact that the people of Lot were punished (Q 7:84; 11:82; 15:73–74; 27:58; 29:34–35; 37:136; 51:32–37; 54:34, 37). The angels announced to Abraham that the inhabitants of "these cities" (Sodom and Gomorrah) would be destroyed because the inhabitants were *evildoers* (Q 29:31). The Qur'an calls the inhabitants of Sodom people who had *done wrong*, and this indicates the nature of their sin. "A plague descended on the city because of the *evil* they committed" (Q 29:34). The messengers who

---

82. Hossfeld and Zenger, *Psalms 3*, 323–24.

visit Abraham speak of a *"people inclined to evil* to whom they have been sent" (Q 51:32). They *have no sense of moderation* (Q 51:34).

But the point that has received the most attention in the history of exegesis is the comment that the people of Sodom *had displayed lust* (Q 54:34–37). Lot says to the attackers: "Do you want commit indecency of such a nature that has never been committed anywhere in the world before now? For you desire men instead of women" (Q 7:80–81; cf. 27:55; 29:29; 26:165–66; 21:74). That lust was a sexual desire of men for men. Just as, in the case of the Bible, the name of the city became a term for homosexual behavior, "sodomy," so the Lot's name (Lût in Arabic) has gradually come to mean something similar in Arabic: *lutiyya* is Arabic equivalent of "sodomy."

But the crimes of the people of Lot were, rather, primarily their refusal to believe, their persistence in wickedness, a sinful behavior that had to be punished despite Abraham's intercession.[83] The sin of Sodom is called grievous (Gen 18:20). "[They] had committed disgusting acts; they were an evil people, who engaged in evil practices" (Q 21:74). What is told about Lot's guests and the men who gathered in front of Lot's house suggests the threat of gang rape rather than a private act, "sodomy," or any other specific homosexual deed. When men approaching men is discussed, it is immediately added: " . . . and [they] rob people on the road and commit reprehensible acts in your assemblies" (Q 29:29).[84]

No other story in the Bible is so frequently referred to as the one about Sodom and Gomorrah.[85] But that does not mean that Sodom's sin was specifically sexual in nature. It was injustice and their total lack of hospitality (cf. Isa 1:10; 3:9; Jer 23:14). It was about the rape of the law (Isa 5:7).[86] They behaved arrogantly and did nothing for the poor and the needy (Ezek 16:49). It is not a coincidence that the fate of the cities was accompanied by the attempt of the inhabitants to attack Lot's two visitors.[87] *Sodom was destroyed because of its lack of hospitality.*

The Destruction of Cities

The rescue of the righteous Lot and the destruction of his surroundings are also used as a point of comparison for other events in history.

83. *E.I.*, s.v. "Lût."
84. Cf. Wessels, *The Torah*, 18, 214, 220–22.
85. Isa 1:9–10; 3:9; 13:19; Jer 50:40; 49:18; Lam 4:6; Ezek 16:46; Amos 4:11; Matt 10:15; 11:23–24; Mark 6:11; Luke 10:2; 17:29; Rom 9:29; 2 Pet 2:6; Jude 7; Rev 11:8 .
86. Brueggemann, *Genesis*, 164.
87. Sacks, *Covenant and Conversation*, 183.

The book of *Jesus Sirach*, probably written around 190 B.C. in Jerusalem,[88] states: "He did not spare the people with whom Lot lived; he abhorred them, rather, for their pride. He was pitiless to the nation of perdition—those people who gloried in their sins."[89]

The author of the book of The Wisdom of Solomon (positioned in the Septuagint between Job and Ecclesiastes) is a Jew from Alexandria with a good Hellenistic education and familiar with the philosophy of his time. The book was most likely written in the first century before or after the start of our era in Alexandria. Those addressed are Jews in the diaspora or dispersion and those in contact with them.[90]

That book states about Lot:

> while the godless perished, [Wisdom] saved the upright man as he fled from the fire raining down on the Five Cities [Sodom, Gomorrah, Admah, Zeboiim, and Zoar], in witness against whose evil ways a desolate land still smokes, where plants bear fruit that never ripens and where, monument to an unbelieving soul, there stands a pillar of salt. For, by ignoring the path of Wisdom, not only did they suffer the loss of not knowing the good, but they left the world a memorial to their folly, so that their offences could not pass unnoticed. (Wis 10:6–8)[91]

In Luke's gospel, Jesus refers to Lot and Sodom when speaking about the coming of the kingdom. When he is asked when that kingdom will come, his answer is: "It was the same in the days of Lot. People were eating and drinking, buying and selling, planting and building. But the day Lot left Sodom, fire and sulfur rained down from heaven and destroyed them all. It will be just like this on the day the Son of Man is revealed. On that day no one who is on the housetop, with possessions inside, should go down to get them. Likewise, no one in the field should go back for anything. *Remember Lot's wife!*" (Luke 17:28–32).

Lot prayed that he and his household would be saved from the acts the people of Sodom committed (Q 26:169), and God delivered him from that city of sin (Q 21:74; 26:170; 27:57; 29:33; 37:134; 51:35; 54:34; 7:83). Lot and his family were saved, except for his wife, who disobeyed and looked back during her flight.[92] She had followed Lot out of Sodom but looked

---

88. *B.W.*, s.v. "Sirach."
89. http://www.catholic.org/bible/book.php?id=28*and*bible_chapter=16.
90. *B.W.*, s.v. "Wijsheid van Salomo/Wisdom."
91. http://www.catholic.org/bible/book.php?id=27*and*bible_chapter=10.
92. Cf. Paret, *Der Koran: Kommentar*, 165. Speyer, *Die biblischen Erzählungen*, 146, 150–58.

back at the destroyed city and was turned into a pillar of salt (Gen 19:26). It was forbidden to look back when fleeing a calamity. We all know what happened to Eurydice when Orpheus looked at her in the underworld: the consequence was that she could no longer be saved from there. In the case of Lot's wife, however, her looking back indicated she longed for a society where sin was fostered, without offering any support for the poor and needy who had no future. "Now this was the sin of your sister Sodom: She and her daughters were arrogant, overfed and unconcerned; they did not help the poor and needy" (Ezek 16:49). The people of Sodom did not provide for the needy! The lesson of the story about the destruction of Sodom is that a society founded on violence, that despises and shuts out the stranger will be razed to the ground and has no right to exist.[93]

Finally, let us look at the *Second Letter of Peter*: "if he condemned the cities of Sodom and Gomorrah by burning them to ashes, and made them an example of what is going to happen to the ungodly; and if he rescued Lot, a righteous man, who was distressed by the depraved conduct of the lawless" (2 Pet 2:6-7).[94] Peter witnessed the transfiguration of Jesus on the mountain (2 Pet 1:16-18; cf. Matt 17:1-8; Mark 9:2-8; Luke 9:28-36) when Moses and Elijah appeared with him. The Messianic promise of the prophets was confirmed there.[95]

Moses as a Stranger

Moses called his son who was born in Midian Gershom (Exod 2:22), which is derived from *ger*, which means "guest" or "stranger." At the same time, it could also be derived from *garash*, which means "driven away." Both meanings are striking. Moses was a stranger, and he had been driven away. He attempted to exercise justice three times. The first conflict was between an Egyptian and a Hebrew (Exod 2:11-12), the second between two of his own people (Exod 2:13-14), and, in the third case, he intervened on behalf of the Midianites to whom he had fled but who were also strangers to him. He defended the girls who had been driven away from a well by some shepherds. These three acts clearly show that Moses was concerned only with justice. This qualified him as a mediator for justice that highly values impartiality: "Do not pervert justice or show partiality. Do not accept a bribe, for a bribe blinds the eyes of the wise and twists the words of the innocent" (Deut 16:19). To do this and act in this way is to image God himself: "For

---

93. Oosterhuis and Van Heusden, *Het evangelie van Lukas*, 164.
94. B.W., s.v. "Lot." Cf. Noegel and Wheeler, *The A to Z of Prophets*, s.v. "Lot."
95. KBS on 2 Peter 1:19.

the Lord your God is God of gods and Lord of lords, the great God, mighty and awesome, who *shows no partiality* and accepts no bribes. He defends the cause of the fatherless and the widow, and loves the foreigner residing among you, giving them food and clothing" (Deut 10:17-18).[96] This is the main theme of the book of Deuteronomy, of the speech that Moses gave before the people entered the promised land: justice and the kind treatment of the vulnerable and needy, including the stranger in society.[97] That "impartiality" is also ascribed to Jesus (Luke 20:21).[98] That quality of "judging by appearances," of "not showing favoritism" is attributed to God in the New Testament and means that God is impartial (Acts 10:34). Paul refers to this repeatedly (Rom 2:11; Gal 2:9; Eph 6:9; Col 3:25).

Abraham as a Stranger— An Example for Jews, Christians, and Muslims

God remembers the covenant he made with Abraham, Isaac and Jacob; his promise lasts for a thousand generations. He says: "To you I will give the land of Canaan as the portion you will inherit." Psalm 105 speaks of this. "When [the Israelites] were but few in number, few indeed, and strangers in it, they wandered from nation to nation, from one kingdom to another. He allowed no one to oppress them; for their sake he rebuked kings: 'Do not touch my anointed ones; do my prophets no harm'" (Ps 105:12-15).

Abraham stayed in the promised land as a foreigner and lived there in tents, as did Isaac and Jacob (Hebr 11:9). The picture of Abraham as someone who was only staying temporarily in a country that was not his is brought to the foreground prominently in the Bible. In Genesis 17:8 we read that he stayed in Canaan as a stranger. "I am a foreigner and a stranger," he says, when he wants to buy a grave in Hebron for Sarah (Gen 23:4). Jacob lived in Canaan as a stranger, like his (grand)father (Gen 37:1). When Abraham stayed in Egypt for a while because of famine (Gen 12:10), God told him that his descendants would stay in a foreign land as slaves (Gen 15:13), where they would suffer oppression for four hundred years (Exod 12:49; Acts 7:6).

The patriarchs and the people who belonged with them were few and lived as nomad strangers in the promised land. The fulfilment of the promise still lay in the future. When the Israelites later arrived in the promised land, with the offering of the first fruits of the land in thankful recognition

---

96. Fischer and Markl, *Das Buch Exodus*, 41–42.
97. Lundbom, *Deuteronomium*, 393 (on Deut 10:18).
98. Attridge, *The Epistle*, 323.

that God kept his promises and gave them the land, the people were asked to stand before the LORD their God and declare: "My father was a wandering *Aramean*, and he went down into Egypt with a few people and lived there and became a great nation, powerful and numerous" (Deut 26:5). The term "Aramean" (in the Septuagint "Syrian") can be viewed as a collective reference to the three patriarchs (Abraham, Isaac, and Jacob) (Num 20:15; Ps 105:12–13). "Lived there" means "living temporarily as a stranger." That was the status of the children of Israel in Egypt (Deut 10:19; 23:8).[99] The description takes up the key terms referring to the patriarchs as "strangers living there" (Gen 12:10; 20:1; 26:3; 26:7–14; 32:5).[100] The wandering points to the nomadic life style of the patriarchs.

This theme is taken up in the letter to the Hebrews:

> By faith Abraham, when called to go to a place he would later receive as his inheritance, obeyed and went, even though he did not know where he was going. By faith he made his home in the promised land like a stranger in a foreign country; he lived in tents, as did Isaac and Jacob, who were heirs with him of the same promise. For he was looking forward to the city with foundations, whose architect and builder is God. (Hebr 11:8–10)

Abraham lived in the land as a stranger that was promised him (Hebr 11:9). Abraham and his descendants, the people of Israel, stayed as strangers in Egypt. "The God of the people of Israel chose our ancestors; he made the people prosper during their stay in Egypt; with mighty power he led them out of that country" (Acts 13:17).

A believer—whether he calls himself Jew, Christian, or Muslim—is a stranger on the earth. He is on his way to his paternal home, his citizenship is in heaven (Phil 3:20; cf. Eph 2:12). But this citizenship already begins on earth. It can be said of the community (whether it be the Jewish *qahal*, the Christian *ekklesia*, or the Muslim *umma*): "We have our home in heaven and on earth we are a colony of citizens of heaven."[101] As a tradition or *hadîth* of the prophet Muhammad states: "Islam started as a stranger and shall end as a stranger. May the stranger experience happiness and glad times."[102]

---

99. Lundbom, *Deuteronomium*, 725–27.
100. Hossfeld and Zenger, *Psalms 3*, 71.
101. Bauer, "Politeuma," 1361.
102. www.al-yaqeen.com.

III

The Language of Canaan and Foreign Tongues

The Circumlocution Office was (as everybody knows without being told) the most important Department under Government. No public business of any kind could possibly be done at any time without the acquiescence of the Circumlocution Office. Its finger was in the largest public pie, and in the smallest public tart. It was equally impossible to do the plainest right and to undo the plainest wrong without the express authority of the Circumlocution Office. If another Gunpowder Plot had been discovered half an hour before the lighting of the match, nobody would have been justified in saving the parliament until there had been half a score of boards, half a bushel of minutes, several sacks of official memoranda, and a family-vault full of ungrammatical correspondence, on the part of the Circumlocution Office.

This glorious establishment had been early in the field, when the one sublime principle involving the difficult art of governing a country, was first distinctly revealed to statesmen. It had been foremost to study that bright revelation and to carry its shining influence through the whole of the official proceedings. Whatever was required to be done, the Circumlocution Office was beforehand with all the public departments in the art of perceiving—HOW NOT TO DO IT.

(*CHARLES DICKENS, LITTLE DORRIT (2003), 119*)

Introduction

IN CHAPTER 19 OF the book of Isaiah in the Bible, Isaiah talks about the Egyptians learning the "language of Canaan" (Isa 19:18). What does Isaiah mean by this? It is certainly not a matter of "Hebrew" as opposed to "Egyptian," i.e., the language of a strange land or people. Rather, it refers to speech habits that are to be contrasted with the "foreign" speech habits or language spoken not only between peoples and countries but also within each country and people. The "language of Canaan" is thus contrasted with the language spoken with unclean lips, a language that is fundamentally hypocritical. And that hypocritical language is spoken primarily at the highest government level.

Charles Dickens gives an example of this in nineteenth-century England. His novel, *Little Dorrit*, is about a family forced to live in a debtors' prison, the Marshalsea, in London, for more than twenty years. (This experience of being confined to a debtors' prison was something Dickens' own father and thus his family as well, underwent.)

In chapter 10 of the first part of the novel, "Containing the whole Science of Government," Dickens writes about "the Circumlocution Office." Here he gives a striking description of how, on the government level, everything possible is done to ensure that nothing is done that the same government says must be done. Language is used—or misused—in this "Circumlocution Office" to that end. Dickens had in mind here the concrete political reality of his time, and the concrete occasions for that can be found in the endnotes in the edition of the novel used here (2003).[1]

If—given this—one wants to read the holy texts of Jews, Christians, and Muslims with a view to their internal cohesion and intertwinings, it is above all necessary to learn the ABCs of the biblical and qur'anic language of Canaan. It is in that language that the Bible and the Qur'an proclaim "the good news," regardless of whether it is expressed in Hebrew, Greek, or Arabic.[2] The foreign language alluded to here is not that of strangers and foreigners but the foreign language of imperialistic masters and oppressors throughout history who can found everywhere in the Bible and the Qur'an: the Nimrods of Asshur, Babylon, and Nineveh, the "Pharaohs" of Egypt, the "princes" and "emperors" of the Greeks and Persians, and those of Rome, Byzantium, and Persia. The latter two were part of the prophet Muhammad's world and time.

---

1. Cf. note 1 in Dickens, *Little Dorrit*, 935: "This chapter was written in September 1855, at the height of Dickens' disgust with the continued obstructions placed in the way of administrative reform."

2. *bashâra, euangelion, bushrâ.*

The Biblical ABCs

In 1941, during the Second World War, K.H. Miskotte's *Bijbels ABC* (The ABCs of the Bible) was published. Miskotte was a minister at that time in Amsterdam and was later appointed professor at the theological faculty of the University of Leiden. His book offers "a general introduction to the basic lines of Holy Scripture" and "is intended to help the reader understand the language of the Bible."[3] Miskotte discusses a number of key terms and takes the Old Testament, the Tanakh, in which the language of the New Testament is rooted, as his starting point. Learning the key terms with their unique meanings and expressiveness is a condition for understanding the message of the Bible—it has its own basic language. Here Miskotte speaks of the "grammar of Scripture":[4] whoever wants to learn to read the Bible has to know the key terms and the grammar of the language of the Bible. Miskotte wanted to introduce the Dutch Christians to this language again, to make it their mother tongue, so it could give them courage in resisting a "foreign language," the language of the Nazis.[5] That kind of foreign language is being heard again in our time, everywhere in Europe and the West as such.

The Language of Canaan in the Prophet Isaiah

The name of Isaiah, "The Lord saves," is characteristic for his prophetic message.[6] This message is strongly influenced by his call vision in the temple, where God's holiness and Isaiah's own sinfulness and that of the people are revealed. This vision is described as follows in Isaiah 6:1–5:

> In the year that King Uzziah[7] died, I saw the Lord, high and exalted, seated on a throne; and the train of his robe filled the temple. Above him were seraphim, each with six wings: With two wings they covered their faces, with two they covered their feet, and with two they were flying. 3And they were calling to one another:
>
> "Holy, holy, holy is the Lord Almighty;
> the whole earth is full of his glory."

---

3. Miskotte, *Bijbels ABC*, 3.
4. Ibid., 67–68.
5. http://www.hervormdnunspeet.nl/drplcm/content/verslag-bijbels-abc-2013 (course instructor: R.H. Reeling Brouwer).
6. Asha'yâ' in Arabic, *Dictionnaire*, s.v. "Isaïe."
7. Ca. 740 B.C.

> At the sound of their voices the doorposts and thresholds shook and the temple was filled with smoke.
>
> "Woe to me!" I cried. "I am ruined! For I am a man of unclean lips, and I live among a people of unclean lips, and my eyes have seen the King, the Lord Almighty."

When the northern kingdom of Israel fell to the Assyrians and the capital city of Samaria was conquered in 722 B.C., Isaiah brought hope for salvation to the Jews of the southern kingdom. The oracle that Isaiah proclaimed about Egypt dates from the time Egypt attempted to seek allies in the Syro-Palestinian region against Asshur (715–701 B.C.). In 671 and 663 Egypt would itself, however, be defeated by the Assyrians.[8]

The oracle in which *the language of Canaan* comes up reads as follows:

> In that day the Egyptians will become weaklings. They will shudder with fear at the uplifted hand that the Lord Almighty raises against them. And the land of Judah will bring terror to the Egyptians; everyone to whom Judah is mentioned will be terrified, because of what the Lord Almighty is planning against them.

In that day five cities in Egypt will speak the language of Canaan and swear allegiance to the Lord Almighty. One of them will be called the City of the Sun.

In that day there will be an altar to the Lord in the heart of Egypt, and a monument to the Lord at its border. It will be a sign and witness to the Lord Almighty in the land of Egypt. When they cry out to the Lord because of their oppressors, he will send them a savior and defender, and he will rescue them. So the Lord will make himself known to the Egyptians, and in that day they will acknowledge the Lord. They will worship with sacrifices and grain offerings; they will make vows to the Lord and keep them. The Lord will strike Egypt with a plague; he will strike them and heal them. They will turn to the Lord, and he will respond to their pleas and heal them.

> In that day there will be a highway from Egypt to Assyria. The Assyrians will go to Egypt and the Egyptians to Assyria. The Egyptians and Assyrians will worship together. In that day Israel will be the third, along with Egypt and Assyria, a blessing on the earth. The Lord Almighty will bless them, saying, "Blessed be Egypt my people, Assyria my handiwork, and Israel my inheritance." (Isa 19:16–25)

---

8. *B.W.*, s.v. "Jesaja."

There are six oracles or prophecies in this passage. The word "oracle" comes from the Latin *orare*: "pray," "beg," "speak." In an oracle or prophecy, God gives an answer to a question, especially in times of personal or national crisis. This "prophetic" declaration is passed on by a herald or messenger who goes into states of ecstasy and uses formulaic sayings like "Thus says the Lord. . . . "[9] The oracles in the book of Isaiah concerns the two great world powers of that time: Asshur, which ruled over the area that now includes Iraq, and Egypt. Judah was caught, as it were, between these two world powers. The oracles all begin with the phrase "In that day."

Let us look at the various oracles in the passage cited above. First, "In that day the Egyptians will become weaklings." The original Hebrew has a phrase meaning "become like women."[10] This is certainly not a woman-friendly expression—here women represent cowardice. A superpower is mocked: Egypt is pathetic, its best period is behind it, is history. All those great macho fighters will be like women! But Judah—that tiny, no-account country—will bring terror to Egypt. That's like Tom Thumb terrifying the giant Egypt—like a mouse that roars. It seems very improbable; nevertheless, there it is in black and white.

"In that day five cities in Egypt will speak the language of Canaan." How, one wonders, will that come about—will Egypt simply, all of a sudden, speak that language? One answer is that it is referring to Jewish communities in Egypt. It does seem logical that they, i.e., the Jews, spoke that language. There were Jews living in the extreme southern part of Egypt on the island Elephantine. They even had their own temple.[11] Moreover, there was a large Jewish community in the north as well, in Alexandria. If that is how this oracle is to be explained, then it would mean that those Jewish communities in Egypt would speak the language of Canaan, thus Hebrew. But this proposal should be rejected, however. Alexandria did not exist of course at the time of the prophet Isaiah. It was not founded until centuries later, in the 4th century B.C., by Alexander the Great. What is this oracle referring to then? It is the Egyptians themselves who would speak the language of Canaan! Does that mean that the Egyptians would then all take a crash course in Hebrew? Of course not. To understand what is meant here we must first know what language the Egyptians spoke until then, and this has to do with the language spoken by their political and economic leaders. What language were they using before? To answer that question, all we

---

9. *ko âmar* YHWH. Noegler and Wheeler, *The A to Z of Prophets*, s.v. "Oracle"; *B.W.*, s.v. "Godswoord."

10. Cf., for instance, the KJV.

11. Cf. Schama, *The Story of the Jews*, Chapter 1.

have to do is look at the first chapter of the book of Exodus, the book of the liberation of the children of Israel from Egypt. At that time a new king came to power in Egypt who did not know Joseph, and he told his people that the Israelites were becoming too numerous and too strong (Exod 1:7; Acts 13:17). This book first lists the names of the sons of Jacob, mentioning that there were originally 70 descendants (Exod 1:1–5) but then states immediately that they became very numerous and strong, so much so that they were filling up the land. For the first time one could truly speak about Israelites.[12] Pharaoh thinks that there are far too many of them and wonders how he can get rid of them, can make sure that their numbers decrease. He wants to prevent them from growing even more numerous. He thus forces the Israelites to perform slave labor, but that was not enough, for their numbers did not decrease. Despite their oppression, they continue to multiply, increasing to such an extent that the Egyptians became afraid. So the Egyptians make the lives of the Hebrews even more bitter. The king of Egypt even thinks of a new way to oppress them: he attempts to make sure that the Hebrew midwives ensure that all Jewish boys are killed. If a boy is born, he is to be thrown into the Nile: "Every Hebrew boy that is born you must throw into the Nile, but let every girl live." *That* is the language that the "pharaonic" Egyptians spoke at that time.

But why do the Egyptians now suddenly speak a different language? How have they so quickly learned the language of Canaan, the language of their oppressed subjects? The answer: through bitter experience. They did not take a course in the language but were forced to take a course in life. How did that happen? The once so powerful Egypt was trampled underfoot by the other great imperialistic world power, Asshur. The Egyptians got a taste of their own medicine. "I will hand the Egyptians over/ to the power of a cruel master" (Isa 19:4). The Egyptians now remember how God had previously acted in Egypt through the leading of the irresistible leadership of Moses. They know about the plagues, punishments, castigations. Both the Egyptians and the Philistines were subjected to plagues and divine punishments (Exod 7:14—11:10; 12:29-33; Q 7:130-34; 27:12; 43:47-50). Not only large groups but individuals as well could be the recipients of God's plagues (2 Kings 15:5). And these plagues were intended as warnings (Isa 15:3). Hopefully, they would lead to penitence (cf. 1 Sam 5:1—6:21). Moreover, at the same time they had to demonstrate God's greatness, power, and grace (Exod 8:22).[13] That is why the Bible says this about the last of the

---

12. Fischer and Markl, *Das Buch Exodus*, 29. The word "Israel" occurs 125 times in the book of Exodus.

13. *B.W.*, s.v. "Plaag."

ten plagues: "At midnight the Lord struck down all the firstborn in Egypt, from the firstborn of Pharaoh, who sat on the throne, to the firstborn of the prisoner, who was in the dungeon, and the firstborn of all the livestock as well. Pharaoh and all his officials and all the Egyptians got up during the night, and there was loud wailing in Egypt, for there was not a house without someone dead" (Exod 12:29–30; cf. Q 7:127).[14]

The oracle in Isaiah 19:1–4 states three things that will happen to the Egyptians now: (1) God will stir them up against each other, (2) he will bring their plans to nothing, and (3) he will hand them over to a cruel master. In other words, a civil war of sorts will begin. The false gods of Egypt will tremble before God, the hearts of Egyptians will be paralyzed by fear. The oracle in Isaiah 19:2–4 reads:

> I will stir up Egyptian against Egyptian—
>> brother will fight against brother,
>> neighbor against neighbor,
>> city against city,
>> kingdom against kingdom.
>
> The Egyptians will lose heart,
>> and I will bring their plans to nothing;
>
> they will consult the idols and the spirits of the dead,
>> the mediums and the spiritists.
>
> I will hand the Egyptians over
>> to the power of a cruel master.
>> and a fierce king will rule over them.

Egypt's political and military plans will be disrupted because the people will be delivered to the brutal, cruel rulers of Asshur.[15] Now the once so powerful "pharaonic" Egypt will itself be subjected, oppressed, and exploited.[16] Their own Egyptian forbears had made life intolerable for the Israelites centuries ago through forced labor in the kilns and in the fields (Exod 1:14). But now they themselves are getting their own back from Asshur.

How do the Egyptians react to this? What are they going to do? Believe it or not, they are going to do precisely what the children of Israel did all those centuries ago. Just as the Israelites once cried out, so now the Egyptians will cry out in the hope that someone will hear them, someone will save them, someone will liberate them, someone will heal them. What had

---

14. For the plagues that Egypt is to suffer, see Q 7:138–41.
15. *KBS* on Isaiah 19:1–4.
16. Brueggemann, *Isaiah 1–39*, 156–57.

happened to the Israelites when they cried out for help was well known: the God of Israel heard the cry of his people: "The Lord said, 'I have indeed seen the misery of my people in Egypt. I have heard them crying out because of their slave drivers, and I am concerned about their suffering. So I have come down to rescue them from the hand of the Egyptians'" (Exod 3:7–8). The Qur'an also relates how Moses (Mûsâ) was sent by God to rescue his people (Q 37:114–22). He is commanded to lead the people through the sea (Q 20:77; 44:23–24) and is saved along with the people.

It all started with the bitter experience of fear and dread because of the severe oppression that the Egyptians were undergoing: desperate, tortured men, women, and children. In our time, that has been depicted in unmatched fashion by the Norwegian painter Edvar Munch in his painting *The Scream* (Norwegian: *Skrik*): a scream by a desperate and terrified, frightened human being. Munch was walking back to Oslo one evening with friends when they paused on a bridge. While his friends continued on a bit later, Munch himself was captivated by the landscape and the sky with the setting sun. He felt a nagging pain below his heart, and fiery tongues of blood hung above the bluish-black fjord. "I sensed an infinite scream passing through nature." He was overcome by a feeling of powerlessness and depression. That was the feeling behind *The Scream*. The horror-struck figure driven to desperation that he painted in such vivid colors against a landscape of undulating lines is a ghostly figure who fixes his gaze on us. Fear dominates in frantic brushstrokes that show the sound waves of the unrestrained scream. Munch thus depicts spiritual suffering and emotional torment—not only of his own terror but also that of his time and, no less, that of ours.[17]

In the hard school of oppression, the Egyptians are taught, so to say, the grammar of the language of Canaan: the grammar of redemption, liberation, and healing. And what is the effect of this? What is the result of the screaming of the descendants of the former oppressors when they in turn call out for help? How does God respond to the cry of the Egyptians? Does he say, "It's your own fault!"? Does he let them stew in their own juices? Isn't that the first thing their former victims would think and feel? But that is not what happens. God also hears the Egyptian people crying out for help. He does not say what General (later President) Charles de Gaulle once said in a time when France had half a million soldiers in Algeria: "Oh, blood dries quickly." Water under the bridge, so to say. But the shed blood of the countless Abels in the world throughout history right up until the present continue to cry out to God. He does hear and see it. He does indeed. And if God hears, that means that he also does something. He rises up in judgement.

17. Cf. Wikipedia.

That does not mean that he just strikes out, that he just avenges himself like we people say in our human language and do. God is, after all, not a human being (Hos 11:9; cf. Num 23:19–20)!

"He will arise in judgment" means that he will set this world right. The Hebrew words that are often translated in English as "repay" or "avenge" can best be translated in the true language of Canaan by "rectify" or "remedy" (Zenger: *Wiedergutmachung*). God rises up to redeem, liberate, and heal all his oppressed, enslaved, humiliated, suppressed, trapped, permanently disabled, poor people. Their number increases daily—in the world of that time and in our world as well, in the modern West. Those people are not deported or thrown off the earth. Just as the Lord cannot hear the cries of his oppressed Israelite slaves without being moved to act, so he also, in Isaiah's oracle, is stirred by the cries of the desperate Egyptians. Indeed, he is moved by their cries. The God the children of Israel came to know so long ago is now fully recognized by the Egyptians.

The Lord will reveal himself to Egypt: "So the Lord will make himself known to the Egyptians, and in that day they will acknowledge the Lord. They will worship with sacrifices and grain offerings; they will make vows to the Lord and keep them" (Isa 19:21). Just like the Israelites, they become servants (servant: *'ebed* in Hebrew; *'abd* in Arabic) of God. The acts of serving and worshipping are connected:[18] they are both directed to God. Instead of ruling, the Egyptians serve. Israel is called the servant of God (Isa 41:8), which points to a particular relationship between God and his people. And that relationship will also now obtain for other peoples. In any event, five of those cities involved in the civil war in Egypt have learned to speak the language of Canaan. The oracle suggests that a socio-economic, political, and military harmony will arise between former enemies. They will worship together the same God both mocked and resisted for so long. The God who healed the Israelite slaves will now heal the sick Egyptians: "he will respond to their pleas and heal them" (Isa 19:22). And so he will heal all peoples!

If this is not astonishing and incredible enough, the following oracle also says something unprecedented about the other major power, Asshur itself: "In that day there will be a highway from Egypt to Assyria. "The Assyrians will go to Egypt and the Egyptians to Assyria. The Egyptians and Assyrians will worship together" (Isa 19:23). Take note: the two superpowers who fought unceasingly for military and economic supremacy will worship the Lord together. There were two major traffic routes between both powers, routes that were used for moving troops and goods. The relative positions of

---

18. In Arabic *'abd* (servant) and *'ibâda* (worship) are connected, just as *'ebed* and *'aboda* in Hebrew are.

THE LANGUAGE OF CANAAN AND FOREIGN TONGUES 85

both powers were usually designated as "the South" (Egypt) and "the North" (Asshur). Both countries fought unceasingly for control but were inevitably also each other's trading partners. That means that they had to cross the region where Judah lay. According to this oracle, the connections would no longer be a source of terror but would be transformed into a "highway" made for easy and unobstructed travel. Why? So that God will bring these two powers "onto the high road of his law and divine justice," to allude to Vondel's (Dutch) translation of Psalm 23 into the "language of Canaan."[19] On that road the new language (the language of Canaan) will be spoken. It is not the language of economic self-interest (with its own toll rates), like the desire expressed today to close up "fortress Europe" as tightly as possible against foreigners who wash ashore on Lampedusa: "There are far too many of them"; "We have to find a way to get shot of them as quickly as possible." The language of Canaan is not the language of "the ideology of national security." It is not the language of "How do we fix it so that the rich keep getting richer and the poor poorer?" No, the language of Canaan is a completely different language. It is the language of justice, of peace, of dignity and security for all. Security is "indivisible:" a person cannot be secure alone. Instead of ruling and dominating, which is what the leaders of Egypt and Asshur do and all rulers since them have done and continue to do up to the present, they now begin to serve.

"In that day Israel will be the third, along with Egypt and Assyria, a blessing on the earth" (Isa 19:24)—blessed by God and a blessing for others. The oracles end with this. This series of oracles speak of fear, alarm, and terror and end in a vision of reconciliation. And v. 24 here is the high point of the most daring expectations from the whole Bible. Israel's old enemies are renamed in this language, given new identities, with, in fact, the favorite names, the pet names, that were first used for the people of Israel: "Blessed be Egypt my people, Assyria my handiwork, and Israel my inheritance" (Isa 19:25).[20] Titles that seemed to be exclusive to Israel will now be given to other nations. Foreign peoples will be adopted by God as his people as well. This is a vision that encompasses the whole inhabited world. That means that Israel's own alleged primacy, its exclusivity or privileges, must be given up. All peoples of the world turn out to be God's chosen people. Former enemies are taken up into God's "community."[21]

---

19. Hymn 23a:2 ("D'Almachtige is mijn Herder en geleide") in het *Liedboek, zingen en bidden in huis en kerk*.

20. "Be very concerned about" (Ps 17:14; Isa 57:6). Israel is the Lord's portion (Deut 32:9); the Lord is Israel's portion (Ps 16:5; 73:26; Jer 10:16, etc.). Listening to Jesus, which Mary chose to do, is "the better part" (Luke 10:42).

21. Brueggemann, *Isaiah 1–39*, 161–66.

The Grammar of the Exodus

Psalm 114 is the psalm of the exile of the people of Israel in Babylon. It belongs to the collection of the so-called Hallelujah psalms (Pss 113–118), which are called this because of the first word in these psalms ("Hallelujah"). These psalms were sung in home celebrations to commemorate the Exodus from Egypt. When Jesus celebrated his last supper with his twelve disciples, the first two were sung when they drank from the cup (Matt 26:30) and the last to close the meal. Then they went to the Mount of Olives (Mark 14:26). These psalms are still sung today during the Passover celebration. On that day the children, after all, have to be taught: "I do this because of what the Lord did for me when I came out of Egypt" (Exod 13:8). Since Abraham, parents have been very explicitly called upon to pass on their experiences to their children. Abraham, the father of *all* believers, was chosen, after all, to teach his descendants to keep "the way of the Lord" by doing what is right and just. Moses is told to tell his children and grandchildren how God dealt with the Egyptians and what signs he performed so that they would know that God is the Lord (YHWH) (Exod 10:2).

That is the background of the use of this psalm in the Passover celebration. It is why the children are instructed by means of a "catechism" during this celebration. When they ask: "What does this ceremony mean to you?" (Exod 12:26), their father (or mother) must answer: "We were slaves of Pharaoh in Egypt, but the Lord brought us out of Egypt with a mighty hand" (Deut 6:21).[22] The parents have to testify to the saving acts of God.

This custom is also found in "black" church services in the United States. It is always moving when the preacher asks the congregation for their approval of the testimony he gives: "Are there any witnesses?' and people everywhere in the congregation respond with "Yes!"

The Exodus from Egypt is the subject of the first few lines of Psalm 114:

> When Israel came out of Egypt,
>   Jacob from a people of foreign tongue,
> Judah became God's sanctuary,
>   Israel his dominion.
>
> (Ps 114:1–2)

The Exodus, leaving Egypt after a stay of 430 years (Exod 12:40–41), meant a break with the world that Israel had known up to that time. They now left that behind because an end had come to that existence. They had

---

22. Fischer and Markl, *Das Buch Exodus*, 137.

escaped affliction and danger; they were truly liberated and free. Moreover, they left to start something new: "The Lord's divisions left Egypt" (Exod 12:41). When Moses and Aaron were told to lead the Israelites out of Egypt by their divisions (Exod 6:26), "divisions" does not, of course, mean military divisions. Rather, the reference is to the procession of the people on the way to Sinai, where they would receive the Torah.[23]

The psalm relates what happened: the sea fled, the Jordan turned back. For whom did they do so? They did so because of the Lord before whom all should tremble, because of the God of Jacob (Ps 114:2-7). The psalm sings about what they attempted during the first Exodus and still remains relevant. Israel was liberated from "a people of foreign tongue" (Ps 114:2). This was a people whose language they did not understand and to whom they could not make themselves truly understood. Isaiah speaks in those terms of the liberation, the saving, of Jerusalem from the Assyrian people, whose language the Jews did not understand: "You will see those arrogant people no more,/ people whose speech is obscure,/ whose language is strange and incomprehensible" (Isa 33:19). The latter is referring to the language of the Assyrian soldiers. If political enemies use foreign languages, they can use that to intensify hostility and exclude any kind of mutual understanding. During the siege of Jerusalem by the Assyrians during the time of King Hezekiah,, the latter's emissaries asks the commander of the Assyrian army to speak in Aramaic and not in Hebrew so that the people would not become discouraged by what was said (2 Kings 18:26, 28). The statement, "a nation whose language you will not understand, a fierce-looking nation without respect for the old or pity for the young" refers in the first instance to the Assyrians (Isa 28:11; 33:19) but can also refer later to the Babylonians: "a people whose language you do not know,/ whose speech you do not understand" (Jer 5:15).

"Judah will no longer see arrogant occupiers who speak a strange, arrogant, intimidating language. The land is freed now for the cadences of Yahweh. The language of faith—Judah's 'mother tongue'—is now the only sound heard."[24]

Israel experienced the fact of Egypt speaking a foreign language as a symptom of strangeness, of hostility, and as life-threatening. The Egyptians were, in their eyes, a people they could not talk to. "Israel in Egypt" represented homelessness, helplessness, isolation, and the Hebrews' existence as pariahs. Setting off to start a new life is Israel's true existence.[25]

23. *KBS* on Exodus. 6:26. Zenger, *Stuttgarter Psalter*, 124, 128.
24. Brueggemann, *Isaiah 1-39*, 265. Cf. Lundbom, *Deuteronomium*, 789.
25. Zenger, *Stuttgarter Psalter*, 129.

The first two-line strophe in Psalm 114, which talks about the Exodus, is followed by the second strophe about Israel's entrance[26] into the land. Something unexpected happens, a wonderful new context, a new covenant after their hard life in Egypt. Israel itself is now God's sanctuary, his dominion (Ps 114:2). God brought them "to his holy land" (Ps 78:54), for after their redemption from Egypt, God led them through the desert to his holy dwelling (Exod 15:13). A Dutch translation (Oussoren) speaks of God leading this community in his "friendship" to the pastures of his sanctuary, which refers to the temple of Jerusalem and the area surrounding it (cf. Jer 25:30; 31:23).[27]

The Exodus ends with Israel entering the Promised Land.

After the destruction of Jerusalem Enoch speaks of a new Jerusalem and develops the notion of "a new house greater and loftier than the first, and set . . . up in the place of the first which had been folded up" (1 En 90:29).[28] According to Baruch, the pre-existent Jerusalem was shown to Moses on Sinai, and the earthly sanctuary would be built following its design (2 Bar 4:2-6; cf. Gal 4:26; Hebr 12:22; Rev 3:12; 21:2, 9; 22:5).[29]

The Qur'an relates how God gives a formerly oppressed people the eastern and western part of the land, i.e., "the whole land that We (God) have blessed." This expression recalls the psalm made so familiar through Christian liturgy: From the rising of the sun to the place where it sets, /the name of the Lord is to be praised" (Ps 113:3).[30] This fulfilled God's promise to the people of Israel (Q 7:137; cf. Gen 12:7; 13:15; 15:18; 17:18; 24:7; 26:3; 48:4; Exod 32:13). In the Qur'an, Jerusalem and the holy or promised land are continually referred to as the "furthest place where you bow down,"[31] in addition to the "nearby sacred place where you bow down,"[32] i.e., the Ka'ba in Mecca. Added to that is "whose precincts God has blessed," a phrase designating the holy land (Q 17:1). Abraham and Lot are saved there (Q 21:71). The wind is made to serve Solomon, and the storm winds hurry at God's command to "the land he has blessed" (Q 21:81).

The Qur'an tells of the dwelling places of Seba (Saba'), known primarily because of the queen of Sheba's visit to King Solomon (1 Kings 10:1-13;

---

26. *eisodos.*
27. Fischer and Markl, *Das Buch Exodus*, 169.
28. http://www.pseudepigrapha.com/pseudepigrapha/1enoch_all.html#CH90.
29. Speyer, *Die biblischen Erzählungen*, 385.
30. Ibid., 348.
31. *al-masjdid al aqsa.*
32. *al-masjdid al-harâm.*

Q 27:2–44).³³ Between the Sabeans and "the cities We have blessed," God establishes towns so that people can travel safely day and night (Q 34:18).

The goal of Israel's election is that Israel "will be the place of his special presence." Perhaps this is what Gerrit Achterberg, a well-known Dutch poet, was alluding to with his "The human being is a place of God for a time" (*De mens is voor een tijd een plaats van God*). It is the Lord of the whole earth as the "God of Jacob" who elects Israel to reveal himself there in such a way that the whole earth will come to know the "God of Jacob."

The notion of the house of Jacob as placed in a hostile world with a strange language expresses the idea that Israel is homeless and threatened. But this condition comes to an end with the first and second Exodus from Egypt and Babylon respectively. Then the sanctuary of the Lord becomes "a place for God," a place for the Lord," the place from which he exercises his dominion over the nations and from where he will give the nations a new language. This has to do with the transformative power that is ascribed to the "God of Jacob." He turns rocks into pools and granite into springs of water (Ps 114:8). That means that God promises to transform the language of the nations.

The same vision can be found in the prophet Zephaniah, one of the nine "minor" prophets who lived before the Babylonian exile.³⁴

Zephaniah prophesied in Jerusalem and lived in the time of King Josiah. He gave the impetus for the reform that Josiah carried out after finding the Book of the Law in the temple (2 Kings 22). This was certainly a form of the biblical book known as Deuteronomy, which contained at least the legislative parts that constituted the basis of King Josiah's reforms (2 Kings 23:1–14).³⁵ Zephaniah imagines the salvation that will occur in terms of the Lord transforming their language: "Then I will purify the lips of the peoples,/ that all of them may call on the name of the Lord/ and serve him shoulder to shoulder" (Zeph 3:9). The new and correct language is characterized by the fact that the people no longer call on false gods (Moloch, "the power of destruction" and Mammon, "the power of money") but serve the true God: do justice and show love. Then the fundamental (Babylonian) confusion of tongues between Israel and the nations is set right, even though they still speak different languages. According to Psalm 114, this will happen when Israel leaves the world of the foreign—i.e., hostile and idol-worshipping—language and truly become the place where God exercises his dominion.

---

33. Cf. Wessels *The Torah*, chapter VI.

34. There are twelve "minor" prophets, who called that because their books are less voluminous than those of the "major" prophets, of whom Isaiah is the "most major."

35. See *KBS* on 1 Kings 22:8.

That is the message: they call themselves citizens of the holy city and claim to rely on the God of Israel" (Ps 114:2). Zenger translates this text as follows (in German): When Israel went out from Egypt, the house of Jacob out from a people of strange language."[36]

It is God who marches at the head of his people during the Exodus through the desert (Ps 68:8). He initiates the departure and gets them moving forward. The line "Judah became God's sanctuary,/ Israel his dominion" (Ps 114:2) is not only about Israel but also about God: God has created the conditions for a new existence. While the gods of the nations had statues and temples for their revelations, the God of Israel reveals himself in the living temple of YHWH, the place where the Lord is praised and thanked in freedom, where the festivals of freedom are celebrated, and where that freedom is also passed on to others. The people become God's sanctuary, the living place of his presence: a sanctuary not for itself but for the nations. In and out of his sanctuary, YHWH begins to change the whole world. The Lord gave Israel the "king's law" so that Israel would be the ideal society, with life, freedom, and brotherhood and sisterhood as fundamental values. Israel was to be a living witness to the fact that saying "yes" to God's dominion would be the basis for this type of society and would make a more humane and just society possible.[37]

Overcoming the Confusion of Tongues

After Easter comes Pentecost, which, as the outpouring of the Spirit of God illustrates, was the opposite of the Babylonian confusion of tongues, the renewal of the common language. Pentecost is celebrated on the fiftieth day after Easter (Lev 23:15-16; Deut 19:9), which, for the Jews, is the "Feast of Weeks," celebrated seven weeks after the Exodus (Exod 34:22; Num 28:26). It is the final feast of the Passover and also a pilgrimage feast. In Jesus' time, this feast brought many pilgrims to Jerusalem (Acts 2:5-13; 20:16; 21:27). The rabbis explained it as the feast of the giving of the law on Sinai. It thus became a day for commemorating the revelation at Sinai.[38]

Acts 2:1-4 describes what occurred at Pentecost as follows: "When the day of Pentecost came, they were all together in one place. Suddenly a sound like the blowing of a violent wind came from heaven and filled the whole house where they were sitting. They saw what seemed to be tongues of fire that separated and came to rest on each of them. All of them were

---

36. Hossfeld and Zenger, *Psalms* 3,187-95.
37. Zenger, *Stuttgarter Psalter*, 130.
38. *B.W.*, s.v. "Pinksteren."

filled with the Holy Spirit and began to speak in other tongues as the Spirit enabled them." The fiery tongues can be associated with the theophany on Sinai (cf. Exod 19:18, where God descends in fire). The Jewish explanation views the heavenly fire as an image of the gift of the Torah, the law of God.[39] The atmosphere is, as it were, electrified by God's presence,[40] and the theophany is accompanied by fire and wind (Exod 19:17-18; 24:16-17; Hebr 12:18). God speaks with a loud voice out of the fire and the dark (Deut 5:22; cf. Exod 24:16). Characteristic of the revelation is that God's presence is perceived only aurally and not visually. God speaks and the people hear. It is said that the people encountered God "face to face," but in that encounter they only heard God speaking (Deut 5:4).[41]

When that sound was heard on Pentecost a crowd gathered and became confused because everyone heard the disciples speaking in their own respective languages. They were astonished and asked in bewilderment: "Aren't all these who are speaking Galileans? Then how is it that each of us hears them in our native language?[42] Parthians, Medes and Elamites; residents of Mesopotamia, Judea and Cappadocia, Pontus and Asia, Phrygia and Pamphylia, Egypt and the parts of Libya near Cyrene; visitors from Rome (both Jews and converts to Judaism); Cretans and Arabs—we hear them declaring the wonders of God in our own tongues!" (Acts 2:7-11).[43] The "Spirit" communicated itself in the community, whereby everyone became a witness to the great acts of God in his or her own language. Through their enthusiasm, driven by the Spirit and bound in one community with each other, they began to communicate.[44]

Everyone heard the Galileans, filled by the Spirit, speaking in their own language (Acts 2:6). This report is connected with the confusion of languages that occurred at the building of the Tower of Babel (Gen 11) and the division of the one human language into many at the time and thus the splitting up of humankind into many nations. This story is about the new reunification of all nations who understand each other via the common language of the Spirit. In other words, at Pentecost the situation that existed at a primal time is now restored at a higher level. One Jewish expectation is that the original common language of the whole cosmos (including the

---

39. *KBS* on Acts 2:3.

40. Fischer and Markl, *Das Buch Exodus,* 218, with a reference to J. Durham.

41. Lundbom, *Deuteronomium,* 240-41.

42. *idiai dialektoi.*

43. Strack and Billerbeck, *Kommentar zum Neuen Testament,* vol. 2, 603-5. These tongues also appeared at Sinai when the law was proclaimed to the nations of the world.

44. *B.W.,* s.v. "Tongen van vuur."

animals) of that primal time would, accordingly, once again become the common language in the end time. While Luke, the author of the book of Acts, saw the Spirit as active, John speaks of the imparting of the Spirit to the disciples: "And with that he breathed on them and said, 'Receive the Holy Spirit'" (John 20:22). That makes one think of God who breathes the breath of life into the human being, turning the human being into a living creature (Gen 2:7; cf. Ezek 37:9). Paul speaks of God's love that is poured out into our hearts by the Holy Spirit (Rom 5:5) and the indwelling of the Spirit in human hearts (Rom 8:9, 11; 1 Cor 3:16).[45]

Maimonides and the Language of Canaan Spoken with Pure Lips

The famous Jewish thinker Moses Maimonides (1135–1204) worked in an Arab world that was dominated by Islamic politics. The major powers of his time were Islamic and Christian. He was born in Cordoba, Moorish Spain, which would be reconquered a few centuries later during the *Reconquista* of the "most Christian monarchs" (Ferdinand and Isabella). Charles V built his palace in the Al-Hamra (Alhambra) in Granada, in the former seat of the Islamic rulers. Both Muslims and Jews were driven out during the Christian reconquest of Spain!

When Maimonides himself had to flee because of a new Puritanical "fanatical" Muslim policy that had been put into effect, he did not turn to "Christian Europe"—for that was even less safe for Jews. He therefore fled from the Arab west, the western part of the Arab world (Maghreb, "Morocco"), to the eastern part of the Arab east (the "Mashriq"), which we call the Middle East. He settled down in Cairo, where he became physician to the famous ruler Saladin who would drive the crusaders from Jerusalem. Aside from being a philosopher and doctor, Maimonides was also a "doctor of souls." At that time (and later as well) he became a guide for countless Jews. These were mostly Jews who were threatened by Christians and Muslims with respect to their identity. Maimonides wondered what he should think about these two movements, which came in one way or another out of "his" Judaism. Should they be seen as enemies? Was reconciliation with them conceivable? Was there a common ground for collaboration, coexistence, and dialogue? Was there a common language? The latter was not a question of a "knowledge of languages"—for he had that in abundance. This Jew wrote his famous *Guide for the Perplexed* in Arabic and knew Hebrew. Rather, Maimonides understood that all three—Jews, Christians, and Muslims—knew the language of the

---

45. Stählin, *Die Apostelgeschichte*, 38.

Scriptures, the revelation of God to Moses and the revelation to Jesus and, as far he himself was concerned, the revelation of God to Muhammad as well. That can be determined from what he wrote on the relationship between Jews, Christians, and Muslims: "The plans of the Creator transcend the ability of human minds to fathom them. 'For his thoughts are not our thoughts,/ neither are our ways his ways'" (Isa 55:8). In other words, he admits that he does not understand it completely either. But he obviously believes that God deals in unsearchable ways with all three: Jews, Christians, and Muslims. "Our human ways are not his, God's, ways." But then he continues:

> Everything that has to do with Jesus of Nazareth and the Ishmaelite [i.e., Muhammad] who came after him, clearly served the way of the king Messiah to prepare the whole world to worship God as one, as it is written:

"Then I will purify the lips of the peoples,
  that all of them may call on the name of the Lord
  and serve him shoulder to shoulder"
(Zeph 3:9)

Maimonides used that common language himself, the language that can be spoken only with pure lips. He saw a common vision for the future.

That question that can asked of us today is whether Jews, Christians, and Muslims can also learn to speak that language, if they can (re)learn it, and develop a common vision for our torn world where the clash between cultures and religions, in particular, the clash between Judaism, Christianity, and Islam, is seen as the cause of all misery. Ida G. Gerhardt wrote in a different context: "And I believe that you, particularly in poetry, 'cannot serve two languages.'"[46] Leaving aside what Gerhardt herself meant by this, if the world is to be habitable, it should be clear which language must be served.

The Arabs in Northern and Southern Arabia

The Arab Peninsula was divided for centuries between "Arabia Felix" in the south, which was called "happy" because it was watered by the monsoons from the Indian Ocean and was thus fertile, and "Arabia Deserta" in the North. That corresponds with the traditional division of Arabs into southern Arabs, who descended from Qahtân, thought to be Joktan in the Bible (Gen 10:25–29; 1 Chron 1:19–23),[47] and the northern Arabs, which claimed to

---

46. Koenen, *Dwars tegen de keer*, 516.
47. This is the line of Shem, which leads to Abraham. The line appears in the table

descend from 'Adnân and, via him, from Ishmael, the son of Abraham.[48] According to a popular tradition, Ishmael was the first to speak Arabic.[49]

There was a strong Jewish presence in southern Arabia. Most likely, they had come to Arabia after the destruction of Jerusalem in 70 A.D., and after the Jewish revolt in 135. The famous Rabbi Akiba was said to have visited the Jews living there. The fact that there were reports of the persecution of Christians points to the quite large influence Christians already had then as well.[50]

Both the northern and the southern tribes were divided into "people of the house"[51] or "people of the goats,"[52] i.e., Bedouins from the desert, the wilderness.[53] "Arab" means Bedouin. The Bedouins of the northern and central deserts are the "sons of 'Adnân."[54] The Arabs from the north are viewed as "Arabized Arabs," whereas the Arabs from the south are seen as the "true" Arabs. They are seen as the descendants of Shem, the son of Noah (Gen 5:32), who was with Noah in the ark.

The Arabs from the south are also called "the lost or distant Arabs." Their identity has become lost in that of other peoples who are explicitly named in the Qur'an: the people of 'Âd and Thamûd. The Arab prophet Hûd was sent to the people of 'Ad, and Sâlih to the people of Thamûd. Both prophets were rejected, however. According to commentators on the Qur'an, the children of Israel fought against the descendants of the tribe of 'Âd in the desert after they had left Egypt, who are thus traditionally located in the south.

After Muhammad's death in 632, various disputes arose between the emigrants (*muhadjirûn*) who originally followed Muhammad from Mecca to Medina (Arabs from the north) and the Muslims from Medina who were called "helpers" (*ansâr*). After settling in Medina (which means "city"), conflict with the native Muslims of the city arose. The latter originally came from the south. Later, after the death of Yazîd I, the son of the founder of the dynasty of the Umayyads in Damascus, a dispute arose between the Qays, a north Arab tribal group, and the Kalb, a southern tribal group. This dispute lasted the whole of the Umayyad caliphate in Damascus, i.e., until 750 A.D.[55]

---

of nations as part of the family of the human race. Shem is given special attention in the next chapter, Gen 11:10–29. Cf. Brueggemann, *Genesis*, 92.

48. The name 'Adnân appears in Nabatean inscriptions from northwest Arabia and also in Thamudic. It travelled to the south via the myrrh route. *E.I.*, s.v. "'Adnân."

49. Kramers, *De taal van den Koran*, 7.

50. Attema, *Het Oudste Christendom*, 7.

51. *ahl al-madar*.

52. *ahl al-wabar*.

53. *badîya*.

54. Glassé, *The Concise Encyclopaedia*, s.v. "'Adnân."

55. Glassé, *The Concise Encyclopaedia*, s.v. "Arab."

Ethiopia was reported to have had a strong influence on the Christians in southern Arabia.[56] The contact between Muhammad and the Christians can be seen from the "Ethiopian loanwords" found in the Qur'an. Jesus' apostles, for instance, are called *al-hawâriyyûn* (Q 3:45; 5:112; 61:14), "hell" is called *jahannam*, the "devil" *al-shaytân*, and the word *at-tâjût* is used for "idols." The devil is "cursed" (*râjîm*) (Q 3:31; 15:17, 34; 16:100; 81:25; 38:78) and "hypocrites" are called *al-munâfiqûn*. God is called *fâtir* ("Creator"). One could also think here of the Ethiopian loanword for "pulpit" (*minbar*) and for "holy book" (*mishaf*). The widely used name for God, *al-Rahmân*, is also often used in the Qur'an.[57] The title of the fifth chapter of the Qur'an is called *'al-ma' ida*, an Ethiopian word for "the table of the Lord."

When the Bible tells of the Exodus of the people of Israel from Egypt it relates that "many other people" went with them (Exod 12:38). These people, that "ragtag collection of various peoples," are called *'ârab* in Hebrew, the same word used for Arabs! "The Arabs have thus been intertwined with Israel right from the start."[58] The mixed bag of people accompanying the Israelites is proof that God wants to grant universal freedom and that others may and can join Israel on its road to freedom.[59]

In pre-Islamic North and South Arabic inscriptions, the word *'ârab* (whose adjectival form is *'ârâbî*) originally meant "nomads of the Syro-Arabian desert." The inhabitants of Dedan—descendants of Ham (Gen 10:7) or Abraham and Ketura (Gen 25:3)—and Tema are nomads who took part in the caravan trade on the routes along which myrrh was transported (I Kings 10:14-15; 2 Chron 9:12-14; cf. Is 21:13; Ezek 27:20-21; 38:13). Isaiah addresses Arabia in his prophecy (Isa 21:13-15). The oasis of Dedan, which appears in the table of nations, is mentioned by the prophets between 700 and 580 B.C. Thus, it is vividly related how a considerably sized caravan of Dedanites, probably travelling along the great trade route from Gaza to Medina, is attacked by an army equipped with swords, bows, and arrows. The Dedanites had to flee to the oasis of Tema off the main route, whose inhabitants the prophet calls to treat them with Eastern hospitality. Caravans from Dedan traded with Tyre, and the Dedanites were viewed as merchants of some importance (Ezek 27:15). Like the Sabeans, they were seen as an important trading people in southern Arabia (Ezek 38:13). The prophet Jeremiah warned the Dedanite caravans to avoid the region of the Edomites

---

56. See the chapter "The Desert and the City" below.

57. Attema, *Het Oudste Christendom*, 13-14.

58. Barnard, *Een winter,* 57 and the note on that page; Köhler and Baumgärtner, *Lexicon,* s.v. "'Arab."

59. Fischer and Markl, *Das Buch Exodus,* 141.

living north of them because of the judgment that was coming to Edom (cf. Ezek 25:13).[60] Dedan is the city of this people located south of Edom; it is now an oasis in northern Hijâz.[61]

The Grammar of the Hijra

Just as Abraham left Ur of the Chaldeans and broke with King Nimrod, the king of Ashur, Babylon, and Nineveh, just as Lot left Sodom and Gomorrah before these cities were "overthrown," just as Moses led the children of Israel out of Egypt, and just like Jesus' Exodus in Jerusalem,[62] so Muhammad left the idolatrous Mecca and led his community to Medina in the year 622.

Muhammad came with a message that confirmed the message of the Bible, both the Tanakh (*Tawra*) as well as in the New Testament (*Injîl*). In particular, Abraham, Moses, and Jesus also have an important place in his message. All those Exoduses are also found in the Qur'an,[63] and they always involve a departure from a world that speaks a foreign or strange language. In Muhammad's time, that world was that of the leaders of the idolatrous and unjust policy makers of his hometown, Mecca, and in the wider world that of the imperialistic powers of the East Roman or Byzantine Empire on the one hand and the Persian Empire on the other. The city of Constantinople, founded by Constantine the Great and named after him, was seen as the "second Rome" and was known in Arabic as Rûm (cf. Q 30).

It is said that Muhammad's great-grandfather received a letter from the Kaysar (the usual name in Arabic for the Byzantine emperor) with a letter of safe conduct for the merchants of Mecca who wanted to visit Syria. For the Ghassanids and the inhabitants of northern Arabia, the Byzantine emperor was the supreme ruler, just as Kisrâ, the king of the Persians, was that for the Lakhmids and all the inhabitants of the area that stretched to the Persian Gulf. For later Arab poets, the Kaysar and Kisrâ were still frequent symbols for power and wealth.

Although the word Kaysar does not occur in the Qur'an, it is mentioned in the biography of the prophet Muhammad, in the traditions, and in commentaries on the Qur'an. The famous Byzantine emperor in Muhammad's time and that of his first two successors, the caliphs Abû Bakr and 'Umar,

---

60. Attema, *Arabië*, 35–36.
61. *B.W.* s.v. "Dedan."
62. On the mountain of the transfiguration, Jesus spoke with Moses and Elijah about the end of his life: about his going away, his departure, or—as literally stated in Greek—his "Exodus in Jerusalem" (Luke 9:30–31).
63. Cf. Wessels, The *Torah*, chapter IV.

THE LANGUAGE OF CANAAN AND FOREIGN TONGUES 97

was Heraclius, called the "great Caesar"[64] or "King of the second Rome."[65] In 614 the Byzantines suffered a defeat at the hands of the Sassanid Persians, whereby the city of Jerusalem was captured. In 622 Heraclius opened an offensive against the Persians and won a decisive battle in Nineveh in 627. In 630 he was able to retake the city of Jerusalem, the same year in which Muhammad captured Mecca! The Qur'an alludes to this last event in its 30th chapter, which is called "Rûm." "The Byzantines were defeated in the near region (the area directly bordering Arabia: Syria/Palestine), but they will, after their defeat, be victorious in turn. The believer will rejoice about that" (Q 30:2-3).[66] That clearly points to the sympathy that the followers of Muhammad clearly felt for the Byzantine Christians at that time.

Muhammad himself sent a brief letter to the governor of Bosra in Syria and via him to the emperor Heraclius. It is said that the emperor asked Abû Sufyân, the leader of Mecca, about the new prophet. Unlike Kisrâ, the Persian king, the emperor thought about converting to Islam, but fear of his subjects prevented him from openly confessing the new religion.

Muhammad was engaged in negotiations[67] to come to an agreement with the still unbelieving Meccan leaders to allow a pilgrimage[68] to Mecca. 'Urwa ibn Masûd,[69] whom the prophet had visited in his camp, told his fellow Meccan citizens: "I have been with Kisrâ in his kingdom (Persia) and with Kaysar in his kingdom (Byzantium) and with the Negus in his kingdom (Ethiopia), but never have I seen a king among his people like Muhammad among his companions."[70] For the Arabs, Kisrâ personified the Sassanid dynasty, which invoked a combination of envy, respect, and fear. They called their capital Ctesiphon (Madâ'in Kisrâ). Kisrâs "secularity" was contrasted with Muslim spirituality. He tore up the letter in which Muhammad invited him to convert to Islam.[71]

---

64. *kaysar 'azîm.*
65. *malik al-Rûm.*
66. Paret, *Der Koran: Kommentar*, p. 388, on Q 30:2-5.
67. *in al-Hudaybiyya.*
68. The *hajj.*
69. He was a leader of Tâ'if, who was the first of his tribe to become a companion of Muhammad. He was killed by his fellow leaders for preaching Islam.
70. *E.I.*, s.v. "Kaysar," 1; Guillaume, *The Life of Muhammad*, 503. The religious and military grounds on which respect for the emperor rested in the pre-Islamic period disappeared in the first centuries of Islam. The new attitude was reflected in the terms for the emperor like *tâghiya* (tyrant) or an expression like *kalb al-Rûm*, the "dog of the Romans," used by Hârûn al-Rashîd in his address to Nicephorus. See *E.I.*, s.v. "Kaysar," 2.
71. *E.I.*, s.v. "Kisrâ."

Clear Arabic

There is a long Muslim tradition that views the Arabic of the Qur'an as a miracle in itself and proof of the truth of the Word of God. The Arabist Achille Ratti, who would later become Pope Pius XI, always talked about the excellence of another classical language, Latin, "The Church, as stated in the Apostolic Letter of 1 August 1922, needs a language that is by nature general and unchangeable, which is not the vernacular. Given that the Latin language is of that nature, it has been determined/designed from on high to be a wonderful aid for the teaching church."[72]

Here I just want to look at the fact that we can also speak of a bilingualism in the Qur'an in the sense of a language of Canaan and a foreign language. Here "foreign language" does not refer to the fact that it is non-Arabic any more than it is the point in the Tanakh that "foreign language" refers to a non-Hebrew language.

The reliable Spirit of God revealed the Qur'an in Muhammad's heart in clear Arabic, just like the language in the old books[73] of previous generations. Was that not a sign for his Arabic contemporaries of the truth of the revelation of the Qur'an and for the fact that the scribes of the children of Israel knew about those? "If We had revealed it [the Book] to non-Arabs[74] and if they had read it or recited it in their own language,[75] they would have not believed it at all" (Q 26:195–199).[76]

The Qur'an is the Arabic Qur'an (Q 11:2; 16:103; 20:113; 26:195; 39:28; 41:3; 42:7; 43:3) and not one in a foreign language (Q 41:44). God made the Qur'an comprehensible in Muhammad's own Arabic language, intending thereby that he could thus bring God-fearing people the good news and warn contentious people (Q 19:97; cf. 44:58).[77] Here the prophet Muhammad did nothing other than other prophets before him had done. The Book of Moses is a guide and proof of the divine mercy that is now confirmed in the Arabic tongue or language[78] to warn the unjust and to bring joyful tidings[79] for the righteous (Q 46:12).

---

72. Kramers, *De taal van den Koran*, 27.
73. *zubur*.
74. *'ajamîna*.
75. *qara'u*.
76. *E.Q.*, s.v. "Arabic Language."
77. Paret, *Der Koran: Kommentar*, on Q 19:97.
78. *lisân*.
79. *bushrâ*.

The word that is used for language is *lisân* ("tongue"), the language in which it was revealed to Muhammad. He is a messenger who is sent to a people using the language of his own people. For the Arabs, thus, that is Arabic: "We did not send a messenger who did not speak the language of the people, so he could make (it) clear to them" (Q 14:4). That was true of earlier prophets as well: they also spoke in the language of their people.

When it is said that the Qur'an was revealed in clear Arabic (Q 26:195), one could say that the Qur'an uses the "language of Canaan" in the above sense. Thus, it is a language that is contrasted with impure, untruthful, foreign, and deceitful language. "We do know that they say: 'It is only people who instruct him [Muhammad].'"[80]

The language referred to as impure is a foreign one,[81] whereas the language of the Qur'an is clear Arabic (Q 16:103).[82] We should look at the word "instruct/teach,"[83] a term that is often used in the Qur'an for God who "instructs" the angels, people, and the elected prophets (Q 55:2; 96:4–5; 2:32, etc.). It is instruction, just like he taught Adam the names of everything in creation (Q 2:31). God taught the prophets the Scripture and wisdom, the Torah and the Gospel, and his laws to humankind in general. God communicates knowledge about what is hidden, for God is said to be the one who has knowledge of what is hidden.[84] It is also said of the demons that they teach people, but what they teach is not *'ilm* (divine knowledge) but magic, so they can lure people into temptation.[85]

What is the precise meaning of the "Arabic language"[86] of the prophetic message over against a foreign language? The translation of the Arabic word *'ajamî*, which is usually translated as "non-Arabic," can be better viewed as "incomprehensible speech." Thus, the most comprehensible translation of "Arabic language" is then "clear language," so that it forms a pleonasm with the word *mubîn*, which means "clear." And what is then clear? God has given all kinds of parables[87] in this Qur'an to warn people. God has revealed an Arabic Qur'an in which there is nothing that deviates from the straight path, nothing that is "crooked" (Q 39:27–28). Sometimes the "people of the book"

---

80. *mu'allamun*.

81. *a'jamî*.

82. *lisânun 'arabiyun mubînun*. Buhl, 164, thinks this statement is unclear. My explanation is a better interpretation.

83. *'allama*.

84. *'alim al-ghayb*.

85. Radscheit, *Die koranische Herausforderung*, 43–44.

86. *lisân* or *qur' ân 'arabî*.

87. *mathâlin*.

especially (Jews and Christians) are reproached for leading believers away from the straight path and putting them on a crooked one (Q 3:99; cf. 7:45, 86; 11:19; 14:3). That is the same reproach Paul made when he encountered a Jewish sorcerer and false prophet, Bar-Jesus ("son of Jesus"), who was an attendant of a certain proconsul, Sergius Paulus, an intelligent man. This sorcerer attempted to prevent the proconsul from becoming a Christian. Paul looked straight at him and said, "You are a child of the devil [intended to be a mocking play on his name] and an enemy of everything that is right! You are full of all kinds of deceit and trickery. Will you never stop perverting the right ways of the Lord?" (Acts 13:9–10).[88] In contrast to the crooked path, the Arabic Qur'an is the "right way," i.e., the true proclamation.[89]

Unfortunately, it is simply always the lot of prophets to have enemies who harass them with lies, fabrications, and false statements (Q 6:112). Paul had similar experiences and warned the community in Rome he was writing to about keeping an eye on those who cause dissension and raise obstacles that conflict with the teaching they had been given. "By smooth talk and flattery they deceive the minds of naive people" (Rom 16:17–18; cf. 1 Cor 1:17, 21; 2:1, 4–5, 13; 2 Cor 11:6).[90]

The long chapter about Joseph begins in the Qur'an with the words: "These are the signs of the clear book." God revealed these as an Arabic recitation or reading, which was done out loud, of course. The Qur'an is not so much read as heard. Muhammad's Jewish authorities claimed to be better informed about the story of Joseph than he was. That is why it is explicitly related by Muhammad: "We [i.e., God] tell you the best story, better than any human authority" (Q 2:3).[91]

The Qur'an that is revealed to Muhammad is clearly seen as something that was said already previously to the messengers before his time. If God had put it in a strange language, then there may have been reason to say: "Why are its verses and details not explained in such a way that everyone can follow and understand it? What does that mean? It's in a foreign language even though the prophet is Arabic": "For those who believe it is right guidance and a source of comfort or healing. But those who do not believe, however, are hard of hearing, stick their fingers in their ears" (Q 41:41–44). They do not listen to it but talk through Muhammad's presentation of it (Q

---

88. "Whoever walks in integrity walks securely,/ but whoever takes crooked paths will be found out" (Prov 10:9).

89. Radscheit, *Die koranische Herausforderung*, 45–46.

90. Ibid., 46–47.

91. Paret, *Der Koran: Kommentar*, on 12:3.

41:26).⁹² "The opposition has nothing to do with the non-Arabic Qur'an and its Arabic proclaimer . . . but with the irreconcilability of obscure and unclear speech with the prophetic claim to point to clear signs."⁹³

This Qur'an was not simply snatched out of thin air, without God being behind it. It is rather a confirmation of the revelation that predated Muhammad. That is why it must not be doubted (Q 10:37; cf. 3:3; 2:97; 5:48; 35:31; 46:30; 6:92). The Qur'an confirms this message from the *Tawra* and the *Injîl*. Just as the Tanakh brings the "good news of God"—and not only the New Testament, as often suggested in Christian interpretations—so Muhammad also brings the good news. He is the joyful proclaimer of that good news, and that message is found in the Qur'an. It turns out that there were Jews and Christians among Muhammad's audience, and that is why it can even be said that, if there is any doubt about what has been revealed, the people of the Book who read the Scriptures before, the *Tawra* and the *Injîl*, can be asked for information about the content of their revelation (Q 10:94).⁹⁴

The Good News of the Tanakh, the Gospel, and the Qur'an

One can see the coherence between the Old and the New Testaments and the Qur'an if one looks at how much all three are characterized by the good news.⁹⁵ The good news is constantly proclaimed in new periods by the prophets. Looking at a few examples of this will help clarify this point.

The book of Isaiah contains messages from various phases of the history of the tribes of Israel. His oracle can also throw light on the connections that run between the three books, namely, the connections between the descendants of Isaac, the patriarch of the Jews, and Ishmael, the patriarch of the Arabs.

One of his oracles concerns the Dumah, Arab nomads who lived in the northwestern part of the Arab Peninsula. It is an oracle, a prophecy about these nomads, who are represented here by their ancestor, Dumah,⁹⁶ the son of Ishmael (Gen 25:14; 1 Chron 1:30). The oracle reads:

---

92. Cf. the translation by Paret, *Der Koran: Übersetzung*.

93. As Paret states—and with him many Western exegetes. See also Radscheit, *Die koranische Herausforderung*, 89, note 371.

94. Paret, *Der Koran: Kommentar*, on Q 10:94.

95. *Bashâra* (Hebr.), *euangelion* (Gr.), *bushrâ* (Ar.).

96. This could be the son of Ishmael (Gen 25:14; 1 Chron 1:30). In this text the name is connected with Seir. The Septuagint translates the term both times by "Idumea" (Edom). *B.W.*, s.v. "Seïr." Seir is place of divine revelation (Deut 33:2; Judg 5:4) and of divine judgment (Isa 21:11; Ezek 35:3, 7, 15).

> A prophecy against Dumah:
>> Someone calls to me from Seir,
>> "Watchman, what is left of the night?
>> Watchman, what is left of the night?"
> The watchman replies,
>> "Morning is coming, but also the night.
>> If you would ask, then ask;
>> and come back yet again."
>
> (Isa 21:11–12)

This double question is directed at a watcher keeping watch and listening to a report about a battle being fought elsewhere. The watcher watches and listens, hoping to hear *good news* about the outcome of the battle. The question is actually: "How late is it?" "Is the night almost over?" The answer is: "It is still night, but it will be day soon. Ask me again later." Question and answer are closely connected with the final battle against Babylon. The watcher is waiting to hear when Babylon is defeated. The *night* thus refers to the long period of oppression under the rule of Babylon, and the *morning* or the new day will bring respite and redemption. The watcher does not doubt that good news will come quickly.

It is a later watcher, according to *Deutero-Isaiah*, who will hear the good news of the defeat of Babylon and pass it on:

> How beautiful on the mountains
>> are the feet of those who bring good news,
> who proclaim peace,
>> who bring good tidings,
>> who proclaim salvation,
> who say to Zion,
>> "Your God reigns!"
>
> (Isa 52:7)

God reigns in Zion as king of the world.[97] The new message that must be proclaimed is shouted by the use of five imperatives:

> Go up on a high mountain.
> You who bring good news to Jerusalem,
>> lift up your voice with a shout,
>> lift it up, do not be afraid;

---

97. *KBS.* Cf. the psalms on God's kingly rule: Pss 47, 93, 96–99.

say to the towns of Judah,
"Here is your God!"
See, the Sovereign Lord comes with power.
(Isa 40:9-10)

The essence of this speech is so decisive because the term "good news [Gospel]" is used for the first time in the Old Testament. This herald has to proclaim the Gospel to the cities of Judah. That message is summarized in the exclamation: "Here is your God!" In their arrogance, the Babylonians built a world without God: "Is not this the great Babylon I [Nebuchadnezzar] have built?" (Dan 4:30)—Babylon with its hanging gardens (one of the seven wonders of the world), which were built in the sixth century B.C. at Nebuchadnezzar's command. Already then they were considered a wonder. But to the exiles as well it seemed that, in their desperation, there was no God. "Look, here is your God." His presence changed everything. This was no longer the path of arrogance on the one side and desperation on the other.[98] The messenger who proclaims these good tidings is more than welcome (Isa 52:7). Mark's gospel opens with Isaiah's words about the messenger of God who now appears in the figure of John the Baptist (Yahyâ), sent to prepare the way (Mark 1:2-4): a voice of one calling in the wilderness,/ "Prepare the way for the Lord,/ make straight paths for him" (Mark 1:3).

This is a reference to Isaiah 52 and a proclamation of the fact that God was decisively present in Jesus, who in turn opposes the arrogance and desperation of a world without God. "'The time has come,' he said. 'The kingdom of God has come near. Repent and believe the good news!'" (Mark 1:15).

Thus, the Qur'an confirms the good tidings (*bushrâ*), the good news. These good tidings will be heard again, now from the mouth of the prophet who confirmed the earlier messages. This good news means the reversal, the transformation of world history.

The Good News Has One Language

There is a tradition about the prophet Muhammad that says that there is no place in Arabia for two beliefs. That has more or less turned out to be true since the death of Muhammad. If one travels to Mecca—which I did only once in my life, in 1974—then at a certain point one starts seeing signs that state that non-Muslims are not admitted into the city. They are then directed to a road that skirts Mecca, a road that is locally called the "Christian road." This practice does not square with the life and practice of

---

98. Brueggemann, *Isaiah 40-66*, 20-22.

the prophet Muhammad himself. The delegation of Christians from Najrân who came to visit him in Medina, under the leadership of their bishop, were welcome to pray in his mosque. Saudi Arabia's constitution is the Qur'an, but nowhere does the Qur'an forbid Jews, Christians, or Muslims to enter Mecca and to go to the house of God built by Abraham, the father of all believers. The point is still: Which language do the Jews, Christians, and Muslims speak—the language of Canaan or a foreign one? Whoever denies a true believer—Jew, Christian, or Muslim—admittance to Mecca speaks a "foreign language."

IV

Foreign Powers and Religion

> Some trust in chariots and some in horses,
> but we trust in the name of the Lord our God.
>
> *(PS 20:7)*

Thus, it is of the utmost significance that the Torah, the law of the theo-polity, was, for all its diversity, always ascribes to Moses and not to David to the humble mediator of covenant and not to the regal founder of the dynastic state.[1]

"The French 9/11"

SOLELY BY CHANCE I had booked a short vacation of about four days in Paris, from 8 to 11 January 2015. It was quite something to be there just at that time. The headline of the first paper I bought in Paris, *Le Monde* read: "The French 9/11." The large demonstration for freedom of expression—the largest demonstration in French history—was held on 11 January. Four Jews had been murdered in a cowardly act in a kosher store on the previous Friday. Close to the scene of the shooting, Ilan Benhanou pulled a small yarmulka out of his pocket and gave it to his friend, "Put this on, will you?" Then he, a thin young man in a black leather jacket, took out his cell phone and began to recite a Hebrew text at a fast tempo in a sing-song voice. Every once in a while he stumbled for a bit. He was able to continue with the text by glancing repeatedly at his cell phone. "That is the psalm of David," an older man with a woolen hat later explained. He had come to watch and had prompted the "cantor" every once in a while. He opened the psalm book he

---

1. Levenson, *Sinai and Zion*, 75.

had taken with him: "Look, Psalm 14. The psalm against fear. We Jews sing this when something serious happens."

The name of the scene of the crime is "Hyper Cachet," written in white letters on a ominous black background. Glass shards in the fenced-off area testified to the violence. "Terror is terror," Ilan said when he put his cell phone and his yarmulka back in his pocket. The man with the psalm book said he was no longer afraid after the hostage-taking of that Friday. "The man who did this was a criminal paid by the Islamic State. We must not be afraid because he claims to murder in the name of Islam. He was no Muslim. He was a criminal."[2]

"The Psalm against Fear"

Psalm 14[3] begins with the words, "The fool says in his heart,/ 'There is no God.'" It is a lament about the criminal activities of the "fools," the enemies of Israel, perhaps the Philistines or Babylonians. Scholars have proposed that there is a word play between *nâbal* ("fool") and Babel![4] The declaration of the fool, "There is no God," is a quote from an earlier psalm, where these words are spoken by a criminal: "God will not seek it out" . . . "There is no God" (Ps 10:4 [NRSV]).[5] That is, there is no God who acts or helps. "He says to himself, 'God has forgotten; / he coves his face and never sees'" (Ps 10:11). The wicked is characterized as someone "who devours my people," a realistic metaphor for the oppression and exploitation of the lower classes:

> [Y]ou who hate good and love evil;
> who tear the skin from my people
>   and the flesh from their bones;
> who eat my people's flesh,
>   strip off their skin
>   and break their bones in pieces;
> who chop them up like meat for the pan,
>   like flesh for the pot?"
> (Mic 3:2–3)

There are

---

2. *NRC*, Friday, 16 January 2015.

3. Psalm 14 = Psalm 53.

4. Hossfeld and Zenger, *Die Psalmen*, 99–100; cf. 1 Sam 25, the story of David, Nabal, and his wise wife, Abigail, who later became David's wife.

5. Hossfeld and Zenger, *Die Psalmen*, 101–2.

> those whose teeth are swords
>> and whose jaws are set with knives
> to devour the poor from the earth
>> and the needy from among mankind.
>
> (Prov 30:14).[6]

The fool's analysis of society denies the order of justice established by God, a line of thinking that assumes that the power and will of God does not intervene in this world. That prevents the world and life from taking shape in accordance with what they truly are. That is why the fool is not a wise man who walks the road of life but a fool who travels the road of destruction. That is, his life in the end becomes shipwrecked. The fool is rich and powerful but misuses his wealth and power for his own interests (cf. 1 Sam 25:2–42; Luke 12:20). He is aggressive toward others, especially the weak and women (cf. Gen 34:7; Deut 22:21; Judg 19:23–24; 2 Sam 13:12–13), and is insensitive to and brutal toward people in need (cf. Isa 32:5–6; Prov 17:7). This assertion by the fool—"There is no God"—which could almost be called his life motto—and the sentence, "He says to himself, 'God has forgotten; / he coves his face and never sees'" are often viewed as expressions of practical atheism (cf. Ps 10:11; 28:5; 64:6; 73:11; 94:7; Job 22:13–14).[7] This way of thinking about God is condemned and combatted both in wisdom literature and in the prophetic tradition because of the fatal consequences it has for society. It does not state nor intend to state that all people are criminal fools but that these fools are so trapped in their evil world because of their violent idolatrous practices that they are actually no longer willing and ready to do good.[8]

Wise Men and Fools

What is it to be Godlike and what is it to be godless? According to Paul, godlessness consists in wise people, the the smart ones in society, refusing—against their better judgment—to believe in the true God and instead becoming guilty of idolatry:[9] "Although they claimed to be wise, they became fools" (Rom 1:22).

---

6. Gerstenberger, *Psalms, Part 1*, 219–20.

7. Also in the prophets in Isa 29:15; Jer 5:12; 12:4; Ezek 8:12; 9:9; Zeph 1:12; Mal 3:14–18.

8. Hossfeld and Zenger, *Psalmen 51–100*, 81–83.

9. *KBS* on Romans 1:18.

In the ancient world the wise person enjoyed high status, but at the same time it was also true that no one could ever claim to be wise. Socrates was considered to be extraordinarily wise precisely because he never claimed to be wise, declaring, in fact, the opposite. The fact that people "claimed to be wise" thus also sounded ridiculous to Paul's readers. Becoming a fool is apparently a divine judgment about people in their alledged superior wisdom. The high point of foolishness is idolatry, a means to suppress the truth: they "exchanged the glory of the immortal God for images made to look like a mortal human being and birds and animals and reptiles" (Rom 1:23). Paul's formulation here alludes to Psalm 106:19–20:

> At Horeb they made a calf
> and worshiped an idol cast from metal.
> They exchanged their glorious God
> for an image of a bull, which eats grass.

The image of the golden calf that Aaron made is the archetype of idolatry in the Bible (Exod 34) and in the Qur'an (Q 2:51, 92–93; 4:153; 7:148–150; 20:88–89, 97). The antithesis between mortal humankind and the immutable God emphasizes the ridiculous, foolish character of this self-deception.[10] The Qur'an almost immediately lists three categories of unbelieving people: hypocrites (Q 2:8–11), fools (Q 2:12–13), and those who joke about God (Q 2:4–16). Characteristic of these three groups is that they believe that they know better. Just like Paul, the Qur'an assumes that they do know the divine message but nevertheless do not follow it. They act as if they believe and thus deceive other, true believers. But they are actually deceiving themselves (Q 2:8–9). "For although they knew God, they neither glorified him as God nor gave thanks to him, but their thinking became futile and their foolish hearts were darkened. Although they claimed to be wise, they became fools" (Rom 1:21–22).[11] "Who other than a fool can scorn the religion[12] of Abraham?" (Q 2:130).[13]

The Human Being: Caliph or King

When God announced to his angels his intention to create humankind, the angels did not respond favorably. "Man will sow corruption and shed blood

---

10. Jewett, *Romans*, 159–62.
11. Schmitz, *Der Koran*, 26–28.
12. *milla*.
13. Paret, *Der Koran: Kommentar*, on Q 2:130.

on the earth." It cannot be denied that they had a point. It is all the more striking that God had such faith in his idea that he nevertheless created humankind. God's intention was that humankind—every human individual, man or woman—would be or become his "deputy" or caliph on earth (cf. Q 2:30; 38:26; 10:14; 35:39; 6:165).

Satan comes onstage after the creation of humankind and tempts humans to choose to be kings instead (Q 20:120). It is precisely that kingship that led to that corruption and shedding of blood the angels refer to. The powerful in the world have usually chosen—and still choose –that kingship. The evildoers and the wicked wreak havoc and disturb the balance in social and political relationships. They commit violence and engage in war.

The Arabic expression for "sowing corruption upon the earth" uses the word *ard* for "earth." Like *eretz* in Hebrew, this word means both "land" and "earth." When Joseph's brothers were accused of stealing a cup, they replied that they had not come to Egypt to sow corruption upon the land: "We are not thieves" (Q 12:73).

"Bringing destruction" characterizes the behavior of the Pharaoh who sows division among the inhabitants of his country. He oppresses one part of the population, such as the children of Israel, whose sons he kills while sparing their women (Q 28:4). And, during a contest of sorts with the Egyptian magicians who serve the court, Moses says: "What you do is magic, and God will bring it to nothing because He will never allow those who sow corruption to thrive" (Q 10:81—God makes straight the crooked roads of corruption that have been built [Q 10:81]). In their turn, Pharaoh's ministers accuse Moses and his people of being the ones sowing corruption on the land because they wanted to abandon the idolatrous habits of Egypt (Q 7:127)![14]

The figures Gog and Magog, the enemies from the north, are held responsible for the heinous violence of apocalyptic proportions. They are also mentioned in the Bible (Ezek 38:2—39:15; Rev 20:7–10). "The man with the two horns" in this story is Alexander the Great, who is asked: "Will you build a rampart between us and them?" (Q 18:94). God wants to avert disaster and does not love those who sow corruption (Q 2:205; cf. 5:64; 28:77). He stands on the side of those who maintain or restore order.[15]

Over against sowing corruption[16] is doing good works or "acting justly or righteously." The name of the prophet Sâlih, who was sent to the people

---

14. Izutsu, *Ethico-Religious Concepts*, 211–13.
15. Paret, *Der Koran: Kommentar,* on Q 2:11, 12.
16. *fasâd* or *ifsâd*.

of Thamûd, is derived from the Arabic term for the latter[17] (Q 7:73-79; 11:61-68; 26:141-59; 27:45-53). That expresses quite well what a prophet was thought to be and to proclaim: to be righteous.[18] Sometimes the verb means "to work toward peace,"[19] "to bring harmony," "to urge people to become reconciled with each other and to come to an understanding" (Q 2:228; 4:35, 114; 49:9-10). The righteous are those who do good deeds (cf. Q 2:220; 4:128; 7:56, 85, 142; 11:46, 90).[20]

Those who believe and do good works[21] are closely associated in the Qur'an. Believing and doing good works are not opposed but are—just as in the Bible—intrinsically connected (Q 2:82). The "good works" are described in summary fashion as follows: worshipping no one but God, doing good to one's parents, close relatives, orphans, and the destitute, being friendly to all, praying,[22] and giving alms.[23] Thus, doing good works is a question of fulfilling both one's religious duties and one's social duties (Q 2:83; cf. 18:110; 2:277; 21:73; 32:24). Thus, faith in the one God is seen as a righteous act. Giving alms is one of the character traits of the righteous person (Q 63:10).

Elijah, Zachariah, John the Baptist, and Jesus were included among the righteous (Q 6:85; cf. 3:46). According to the Qur'an, it is said in the psalms (with reference to Psalm 37):[24] "The righteous servants of God will inherit the earth" (Q 21:105; cf. 39:74; 27:21).[25]

On the Day of Judgment[26] God will determine which side the individual human being stood on (regarding his human project). Here the word *dîn* is used (!), which here therefore means "judgment" and not "religion" (see below). God thus decides if a human being belongs to the party of God, Hezbollah (Q 5:56; cf. 58:22), or the party van Satan (Q 58:19; 4:119),

17. *islâh*.
18. *E.Q.*, s.v. "Good Deeds," 340.
19. *sulh*.
20. *Muhammad, al muslih al-a'zam. E.I.*, s.v. islâh.
21. *salihât*.
22. *salât*.
23. *zakât*.

24. Psalm 37:29. Cf. also verses 9, 11, 22, and 34. "Blessed are the meek,/ for they will inherit the earth" (Matt 5:5). "But for the elect there shall be light and joy and peace,/ And they shall inherit the earth. (1 En 5:7; http://www.pseudepigrapha.com/pseudepigrapha/1enoch_all.html#CH5); Speyer, *Die biblischen Erzählungen*, 449.

25. "Moses said to the people: 'Ask God for assistance and be patient. The earth belongs to God, and He gives it as an inheritance to whom He will among his servants'" (Q 7:128). Cf. Isa 60:21: "Then all your people will be righteous/ and they will possess the land forever./ They are the shoot I have planted,/ the work of my hands,/ for the display of my splendor"; Izutsu, *Ethico-Religious Concepts*, 204-6.

26. *yaum al-dîn*.

whether he or she has followed the straight path,[27] the path of God, or the wrong path, whether he or she built up and preserved the earth or sowed corruption and shed blood on it.

"I'm an Atheist"

We live in a time in which a great deal of terrorism and violence is committed in the name of God and religion. Would it not then be better to become atheists, as many in the West already are? Is it not religion—and especially Islam, as countless people in the West claim—that is the source of the evil in our world? Is it therefore not a good thing that God and his prophets—not only Muhammad but also Moses and Jesus—are mocked?

I was once invited by a group of intellectuals to give a private lecture on the relation between Jews, Christians, and Muslims. Because it was a small group meeting in someone's home, everyone first introduced themselves. I was struck by the fact that many added, "I'm an atheist." This is some way to begin a meeting where one has been asked to speak about Jews, Christians, and Muslims, people who are explicitly thought to believe in God. When it was time for me to give my lecture, I could not refrain from remarking that, from the perspective of the Jewish, Christian, and Muslim traditions, the statement "I'm an atheist" was singularly uninteresting. That is not what these three religions are about. But what are they about then? In the three books on which these traditions rest, it is a question of "the way of God," the Torah: the way that God indicates. What way is that? That's easy enough to summarize in a few words: act justly and show love. The rest is all secondary.

When a few Pharisees and Herodians (supporters of King Herod and thus the Roman emperor) attempted to trip Jesus up with a trick question—namely, whether they should pay taxes to Caesar—they led into their question by saying: "Teacher, we know that you are a man of integrity. You aren't swayed by others, because you pay no attention to who they are; but you teach the way of God [the Torah] in accordance with the truth" (Mark 12:13–14).

And in the psalm that the young Jew recited in Paris, the one who says there is no God is not called an "atheist" but a "fool." He is a a fool because he thinks that he can live without God or his commandments. He thinks that people can live quite easily without acting justly and showing love.

Many in the West see not believing in God as a sign of great "Enlightenment." By that they often want to indicate primarily that, in contrast to religious people, they have nothing to do with what has been done and

27. *sîrat al-mustaqîm*.

still is done in the name of God and religion. And is it not true that religious people are responsible for much of the violence in the world? One could think of Dutch history—the Eighty-Years' War between Protestants and Roman Catholics. Did we not witness something similar in our time in Northern Ireland? And are wars not being fought in the Middle East between Muslims and Jews, between Sunni and Shi'i Muslims? The leader of IS, the Islamic State, comes to mind here: someone presents himself as God's deputy and murders his opponents in a barbaric way by beheading them or burning them alive. It's easy to see why people say: "Please preserve us from this kind of faith in God." Is it not a great blessing to live in a Western civilization where church and state are separated? Isn't that sufficient reason to keep it that way and to implement it throughout the world?

In France especially, the separation of church and state is considered to be of paramount importance. The state does not interfere with the church, and the church does not interfere with the state. In 2004 France introduced a prohibition against wearing external religious symbols: thus, no more headscarves, but also no yarmulkes or crosses. Religion became purely a private matter for the citizen. Religion is allowed, certainly—but not in public, only in one's home. Nobody should be able to notice it or be bothered by it. Does that not protect us from the great threat of Islam, which does not endorse this separation? Is it therefore not better to join a "demonstration of the republic," like the one that took place on 11 January 2015 in Paris, than to follow "the way of God?"

No Separation of Church and State?

With respect to the important achievement of the separation of church and state, the following statement by Jesus is often cited: "Give to Caesar what is Caesar's and to God what is God's" (Mark 12:17). This is seen, therefore, as the Christian foundation for that separation. And here it differs from Islam, which, as is generally and widely believed, does not include this separation between religion and state. A well-known saying in Arabic reads: *islâm dîn wa dawla*, i.e, "Islam and the state together." Examples of this view in recent times—both in theory and in practice—are the shocking acts of the Islamic State in Iraq and the Levant and the Islamic State in Iraq and Syria (IS).[28] The leader, Abu Bakr al-Baghdâdî, appointed himself caliph in 2014 and sees himself as standing at the beginning of an Islamic domination of the world.[29]

---

28. Arabic: *al-dawla al-islamiyya fî al 'Irâq wa sh-Shâm*; abbreviated: *Da' ish*.
29. With the definitive end of the Ottoman (Turkish) Empire after the First World

It is not my intention here to explore in more detail the question how the relationship between religion and the state was expressed in the history of Christianity and Islam. I am much more interested in the question how the relation between religion and politics should be understood from the perspective of the Bible and the Qur'an. Can the words of Jesus I quoted above serve as a basis for the separation of religion and politics? Are the Islamic religion (*dîn*) and the state (*dawla*) truly inseparably connected? The words *islâm* and *dîn* do both occur in the Qur'an, but does "islam" there mean the same thing as "Islam" today? And does the word *dîn* mean "religion" in the same sense as it is currently used? The expression *islâm dîn wa dawla* does not occur in the Qur'an, by the way, nor in the authoritative Muslim tradition (*hadîth*). It has become known primarily as a slogan of the Muslim Brotherhood and has in the meantime become a "dogma" of the Islamists.[30]

"Give to Caesar what is Caesar's"

When Jesus said, "Give to Caesar what is Caesar's and to God what is God's" (Mark 12:17), was he concerned with the relationship between church and state, between religion and politics? That does not seem very likely.

Which state are we talking about, by the way? It was the cruel Roman Empire, which subjugated people after people, including the Franks, i.e., the French! The campaign against the Franks was described by Julius Caesar in his book *The Gallic Wars*,[31] which many students of Latin had to read as their first Latin text. This work has been called a masterpiece of political propaganda. Caesar was interested, namely, in how he came across to his readers and sponsors in Rome.

A well-known French comic book series, *Asterix and Obelix*, is about the period of Roman rule in France. Asterix and Obelix live in a village that was the only one to withstand the Roman invasion. It was able to do so with the help of a magical potion that made the Gauls extremely strong and thus invincible. Asterix is a small man with blonde hair and a moustache. He relies primarily on the superhuman power of the potion he gets from the druid. But the hard reality of the time was, of course, very different. Caesar's conquest of the country for the Roman Empire was violent and thousands were killed. The same thing happened in Palestine. Jesus was born when

---

War, not only did the last caliph disappear but the caliphate also came to an end.

30. Quite a few terms are used for these people: "fundamentalists," "Salafists," "Neo-Salafists." We will not discuss the terms any further.

31. *De bello Gallico*.

Augustus was Caesar, and Augustus' successor, Tiberius (14–37), was in power during Jesus' public ministry. His representative Pilate was the prefect of Judea from 26 to 36 A.D., and King Herod Antipas († ca. 39) was king of Palestine. Herod founded the city of Tiberias, named after the Roman emperor.

The first time the Roman empire is mentioned in the gospel of Mark is in the story of the healing of the possessed man in the city of Gerasa in the Transjordan. Like most of the cities in that region, it was dependent on Rome at the time. There was a Jewish community in the city that belonged to the lower strata of society.[32]

The possessed man, so the story goes, wandered among the tombs all day and night. When he saw Jesus from a distance, he ran and fell on his knees in front of him. He shouted at the top of his voice, "What do you want with me, Jesus, Son of the Most High God? In God's name don't torture me!" Jesus had told him the impure spirit that was in the man to come out him. When Jesus asked his name, he said "Legion . . . for we are many." Then he begged Jesus not to send them out of the area (Mark 5:6–10). After Jesus had healed the man, people came to see what had happened. This man, who had been in the power of Legion they now saw sitting with Jesus (Mark 5:15).

"Legion" was the name of a unit of the imperial Roman army; these units consisted of 5–6,000 soldiers. The headquarters of the Roman army in Palestine was in Caesarea, located in Judea. The garrison in Jerusalem was not very large but was sent considerable reinforcements during feast days and periods of unrest.[33] The declaration by the possessed man, "We are Legion," contains an unambiguous reference to the imperial army. This man who lived among the dead embodies the situation of oppression in which most of the people in the area lived.[34]

Jesus' first public appearance was in Galilee, the area from which he himself came. He was known, after all, as Jesus of Nazareth, an unimportant city on the southern border of Galilee. Nazareth was where Joseph and Mary lived, and Jesus too (Luke 4:24)[35] until his baptism by John the Baptist (Mark 1:9).[36]

Mark relates a political and theological conspiracy among the Pharisees and Herodians against Jesus. The Herodians were supporters of the line of King Herod—it was a political and not a religious group. The Pharisees

---

32. *B.W.*, s.v. "Gerasa"; "Dekapolis."
33. *Bijbelse Encyclopedie*, s.v. "Legioen."
34. Howard-Brook, *"Come Out, My People!"*, 404, plus note 16.
35. But see Luke 2:4 and Jonah 4:44.
36. *B.W.*, s.v. "Nazaret(h)."

enjoyed a great deal of support among the population in Jerusalem. Flavius Josephus, a Jewish historian from the first century A.D. reports that they had such great power over the masses that anything they said against the king or the high priests was immediately believed.[37]

Jesus warned his disciples against the leaven of the Pharisees and Herod (Mark 8:15; cf. Matt 16:6, 11). That is a negative use of the word. Leaven is fermented dough from a previous batch and is thus intended by Jesus to refer to something from yesterday, from the past: the old leaven (cf. 1 Cor 5:7).[38] It also refers to hypocrisy (Luke 12:1).[39]

From the moment that Jesus began his public ministry in Jerusalem, the political and religious center of the country, the situation became tense and dangerous. When he entered the temple with his disciples, he chased out those who were buying and selling goods and services; he overthrew the tables of the moneychangers and the benches of those selling doves. He did not permit anyone to carry merchandise through the temple courts, teaching them: "Is it not written: 'My house will be called a house of prayer for all nations' [Is 56:7]? But you have made it 'a den of robbers.'" When the high priests and teachers of the law heard about this, they sought for a way to get rid of Jesus. They were afraid because the whole population was so amazed at what he was teaching (Mark 11:15-19). That evening Jesus and his disciples left the city for reasons of safety.

We stated above that the Pharisees and the Herodians conspired against Jesus. Jesus himself called it a test, a trap, which calls to mind "the temptation in the desert" by Satan (Mark 1:13), the testing by the Pharisees when they asked him for a sign from heaven (Mark 8:11),[40] and the time they wanted him to say whether a man was permitted to divorce his wife (Mark 10:2). The answer Jesus gave was to expose the hypocrisy of those questioning him (Mark 12:15).[41]

The Herodians were sincere supporters of the emperor, but the Pharisees had other ideas about him. Jesus' followers included those who were openly opposed to Caesar, the so-called "Zealots" (Mark 3:18)—"militants," or "jihadists," we could say, proponents of active resistance against the oppressors, in this case Caesar. The Pharisees and Herodians wanted to set a

---

37. Josephus, *The Complete Works*, 13.10.5.

38. *Bijbelse Encyclopedie*, s.v. "Zuurdeeg."

39. An important number of those who opposed Muhammad are also called "hypocrites" (*munâfiqûn*). Cf. Q 3:167; 58:19.

40. There are also examples in the Qur'an of the prophet Muhammad's opponents asking him for signs (Q 6:37, 19-111, 158; 7:203; 10:20; 13:7, 27; 17:90-93; 20:133; 23:5; 29:50).

41. Howard-Brook, *"Come Out, My People!"*, 404.

"trap" for him by catching him in his words (Mark 12:13). Jesus thus found himself in a very tense and dangerous situation. "*Is it right* to pay taxes to Caesar? *Should* we pay?" The Zealots were opposed and proposed violent measures. They expected the Messiah, the Redeemer, to bring liberation from the foreign ruler and saw paying taxes as an act of blasphemy against God. If Jesus consented to paying taxes, he would be denying that he was the Messiah. If he said that no taxes need be paid, the Herodians could report him to the emperor.

We should look closely at how the interviewers introduce the question in the passage in the Bible: "Teacher, we know that you are a man of integrity. You aren't swayed by others, because you pay no attention to who they are; but you teach *the way of God* in accordance with the truth." These words indicate that they knew that Jesus was not afraid and would honestly state his opinion. But before Jesus answered, he first came with a request: "Bring me a denarius and let me look at it."

This is the key, the essence of this story. Jesus asked to see the image on the imperial coin, and this had nothing to do with the separation of "church and state," a notion that would, by the way, have seemed strange at that time. And it also has nothing to do with "Christian" citizenship in the world of Caesar.[42]

"Bring me a denarius"

By making this request, Jesus forced his questioners to literally put their hands in their own pockets. He asked them to show him a coin, which they promptly produced. A denarius was a silver coin, the most common coin in the Roman Empire, and was also known as a "piece of silver." This brings to mind Judas, who would betray Jesus for thirty pieces of silver (Matt 26:15). But it was not simply a coin: this coin bore, it should be noted, the image of Caesar and an inscription with a clear message.

That was true for the Dutch guilder when it was the currency of the Netherlands. The Dutch guilder had engraved on its side: "God met ons" ("God with us"). But "God is also with our Dutch euro" ("God is ook met onze Nederlandse euro") a Dutch newspaper wrote on the eve of the introduction of the euro. "The Netherlands, a country of ministers and merchants, scored a national success on the European level: the very respectable Dutch guilder could then disappear, for the inscription will be on the two-euro coin. The Secretary of the Department of Finance at the time, Gerrit Zalm, had to lobby hard for this at the EU. To the great satisfaction of the

---

42. Ibid., 404–5.

small Christian right, which fought for the retention of the inscription, the secretary succeeded in keeping God on the coin." Where does the text "God with us" come from? It comes from the apostle Paul, in his letter to the church of Jesus' disciples in the capital city of Rome: "If God is for us, who can be against us?" (Rom 8:31). Was God with the Protestants and against the Roman Catholics? Is God with our euros today? Against whom? On whose side? Such an inscription is not as innocent as it seems.

On the piece of silver Jesus was shown stood the inscription: "Caesar Augustus Tiberius, son of the Divine Augustus." According to a recent study, Augustus was a cross between Mussolini, Hitler, and Stalin. From a strictly Jewish point of view, that inscription is nothing more than straightforward blasphemy. The questioners thus compromised themselves by having this coin with the emperor's image and proclamation on it on their person. They were at a loss for words as they stood there, but not at a loss for coins. And at that moment Jesus answered, briefly and tersely, with those famous words: "Give to Caesar what is Caesar's and to God what is God's."

Does this mean that Jesus introduced a neat division between obligations owed to Caesar and those owed to God? Those owed to the state and those owed to the church? To undersand Jesus' answer properly, we have to know the history of the Jews as Jesus and his questioners knew it. Throughout the centuries, the Jews had to deal with foreign occupiers. In Jesus' day, it was the Romans and before that the Greeks. The latter had conquered large parts of the Middle East under the leadership of Alexander the Great. That was when they conquered Jerusalem. A group, the so-called Maccabees, rose up in revolt against them when the Greeks desecrated the temple by sacrificing a pig on the altar, an unclean animal for Jews. That is how Muslims view it as well. In July 2013 a pig's head was found at the Rahman Mosque in Boskoop (a town in the Netherlands), and one was also found at a mosque in Vienna at Christmas 2014.

For the Jews, this sacrifice of a pig by the Greek occupiers was the final straw, and a group of rebels led by Judah Maccabee decided to strike back. Jews who wanted to live according to the Torah, "the way of God," joined him. The "way of God" for them meant, however, "holy war." The Maccabees eventually reached Jerusalem and, after a bloody struggle, were victorious. But when they entered the temple, they found the high menorah, the seven-branched candlestick, lying on the ground. They put it back up, lit it again, and rededicated the temple. The high priest, priests, and lay people then celebrated the feast of the rededication of the temple. That feast, Hanukkah, is still annually celebrated by the Jews as the "Festival of Lights." When the father of Judah Maccabee was preparing himself for his death, he gave a speech in which he urged his sons to surrender themselves to the way of

God. This speech is important for understanding Jesus' answer about the taxes. Judah Maccabee's father says to his sons: "You shall rally about you all who observe the law, and avenge the wrong done to your people. Pay back the Gentiles in full, and heed what the law commands" (1 Macc 2:67–68).[43] He thus urged them to do two things: "Take vengeance on the Greeks" and "heed what the law commands." With these words he died. What does that mean? Mattathias, Judah's father, instructs his sons to give the Greeks a taste of their own medicine: "Do unto them as they have done unto us." This statement thus has a double motive: the obligation with respect to avenging the Jews on their enemies and their obligations toward God.

"Give to Caesar what is Caesar's and to God what is God's" is therefore to be understood as an echo of the final words of the father of Judah Maccabee. This answer could initiatially sound quite revolutionary: "Get even with the Caesar"; "Give him a taste of his own medicine." But is that what Jesus meant? Jesus was not giving a lecture, giving a pep talk for the troops or addressing some kind of political gathering. He was confronting his questioners with Roman coins in their hands. It could be concluded that he meant to say, "Yes, pay Caesar's taxes"; "Give to Caesar the coins that already bear his image, which you carry around with you all day anyway. You already pay him in that way." It could thus be said that Jesus' answer is anti-revolutionary. But given the tenor of what he meants, that is not the case. Nevertheless, his answer contained a very different revolution from the one the Zealots had in mind, the dedicated "jihadists" of that time, and from that of the Maccabees. It is also very different from the one initiated by Judah the Galilean, a teacher of the law some decades before Jesus, who, like him, came from Galilee. Judah incited the inhabitants of Galilee to rebel, calling the people who paid taxes to Caesar cowards because they also acknowledged mortals (like Caesar) in addition to God as their lord and master. Jesus' answer to the question of paying taxes is crystal clear: "Pay!" But the mysterious and revolutionary quality of Jesus' answer is found in what he meant precisely by "what is Caesar's" and "what is God's," and how those two are related.

Shortly after this interview Jesus would be arrested and brought before Pilate to be judged. Pilate asks him: "Are you the king of the Jews?" Jesus was brought to Pilate because it had been asserted that he claimed to have kingly ambitions and thus in fact preached rebellion against Caesar. Pilate himself does not seem to be too impressed by this schlemiel, this "nobody" who was brought to him accompanied by a whole cohort of soldiers. There is clearly a tone of sarcastic mockery to be heard in his question: "Are *you* the king of

---

43. http://quod.lib.umich.edu/cgi/r/rsv/rsv-idx?type=DIV1andbyte=4219672.

the Jews?" Jesus answers: "My kingdom is not of this world" (John 18:36). But can we not hear a kind of separation of church and state in this answer? Many exegetes hear Jesus saying here: "My kingdom is in heaven." But that is not what Jesus said or meant. The kingdom of God Jesus was talking about is grounded precisely in the world of that time, just as his words are still relevant for the concrete world of today. "My kingdom is not of this world" means "My kingdom is not of the world of the Zealots, fanatics, jihadists, who want to establish the kingdom by violence. Thus, my kingdom is not your world either, Pilate. It is not the world of the Caesars, the world of the network of murder and lies that cares about nothing and nobody, the world of propaganda. It is not the world of exploitation and oppression. My kingdom does not arise through crusades nor through jihad." When these words were written down in the Gospel (of John), it had already become clear that the rebellion to establish God's kingdom by armed struggle had failed dramatically. The Jewish rebellion had been crushed and Jerusalem and the temple had been razed a long time ago.

"My kingdom is not of this world" does not mean that Jesus' kingdom is supernatural. His kingship merely directly opposes the prevailing violent views of the rulers of this world—then and now! Does this mean that Jesus took a passive attitude to injustice and violence? Did he accept oppression? Not at all. Jesus never hesitated to condemn the blood and evil in which this world is drenched. His politics entailed a constant witness to the truth. But of what truth? The truth that all great unjust powers, such as that of the Roman Empire as well as the great powers of today will ultimately collapse like sand castles. Jesus offers a different model, unfolds a vision that is worth considering and reflecting upon. What was it again that Jesus said to Peter (Matt 26:52; cf. John 18:10–11)?[44] "If you take up the sword, you have no part in my kingdom." Jesus came to bring an alternative into the world. If this world claims that injustice, violence, and terror are permanent factors, Jesus teaches the opposite. He claims that this world of violence will pass away. God has said, after all: "I will be there for the oppressed, the enslaved, the poor."[45]

---

44. Cf. Jeremiah 15:2: "And if they ask you, 'Where shall we go?' tell them, "This is what the Lord says:/ 'Those destined for death, to death;/ those for the sword, to the sword; / those for starvation, to starvation; / those for captivity, to captivity.""

45. Wright, *Jesus*, 502–7.

"Give to God what is God's"

"Give to God what is God's" is not a call to be properly pious and keep away from dirty politics. Rather, it concerns breaking with every idolization of the domination of money, terror, and the cynicism of the powerful. Through this statement, Jesus calls us to forswear our veneration for and belief in the abusers of power and to worship exclusively the true God. That is what is revolutionary about his call. That is the challenge that lies hidden here: to follow him in the actual revolution against the blasphemous worship of the networks of money, lies, and violence.

The coin Jesus looked at stated that Caesar Tiberius was the son of the divine Caesar (Augustus). But how very differently the Torah, "the way of God," thought about that. What was it that Moses, the first great liberator of God's people, had to say to the Caesar of his time, the Pharaoh of Egypt? "This is what the Lord says: *Israel* is my firstborn son" (Exod 4:22). The Egyptians believed that a deity adopted Pharaoh as his son and thus began a special, protective, and close relationship with him. Thus, the message that Moses' announcement to Pharaoh brings is: "Israel is my son, my firstborn. That privilege is not reserved for the one at the top but for the whole community." Furthermore, "firstborn" indicates the very special and intimate relationship between God and the people. This relationship is thus described here in terms of the metaphor of parents and children: "because I am Israel's father,/ and Ephraim is my firstborn son" (Jer 31:9).[46]

This expresses good tidings. What does Moses say to the people? "The Lord your God, who is going before you, will fight for you, as he did for you in Egypt, before your very eyes, and in the wilderness. There you saw how the Lord your God carried you, as a father carries his son, all the way you went until you reached this place" (Deut 1:30–31). And how do the prophets express it after Moses? "To them I was like a father who lifts a little child to his cheek, and teaches them to walk" (Hos 11:1–3; Isa 1:2; Jer 31:20). For about forty years [thus the span of a human life] he carried them in the wilderness (Acts 13:18; Isa 46:3–4; 63:9). He is like an eagle who carries its young on its wings (Exod 19:4; Deut 32:11) or a nurse who takes a nursing child to her breast (Num 11:12).

If we ask what the relevance of this message is for the distressing, frightening, threatening, terrifying world of terror today, then the same words still need to be heard: "Give to Caesar what is Caesar's and to God what is God's." But how different is this from the message that is usually understood here? Here Jesus calls us to follow his "agenda." In its original

---

46. Fisher and Markl, *Das Buch Exodus*, 75.

Latin form, the word "agenda" meant "what had to be done." Thus, follow the revolutionary agenda of Jesus' kingdom—it is completely different from that of Judah Maccabee two centuries earlier or that of Judah the Galilean two decades before Jesus. It is a question of total obedience to and imitation of the God of Israel and of his servant, Jesus. This Jesus was born to be king. He came to fulfill the way of God; he is the Torah become flesh and embodies its purpose in himself: doing justice and showing love. In this Jesus is a reflection of the generous love of God for the whole world, and the express "image" of God's being (Hebr 1:3; KJV). His agenda is completely devoid of violence: "But I tell you, do not resist an evil person. If anyone slaps you on the right cheek, turn to them the other cheek also" (Matt 5:39). "There is no violence in God" (Diognetus). Jesus himself perceived the dawning of the kingdom of God, the empire of justice and love, as very close by. He definitely believed in that. He preached, lived, and expressed that in his entire existence. There is only one power—both extremely tender and extremely strong—and that is the superior power of love.

"The fool says in his heart, 'There is no God'"—the psalm recited in "Paris." But what does the fool, the idiot in Dostoyesky's novel of the same name say: "Love is capable of melting ice, ending ice ages, and planting forests in deserts. Gentleness is the most productive violence on earth."[47]

Islam—Religion and State in One?

What does the Qur'an tell us about the relationship between religion and the state, between religion and politics? The different terms in the Qur'an must be understood and explained in their own context. What are we to understand by "islam" and "religion"?

Shortly before his death, the prophet Muhammad made his final pilgrimage[48] to Mecca, which has become known as the "Farewell Pilgrimage." On that occasion he spoke these memorable words: "Today [or "these days"] I have completed your religion so that nothing is lacking" and "I have sanctioned islam as your religion"[49] (Q 5:3). This statement is of major importance, also because it probably is one of the latest texts of the Qur'an, from Muhammad's last year and thus indicates precisely how people thought about this subject at the end of Muhammad's activities. In any case, this statement has continued to have an impact throughout the centuries.

---

47. Cited by Drewermann, *Das Markus Evangelium*, Part II, 270.
48. *hajj*.
49. *din*.

When the Qur'an uses the word "islam," it does not mean the same as how the term is commonly used today and what the newspapers report on daily. In the discussion on terrorist acts, such as the attacks on 9/11, it is often and correctly claimed by Muslims that islam means "peace" and that the perpetrators of those attacks were not Muslims. That is a correct observation in the sense that this is also what the Qur'an says. But it should be added immediately that those who committed these acts did consider themselves "Muslims" and were convinced that their acts were or are "Islamic." They assumed that their acts could be justified by appealing to the Qur'an.

What did Muhammad mean when he spoke of the completion of islam? To understand that, we need to look at the basic meaning of the verb[50] from which the word islam derives.[51] The stem of the verb (*slm*) means: "to surrender oneself to" (i.e., to God). When used by Muhammad, it means: "to belong to God or to serve him alone." The words *islâm* and *muslim* can be formed from the three consonants of the stem. But those are not as such designations for the contemporary understanding of *Islam* and *Muslims*. The word *salâm*, which is also formed from this root, means "peace," just like its Hebrew cognate, *shalom*. A definitive translation of who or what a Muslim is thus reads: "he or she who completely surrenders oneself to God in complete trust and thus finds peace with God and with fellow human beings." That is the islam that Muhammad speaks of in his farewell. The concept "islam" was originally based on the conception of the human being as someone who has "surrendered" himself to God as God's servant.[52]

God's Religion

The second half of the sentence that is articulated at the Farewell Pilgrimage reads: "Now I am content (or "have pleasure in:) that you have islam as *dîn*, as religion" (Q 5:3). With the Jews in mind, the Qur'an says: "The religion of God is 'surrender (*islâm*)'" (Q 3:19). This concerns surrender to God. The "religion" (*dîn*) of God is not the same as Islam, but that religion (*dîn*) does belong to God. The religion of God is "surrender." The call that Muhammad makes to the Jews and Christians of his time—and thus also to those of our time—at his farewell is not to convert to his new religion, Islam, but to see, to understand, to believe that all (Jews, Christians, and Muslims) are called to convert to the religion of God, to surrender themselves to him, to serve him and thus follow his religion (*dîn*). The statement in the Qur'an

---

50. *aslama*.
51. D.Z.H. Baneth, cited by Cuypers, *The Banquet*, 77, note 33.
52. Izutsu, *God and Man*, 226.

at Muhammad's farewell speech is thus not a call for Jews or Christians or whoever to "surrender" themselves to Islam, to convert to Islam, to become Muslim in the current sense of the word. The *dîn* of God can never, per definition, be equated with Islam.[53]

"To him belongs everything in heaven and on earth. To him belongs religion forever"[54] (Q 16:52). On the one hand, this means that God has absolute power, but it also means, on the other hand, that creatures are required to show absolute obedience. The image used here for "religion" is that of a servant who submits completely to a mighty king. "Whenever you doubt my religion (*dîni*), let it be said to you: 'I do not serve them that you serve in addition to God'" (Q 10:104). "Say: 'I [Muhammad] am commanded to serve with a sincere faith [*dîn*]'" (Q 39:11). This shows that there is an internal connection between "religion" and "serving" (which also comes through in the Dutch word *godsdienst*, which is usually used as a translation for "religion"). Originally, *dîn* had to do with the religion of each individual believer.[55]

To understand what the *dîn Allâh* is, we need to know what the "religion of God" is being contrasted to. Sayyid Abû-l-A'lâ Mawdûdî (1903–1979) sees the expression *dîn Allâh* as opposed to and contrasted with the "religion of the king."[56] That is an important detail in both the Bible and the Qur'an. There are "kings" in the various kingdoms of the world that see themselves as the "son of God" or even as God himself. Nimrod, the king of Asshur and Babel in Abraham's time, and the Pharaoh of Egypt in Moses' time are the most striking examples of this. Abraham disputed with Nimrod (cf. Gen 10:8–9), who claimed that God had given him the kingship. When Abraham tells Nimrod that it is God who decides over life and death, the king answers that it is he himself who has that power, thus making himself God's equal. Abraham then challenges him by saying: "If God makes the sun rise in the east, why don't you make the sun rise in the West if you are God?" (Q 2:258).

Pharaoh of Egypt also compared himself in turn with God. He said: "There is no God other than me!" (Q 28:38) and declares to Moses, "if you follow any other god than me, I will surely put you in prison" (Q 26:29). The Qur'an also states about Pharaoh: "Have you [Muhammad] not heard the story of Moses? His Lord summoned him in the holy valley Tuwâ: 'Go to Pharaoh for he has become a tyrant. Tell him: Do you intend to act uprightly

---

53. *E.Q.*, s.v. "Religion."
54. *dîn*.
55. Izutsu, *God and Man*, 224–26, 229.
56. *E.Q.*, s.v. "Religion."

so that I can lead you to your Lord and will you fear him?' And Moses showed him the great miraculous signs, but Pharaoh denied them and was disobedient. Then Pharaoh called his sorcerers and called out: 'I am your lord, the most high'" (Q 79:15-24).

To his own fellow citizens, the unbelieving Meccans, Muhammad had to state that his Lord had told him that they should serve no one else but God: "I am commanded to 'surrender' myself to the Lord of all men" (Q 40:66; cf. 10:72; 6:71). In that respect, Muhammad stands in the line of all prophets before him, such as Noah, who said: "I am commanded to belong to those who have surrendered themselves to God" (Q 10:72). And, thus, that also obtains for Muhammad in Mecca: "I am commanded to do nothing else than serve the Lord of the place He has declared holy [Mecca, the place where the Ka'ba is located)], to whom everything in the world belongs. And I am even commanded to join those who have surrendered themselves to God and to present the Qur'an to the world" (Q 27:91-92). Muhammad has to be the first of those who have surrendered themselves to God[57] (Q 39:12; cf. 6:14; 6:163).[58]

God commanded him to do nothing other than serve him by orienting himself completely to him as a "seeker of God"[59] and to observe spiritual and social obligations.[60] That is the well-established, indisputable, proper religion[61] (Q 98:5; cf. 10:104-5). "Then turn your face to religion as a seeker of God. That is your true religion" (Q 30:30).

Hanîf is the term for the faithful representative of the Abrahamic tradition in the time of ignorance,[62] the period that preceded the coming of Muhammad.[63]

Abraham's Religion

There is yet another expression that is found in the Qur'an, namely, that for the "religious community": "the *milla* of Abraham." The term *milla*, "religion," is said to have been possibly introduced by the Jews in the Hijâz. It

---

57. *al-muslimîna*.
58. Moses is called the first of the believers.
59. *hanîf*.
60. *salât* and *zakât*.
61. *dînu l-qayyimati*.
62. *djahiliyya*.
63. Glassé, *The Concise Encyclopaedia*, s.v. "Hanîf"; cf. Paret, *Der Koran: Kommentar*, on Q 2:135.

can be translated in the sense of "way."[64] The word is sometimes used for "pagan religions," namely, the people of Shu'ayb (Jethro). They wanted to drive him out of the city if he did not return to their religion[65] (Q 7:88–89). The term acquired a special meaning in the time of Muhammad's activity in Medina, where the Qur'an mentions the "religion of Abraham" eight times (Q 2:130, 135; 3:95; 4:125; 6:161; 12:38; 16:123; 22:78).[66]

"Abraham was himself a community[67] who surrendered himself to God" (Q 16:120). He is the prototype of the community of true Muslims. Ishmael is also part of this "Abrahamic community."[68] When he lays the foundation for the house of God (a reference to the Ka'ba in Mecca), which was built by Abraham and his son Ishmael, Abraham prays: "Our Lord, make both of us 'people who have surrendered themselves to you'" (Q 2:128). Abraham transmitted the "religion"[69] to his sons: Ishmael, Isaac, and also Jacob (Q 2:132). This shows how much the true religion designated by words like *dîn* and *milla* is not Islam. The "true" Muslims are the followers of Abraham, Ishmael, Isaac, and Jacob, "the people who have surrendered themselves to God."

Shortly before Jacob died, he said to his sons: "Who will you serve after I die?" They said: "We will serve your God, the God of your fathers Abraham, Ishmael, and Isaac as the only true God. To him we will surrender ourselves" (Q 2:133).[70] Abraham was not a Jew nor a Christian but a *hanîf*, "someone who surrendered himself to God" (a "Muslim") (Q 3:67).[71] "Those to whom Abraham was the closest were those who truly followed him *and* this prophet [Muhammad]" (Q 3:68).

It can rightly be stated that Islam is a "religion" that has developed from individual salvation in the Meccan period into a religion with social and political codes.[72] Nevertheless, this is formulated too strongly if it is tak-

64. Jeffery, *The Foreign Vocabulary*, 268–69.

65. *milla*.

66. *E.I.*, s.v. "Milla." With the article, *al-milla*, but that is post-Qur'anic and means the true religion as revealed by Muhammad. These words are sometimes used as *ahl-milla*, the adherent of the Islamic religion (Tabari), just as *ahl al-dhimma* is also used for non-Muslims.

67. *umma*.

68. Paret, *Der Koran: Kommentar*, 294 on Q 16:120.

69. *milla*.

70. The "blessing of Jacob" can be found in Genesis 49. Cf. also Deuteronomy 33 for the "blessing of Moses." Deuteronomy 33:4: "the law that Moses gave us, the possession of the assembly of Jacob."

71. Q 16:120; 2:135; 6:161; 16:133; 4:125; 10:105; 30:30; 22:31; 98:5.

72. *Dictionnaire*, s.v. "Religion."

en to mean that Muhammad introduced a new religious-political system, an "Islamic *sharî'a*" on whose basis a political state or a republic could be formed as an "Islamic form of government" set up by Muhammad. That is not what the Qur'an is concerned with. The religion the Qur'an talks about is "God's religion"![73]

This explicitly concerns the orientation that God announced to Muhammad and that the prophet passed on in his time: "'The Lord led me on a straight path,[74] a firmly anchored religion,[75] the religion of Abraham the seeker of God, who did not join the idolaters.' Say: 'My prayer and my pious exercises and my life and my death are for God the Lord of the worlds. He has no equal. I am thus commanded, and I am the first of those who have surrendered themselves to God'" (Q 6:161–62).

This talk of the *millat Ibrâhîm* introduces a new emphasis that becomes central in the so-called Medina period (622–632): the unity of God becomes the unity of the growing Muslim community,[76] of those who surrender themselves to God, thus Muslims in the true sense of the word.

"Religion"[77] does not revolve only around the personal but also around the collective connectedness and surrender to God's true way. "Religion"[78] thus means religion in the sense of prescribed behavior in a specific community of "people who have surrendered themselves to God" or *muslims*. There is only one religion, God's unchangeable "religion" (thus not unchangeable Islam, as is often claimed—and not only by extremists).

That community does exist on earth concretely in various degrees of purity. Here is where the corruption of the Scriptures by the Jews in Medina comes in. Some of the Jews twisted the verbal content so that a different twist could be given to the meaning. A well-known example of this is that the Jews said: "We hear and do not obey" (Q 4:46). The Jews in Medina mocked Muhammad's message by using a Hebrew play on words: they twisted the Arabic *sami'a nâ wa-'asaynâ* ("We hear and obey") by pronouncing it as *shâma'anû we-'aînâ*, which sounds like completely the opposite is being said in Arabic: "We hear and are disobedient."[79] But this twisting of words and their meaning is not solely characteristic of *the* Jews or *the* Christians, as would often be later claimed. It is rather something that every hearer can

---

73. *dîn Allâh.*
74. *sîrat al-mustaqîm.*
75. *dînan qiyâman.*
76. *umma.*
77. *dîn.*
78. *dîn.*
79. Stillman, *The Jews of Arab Lands*, 150. E.Q., s.v. "Corruption."

do, including, for example, "nominal" Muslims. And that is what the text is saying. It is not yet a point of discussion in the Qur'an as to whether the text of the Scripture has been tampered with. But that does come out later in the relationship between the people of the Book (Jews and Christians) and Muslims.[80] Then the question of changing or corrupting the text of the *Tawra* and the *Injîl* is made explicit.

The religion described is connected with the unity of God[81] and is characteristic of the community[82] that surrenders itself to God. It is often concluded on this basis that the Qur'an is saying: "The religion of Muhammad has come to restore religion to its original purity." But that does not mean that it is not stated per definition that the Muslim community and Islam only are good and Judaism and Christianity are not or are no longer. That is how it was and is often explained, but the Qur'an (and the Bible) only critiques "Jews," "Christians," and "Muslims," who deviate from the right path, and the Qur'an warns the followers of Muhammad that they can fall into the trap that Jews and Christians have fallen into.[83]

It is thus not a question of Islam in the sociological sense, an Islam that is thought to replace Judaism and Christianity. "Pure" Judaism and Christianity are, according to the Qur'an, also "islam." The *dîn* is the *milla* of Abraham and remains the orientation point for "nominal" Jews and Christians as well as for "nominal" Muslims. It is not Islam that is the criterion but the *milla* of Abraham. God's *dîn* is and remains the criterion for all.

80. *tahrîf.*
81. *tawhîd.*
82. *umma.*
83. *Dictionnaire*, s.v. "Religion."

V

The Foreign King
Joseph in Egypt as a Role Model for Muhammad

But for Brueggemann the gospel is wholly political because the Bible is wholly political; and the gospel is wholly personal because the Bible is wholly personal. The personal is the political and the political is the scriptural.[1]

Introduction

THE FIRST PART OF Thomas Mann's tetrology *Josef und seine Brüder* (*Joseph and his Brothers*), a novel about the longest cycle in the Pentateuch, was published in 1933 in Germany, the same year Hitler came to power in Germany. Mann spent 16 years working on this novel, which he considered his magnus opus. With this mythical story from the Jewish-Christian tradition, Mann wanted to offer an alternative to the totalitarian mythology that the Nazis were using to justify their anthropology of Übermensch and Untermensch.[2] His work was intended as "a great show of sympathy for the old Jewish world of the patriarchs." On 17 November 1942, in a speech before the Library of Congress in Washington called *The Theme of the Joseph Novels*, Mann stated the following about the word "myth":

> [T]he word "myth" has a bad reputation nowadays—we only have to think of the title of the book, which the "philosopher" of German fascism, Rosenberg, the preceptor of Hitler, has given to his vicious [sic] textbook: "The Myth of the 20th Century."[3]

---

1. Samuel Wells in his foreword to Brueggemann, *The Collected Sermons*, XII.
2. www.jozefenzijnbroers.nl.
3. Rosenberg, *Der Mythus des 20. Jahrhunderts*.

So often, in the last decades, had the myth been abused as a means of obscurantic counter-revolution that a mythical novel like the Joseph, upon its first appearance, inevitably aroused the suspicion that its author was floating with the murky stream. This suspicion had to be discarded for at a second glance a process could be observed similar to what happens in a battle when a captured gun is turned around and directed against the enemy. In this book, the myth has been taken out of Fascist hands and humanized down to the last recess of its language,—if posterity finds anything remarkable about it it will be this.[4]

Some people were inclined to regard "Joseph and His Brothers" as a Jewish novel, even as merely a novel for Jews. Well, the selection of the old testamental subject was certainly not a mere accident; most certainly there were hidden, defiantly polemic connections between it and certain tendencies of our time which I always found repulsive from the bottom of my soul; the growing vulgar anti-semitism which is an essential part of the Fascist mob-myth, and which commits the brutish denial of the fact that Judaism and Hellenism are the two principal pillars upon which our occidental civilization rests. To write a novel of the Jewish spirit was timely, just because it seems untimely.[5]

In this chapter the story of Joseph will be central, and we will look especially at his importance as a ruler. This is an important aspect within the story itself as well as within the whole of the Bible. The same obtains, for that matter, for the Qur'an: the story of Joseph has been of major significance for understanding his "political" role. Dreams and their interpretation are crucial in the Joseph cycle, but it is also good to clearly see how the dreams cast light on the role of other prophets, including Muhammad.

The Man Born to Be King

During the Second World War Dorothy Sayers, a well-known British writer, wrote a radio play cycle on the life of Jesus called *The Man Born to Be King*. The first play was aired shortly before Christmas in 1941 and the last in October 1942. There was a broadcast once every four weeks, twelve in total. The following titles appear in the cycle: *Kings in Judea*, *The King's Herald* (John the Baptist), *The Heirs to the Kingdom*, *Royal Progress*, *The King's*

---

4. Mann, *The Theme of the Joseph Novels*, 21.
5. Ibid., 14.

Supper (the Last Supper), *The Princes of This World* (Herod and Pilate, the representative of Caesar who had Jesus, the "King of Sorrows," whipped, condemned, and crucified). Finally, *The King Comes to His Own*: He is the true "king of the Jews." The message of this cycle can be summarized as follows, using the words of the Bible: "These [signs] are written that you may believe that Jesus is the Messiah, the Son of God, and that by believing you may have life in his name" (John 20:31). Jesus' name, after all, means: God saves, redeems, liberates."

There was another young man in the Scripture who was born to be king: Joseph, one of the twelve sons of the patriarch Jacob. As a child, he dreamed of being king—and that is what he did indeed become and managed thereby not only to save his family but also the Egyptians.

His brothers quickly understood the essence of his dreams as a child: "Do you intend to reign over us? Will you actually rule us?" (Gen 37:8). The words "king," "kingdom," and "rule" occurred earlier in the stories of the patriarchs. Abraham was told: "I will make you very fruitful; I will make nations of you, and *kings* will come from you" (Gen 17:6), and Abraham's grandson Jacob is told the same thing at Bethel: "I am God Almighty; be fruitful and increase in number. A nation and a community of nations will come from you, and *kings* will come from your body" (Gen 35:11). For the first time in the Bible, however, we encounter words that have to do with political power. "With the dream of Joseph, something new enters the awareness of Israel."[6] "So then, it was not you who sent me here, but God. He made me father to Pharaoh, lord of his entire household and ruler of all Egypt" (Gen 45:8).

These dreams are dreamed by the *powerless* in the family. They are dreams that represent the imagining of new political possibilities that threaten the existing (old) political order directly and bring it into question.[7] A new imagination comes into power, like that written on the walls in Paris in 1968 ("L'Imagination au Pouvoir").

Both in the Bible and in the Qur'an, the story of Joseph plays an important role. The long closing section of the first book of the Bible (Gen 37–50) is devoted to Joseph and is the longest story in the Bible about one figure. The same is true in the Qur'an. Although the stories about Abraham, Moses, and Jesus are related in various chapters, there is one entire chapter, the twelfth, devoted to Joseph (Yûsuf), That story is called "the best of stories" (Q 12:3).

---

6. Brueggemann, *Genesis*, 301.
7. Ibid., 302.

The prophet Muhammad was sometimes challenged by Jews to prove that he truly was a prophet and able to tell the story of Joseph: "Ask Muhammad why Jacob's family moved from Syria [Palestine is part of that] to Egypt?" And the prophet could explain this to the Jews, for "God would never send any prophet without telling him the story of Joseph, as He told it to our prophet Muhammad."[8]

Joseph as a Stranger in a Strange Land

It is striking how favorably Egypt is presented in the narrative cycle about Joseph. The period of Solomon's reign has sometimes been referenced in connection with this, since there were also good relations at that time with the Egyptian court.[9]

That did obtain for King Solomon, who was married to the daughter of Pharaoh. That could also explain the interest that is apparent in the story of Joseph for a foreign country, a foreign people, and the foreign court of the king. "There is no other narrative in the Old Testament where becoming acquainted with a foreign country is reflected in such a direct and lively fashion."[10] Foreigners like Joseph's brothers could be received at court but could also be suspected of espionage. Their youngest brother, Benjamin, was even imprisoned. At the end of the Joseph cycle, the dead Joseph is paid the honors that were typical of Egypt, such as the embalming of his body (Gen 50:26).

The portrait given to the country and the people bears all the characteristics of a first encounter. There is no mention of fear or of condemnation of what is foreign. When Joseph commands that his brothers be served dinner, it is striking that a separate table is set for his brothers, "because Egyptians could not eat with Hebrews, for that is detestable to Egyptians" (Gen 43:32). This was something that Israelites themselves did not experience toward the Egyptians at that time.[11]

After the history of the patriarchs, Abraham, Isaac, and Jacob (Gen 12:36), the narrative cycle about Joseph is, as it were, an "addition" to the book of Genesis. That is, by the way, also what Joseph's name means. When

---

8. Cf. *E.Q.*, s.v. "Jews and Judaism"; Johns, "Joseph in the Qurân," 31.

9. Gerard von Rad placed the story in the tenth century, the century of King Solomon, because of the keys that that century offered for interpreting the story. Cf. Brueggemann, *Genesis*, 292.

10. Westermann, *Genesis* 3, 18.

11. Ibid., 18.

he was born his mother Rachel called Joseph, thinking, "May the Lord add to me another son" (Gen 30:24).

For the first time a story is told of someone who is separated from his family by violence and has to live as a slave among strangers in a strange land. And in that land he is also accused of an alleged offense and sentenced to prison. He has no rights and no advocate other than "the God of his fathers" "who is with him." The latter is apparent from the friendly way in which people with whom he has to work approach him, first in Potiphar's house and then in the prison. Because he finds "favor in God's eyes," he can rise to a high position again. That God is with him does not mean that He is against the others, the strange Egyptians. The latter are helped precisely for Joseph's sake. That can also be noted much later when Israel ceases to exist as a state and the people live in exile in Babylon. Then the prophet Jeremiah writes in a letter to the exiles: "Also, seek the peace and prosperity of the city to which I have carried you into exile. Pray to the Lord for it, because if it prospers, you too will prosper" (Jer 29:7). The Jews in exile have to work for the prosperity, the *shalom*, of the empire and its capital city. The prosperity of Judah depends on the prosperity of Babylon.[12]

That God is with Joseph can be seen from how He makes him successful at everything he does. He is given great responsibilities in Potiphar's house, which he relates to Potiphar's wife with great respect. That is also the reason why he resists her advances: "With me in charge . . . my master does not concern himself with anything in the house; everything he owns he has entrusted to my care. No one is greater in this house than I am. My master has withheld nothing from me except you, because you are his wife. How then could I do such a wicked thing and sin against God?" (Gen 39:8–9). Joseph remains true to the God of his fathers, the God who is with him and against whom he has no intention of sinning.[13]

The "Joseph Drama" in the Qur'an

To come to a proper appreciation of this longest and "best of stories" about Joseph in the Qur'an, we really have to get into the story, especially the *dialogues*. The intonation of the voice of someone speaking or reciting the story is the best means to acquire this effect.[14] The word "Qur'an" does

---

12. Brueggemann, *Jeremiah*, 257. This positive attitude with regard to Babylon is very different from the deep hatred found in other places, including Jeremiah (e.g., in chapters 50 and 51).

13. Westermann, *Genesis 3*, 66–67.

14. This is explained in a splendid essay by Antony Johns, subtitled: "Dramatic

mean: "what must be recited/declaimed." When Muhammad was called as a prophet, he heard a voice that commanded him: "Recite," "Declaim." The Arabic word here is *'iqra* (Q 96:1), and that is where the word "Qur'an" is derived from. The role the reciter plays is crucial for the proper understanding of the difference between the rhetorical idiom of the Joseph story in the Bible and in the Qur'an. The way in which the *voices* of Joseph, Jacob, and his brothers are intoned reveals the oscillation and tension of the story. One example of such is the exclamation of the water bearer who finds Joseph in the well: "What luck! Here is a young man!" (Q 12:19).[15] Another example is the scene in which Joseph is pursued by Potiphar's wife, who was later—under the influence of the Hebrew *zalikha*—called Zulaykha: "She raced with him to the door—he in an attempt to get away and she to stop him. She ripped his shirt from behind while trying to do so. Suddenly, there was her husband, standing in front of them. And she said, without hardly losing a breath, "Whoever tries to do your family harm deserves nothing other than to be put into prison or to be severely punished" (Q 12:25).[16] Her terse style here expresses both her confusion and her guilt feeling.[17]

The story is composed in scenes that follow one another in quick succession, whereby the events are always communicated via dialogues.[18] The description is spare, and the connections between one scene and another are minimal. The explanations are dramatic and not descriptive or narrative. What connects the different scenes is the voice of God, both at the beginning and at the end with a beautiful peroration: "There is truly something in the account of the messengers for those with understanding to think about. And it is not a fictitious story. This story [as is true of the whole Qur'an] is a confirmation of what existed prior to it and clearly explains everything in details: a true guide and mercy for people who believe" (Q 12:111).

The Joseph story could be said to be "a play of voices." As such, it is not unique in the Qur'an. There are several striking examples of dialogues, such as the one between the angel Gabriel (Jibrîl) and Mary (Q 19:18–32; cf. Luke 1), the mother of Jesus, or that between Abraham and his father (Q 19:41–48). The Qur'an is a mosaic of voices, and that comes to the fore in the Joseph chapter in a particularly clear and explicit way.

Dialogue, Human Emotion and Prophetics Wisdom" (Johns, "Joseph in the Qurân," 29–55). Cf. Agten et al., *Bibliodrama*, in connection with the so-called bibliodrama.

15. Johns, "Joseph in the Qurân," 31; *yâ bushrâ hâdhâ gulâm*!
16. Cf. the translation by Paret, *Der Koran: Übersetzung*.
17. Johns, "Joseph in the Qurân," 33.
18. Ibid., 31.

There is the voice of God or of Gabriel as a messenger for God, who draws a lesson from the episode that has just been concluded. After Joseph (Q 12:33) is placed in charge of the storage barns in Egypt, we read, for example: "And so We gave Joseph power in the land (Egypt) to live where he wanted. We bestow mercy on whom we bestow mercy. And We reward those who do justice" (Q 12:56–57). This allows those who hear this story to draw a conclusion about the providence of God.[19]

The way in which the spoken word is used indicates how the story was presented to those who heard it. It is also suggested that Muhammad did it that way originally. In his volume with stories about the prophets, Al-Kiå'i cites the tradition about how Muhammad was challenged to tell the story of Joseph and his brothers and how he recited it and thus raised and lowered his voice at the right places.[20]

The Joseph Cycle in the Bible: His Dream and the Dreams

Joseph is a master dreamer. "Here comes that dreamer," his brothers say (Gen 37:19). Joseph did not get his penchant for dreams from a stranger. After all, his father Jacob had the dream of a ladder[21] reaching from the earth to heaven (Gen 28:18).[22]

The whole Joseph cycle revolves around the great dream of "ruling." Also, the dreams of the butler and the baker in the prison with Joseph that he is able to interpret are also related to this. Then there are the dreams Pharaoh has. All those dreams serve to bring about Joseph's own great dream and help him to gradually come closer to its fulfillment. The butler will become the link to Pharaoh's court, but Joseph nevertheless remains powerless and helpless behind in the prison. He had asked the butler: "When all goes well with you, remember me and show me kindness; mention me to Pharaoh and get me out of this prison" (Gen 40:14). Here he shows his dependence on the butler for his own freedom and humbly asks him to put in a good word for him and to *liberate him from prison* (sic!). "For I was forcibly carried off from the land of the Hebrews, and even here I have done nothing to deserve being put in a dungeon" (Gen 40:15) He needs help for his "Exodus." But the butler forgets about Joseph—out of sight, out of mind

19. Ibid., 32–33.
20. Ibid., 34. Cf. *Al-Kisâ'î, Tales of the Prophets*.
21. *mi'râdj*; cf. Q 17:1.
22. Marc Chagall uses "Jacob's ladder" in a number of his paintings as a symbol of the connection between heaven and earth.

(Gen 40:20–23), just as "Egypt" will later forget Joseph when a new king comes to power who did not know Joseph (Exod 1:8).[23]

When Joseph was a young boy, his brothers were quite jealous of him because their father favored him. Jacob gave him a coat of many colors, and this act could only spoil a young boy. Joseph dreamed that his brothers' sheaves reverently bowed down before his. He just did not know when to stop. And the next time he had a dream he just had to tell his brothers: "the sun, moon, and eleven stars were bowing down to me." That went too far even for his father: "Will your mother and I and your brothers actually come and bow down to the ground before you?" (Gen 37:10). Initially, no one knew what the dreams meant, what the connection between dream and reality was.

After Joseph is sold to Egypt and rises to a high position there, the famine in Canaan leads to the encounter between him and his brothers (Gen 45). It is a drama that is greater than all the various players involved. After playing cat-and-mouse with them for a long time, whom he did recognize, Joseph can no longer contain himself: "Have everyone leave my presence!" he calls, upon which his entourage of Egyptian officials left by a side door. As soon as that happened, Joseph bursts out in tears, so loud that Egyptians heard it anyway—indeed, the sound even reaches Pharaoh's palace: "I am Joseph! Is my father still living?" He is the one whom his brothers had previously dumped into the well and then sold as a slave while his brothers showed his father the bloodied "king's cloak" to convince him that Joseph had been attacked and devoured by a wild animal. But now the one thought dead stands before them, in the flesh, alive, in power and splendor! The dream was fulfilled; his young man's dream has become reality; "I am . . . Joseph."

"I am." "I am" is the standard phrase for a disclosure, a revelation. The phrase is also used by God himself. "I am the first and the last" (Isa 44:6). "I am the Lord and there is no other" (Isa 45:6). When Moses *sees* a burning bush and then *hears* a voice that calls "Moses, Moses," he answers, "Here I am." And when Moses asks. "Whom shall I say has sent me? What is your name?" he is given an answer consisting of one word with four consonants: YHWH. That can be translated as "I am . . . who I am." "I will be who I will be; I will be with you."

"*I am . . . Joseph!*" This is thus more than an introduction, more than: "May I introduce myself? I'm Joseph." With that statement—"I am Joseph! Is my father still living?"—the whole situation changes in an instant. Suddenly, the brothers have to shift to a reality from an allegedly dead brother to one in which that brother is alive and powerful no less. But as soon as

---

23. Brueggemann, *Genesis*, 324–25.

Joseph reveals who he is, their feelings of guilt come back with a vengeance and his brothers are overcome with great fear and terror. They had every reason to be after all that they had done. They became even more worried by what Joseph had done before he revealed his identity to them, such as hiding the cup in Benjamin's sack so he could put him in prison as a thief. They knew that they were guilty, as the spokesperson Judah immediately confessed to the act. After the cup has been found in Benjamin's sack, he spoke up: "What can we say to my lord? . . . What can we say? How can we prove our innocence? God has uncovered your servants' guilt. We are now my lord's slaves—we ourselves and the one who was found to have the cup" (Gen 44:16). And Judah was thinking then not of the alleged theft but of the guilt they themselves bore as brothers for what they had done. Judah was even prepared to stay behind with Joseph as a slave so that Benjamin could return home to his father. He would not have been able to bear the pain his father would otherwise have suffered because of the loss of another son (Gen 44:33–34).

It is precisely that declaration by Judah that renders Joseph unable to contain himself any longer, and he abandons his air of powerful ruler. He is overcome by emotion. That is why he first dismisses his entire court, thus indicating that there will be no day of reckoning. He wants to put the past behind him for good and invites his brothers to do the same.

"*I am your brother Joseph.*" With that Joseph implicitly says: "Don't be afraid. Don't reproach yourselves." The family bond appears to be stronger than his Egyptian success story. He restores the family connection not by making a sovereign declaration along the lines of: "Do you understand who's standing in front of you? You know who I am!" Nor does he introduce himself by the royal name he was given by Pharaoh and that gave him power over all of Egypt: Zephenath-Paneah (Gen 41:45). No, he screams it through his tears: "I am *your brother* Joseph." The tears of Joseph and his brothers are signs of the reconciliation of brothers. The kiss Joseph gives his brothers is thus not a kiss of betrayal but the seal of forgiveness.[24]

"God intended it for good"

Then came the important moment, the high point of everything that had happened. Joseph indicated the deepest basis for his undoubtedly generous attitude. He indicates three reasons. First: "it was to save lives that God sent me ahead of you" (Gen 45:5); second, "God sent me ahead of you to preserve for you a remnant on earth and to save your lives by a great

---

24. Ibid., 343–51.

deliverance" (Gen 45:7); third, "it was not you who sent me here, but God" (Gen 45:8). It is on this basis that Joseph embraces his brothers, gives them food, welcomes his father from Canaan soon after, gives his family land, and allows them to build up a new existence under his protection.

But the brothers know better, namely, that God did not send Joseph to Egypt—they themselves did, out of jealousy, hate, and fear. Joseph's speech now brings about a complete turnaround in their fate: the guilt of the brothers, the father's sorrow, and Joseph's vengeance together become a means for the ending, for the revelation of what/who was actually behind everything that had occurred. The action of the Hidden One: "it was to save your lives and many others that God sent me ahead of you." Joseph makes it clear to his brothers that not only their family but also the Egyptians are suffering from hunger! And that has been going on for two years and would go on for five more. Through his interpretation of Pharaoh's dreams and through building storage barns Joseph has opened up new prospects, a way to escape the famine for both the Egyptians and his own family. It is not only the survival of the Egyptians and the Hebrews that God has in mind but the salvation of all nations. God's intention, his plan, his hand, is at work, in and through the "dirty hands" of people: "it was not you who sent me here, but God. He made me father to Pharaoh, lord of all his entire household and ruler of Egypt" (Gen 45:8). The brothers were so busy at the time with their own plotting that they failed to see that another plan was being implemented: the plan to give life to this world of hunger and death, for their own family and for the family of the world.

Joseph had dreamed he would be king. That was the work of God's hand, not of Pharaoh. No one else could and can take credit for that. God had placed the royal power in Joseph's hands. Apparently, God's plans, the things he wants to achieve by his hand, are carried out in concrete history by the hands of people.[25]

Does Joseph's explanation allay his brothers' fear? Do they now accept the reality of the dream—for themselves, for the Egyptians, *and* for the world? Immediately after their father Jacob dies their fear returns. They are afraid that Joseph will still take revenge. They literally throw themselves before him, precisely as Joseph had dreamed: "We are your slaves." The brothers do not dare trust the dream. But the most impressive words in the whole Joseph narrative are now immediately stated by Joseph: "You meant evil against me, but God meant it for good" (Gen 50:20; RSV). That is where the whole of Joseph's story finishes.

---

25. Ibid., 343–51.

These are magnificent words to conclude the Joseph cycle and thus the whole book of Genesis. What is said here at the conclusion goes back to the opening of the Bible: "God saw all that he had made, and it was very good. And there was evening and there was morning—the sixth day." The words that Joseph speaks in 50:20 are the decisive climax of his story. And it is immediately a programmatic confirmation of the good news, of, one could say, the whole Bible. The evil plans of humans never ever frustrate God's plans. His plan is implemented (in a hidden fashion) even by evil: the plan for the world, for good, for life, *l'chaim*.[26]

The Nature of Joseph's Kingship

The whole Joseph cycle is directed at the great dream of ruling. Joseph ascends the throne—in Egypt no less! The story begins with a royal proclamation by the Pharaoh: "'You shall be in charge of my palace, and all my people are to submit to your orders. Only with respect to the throne will I be greater than you.' So Pharaoh said to Joseph, 'I hereby put you in charge of the whole land of Egypt'" (Gen 41:40–41). Joseph received emblems that belonged to his position: the ring on his finger, fine linen robes to wear, and a gold chain around his neck (Gen 41:42). This was followed by a public announcement: "He had him ride in a chariot as his second-in-command., and men shouted before him, 'Make way!' Thus, he put him in charge of the whole land of Egypt" (Gen 41:43). And Joseph was also given a royal name (Gen 41:45) and finally had his status sealed by marriage to the daughter of the priest of On (Heliopolis), one of the most powerful families in Egypt.[27]

But what is Joseph's attitude to the Egyptian kingdom? One should be aware of how much Egypt is connected to the misery that the people of Israel went through and the way in which Moses became the leader of the Exodus at God's initiative. Here it is very important to look at Joseph's character, given that he was placed in a very close relationship with Pharaoh. Did he thus become tainted by "power"? The story says more about that than a superficial reading might convey to the reader. Joseph was thirty when he entered the service of Pharaoh, the king of Egypt. After his appointment he left Pharaoh's palace and travelled throughout the land of Egypt. "During the seven years of abundance the land produced plentifully. Joseph collected all the food produced in those seven years of abundance in Egypt and stored it in the cities. In each city he put the food grown in the fields surrounding it. Joseph stored up huge quantities of grain, like the sand of the sea; it was

26. Ibid., 376.
27. *KBS* on Genesis 41:45.

so much that he stopped keeping records because it was beyond measure" (Gen 41:46–49). Joseph proves to be a smart, one could say crafty, ruler and is completely devoted to Pharaoh's concerns. He is prepared to sacrifice the interests of individuals to the property of the crown: "When all Egypt began to feel the famine, the people cried to Pharaoh for food. Then Pharaoh told all the Egyptians, 'Go to Joseph and do what he tells you.' When the famine had spread over the whole country, Joseph opened all the storehouses and sold grain to the Egyptians, for the famine was severe throughout Egypt" (Gen 41:55–56). This shows Joseph's dexterity as an administrator. But Joseph does not present himself as a disinterested figure. And it is immediately clear what dangers a person is exposed to when he become entangled in the interests of a great imperial power. The Egyptian kingdom that Joseph leads in the name of Pharaoh does offer food but at the same time demands the lives of its subjects in return. Exploitation, oppression, and slavery are a constant threat. Joseph is a factor in the emergence of a situation in which his people will find themselves soon enough. He helps set the stage on which the cry for liberation would later be heard. The inhabitants of Egypt are turned into slaves, and they lose their freedom. Joseph is certainly crafty, but that is a highly dubious honor.

The program Joseph proposes to Pharaoh is thus not far removed from the imperialistic politics of Egypt that the children of Egypt will quickly complain of (Exod 5:5–19) with a Pharaoh who did not know Joseph (Exod 1:8).[28] And what Joseph does is completely at odds with the Torah will later command: "If any of your fellow Israelites become poor and are unable to support themselves among you, help them as you would a foreigner and stranger, so they can continue to live among you. Do not take interest or any profit from them, but fear your God, so that they may continue to live among you. You must not lend them money at interest or sell them food at a profit. I am the Lord your God, who brought you out of Egypt to give you the land of Canaan and to be your God" and "If a foreigner residing among you becomes rich and any of your fellow Israelites become poor and sell themselves to the foreigner or to a member of the foreigner's clan, they retain the right of redemption after they have sold themselves" (cf. Lev 25:35–38; 47–48). If we follow Joseph's acts in Egypt, we will be struck by the parallel with what will happen in the monarchical period. Solomon, especially, will press workers from all of Israel into forced labor for the "holy task" of building the temple in Jerusalem. They are slaves (!), totaling 30,000 men. "He sent them off to Lebanon in shifts of ten thousand a month, so that they spent one month in Lebanon and two months at home. Adoniram

---

28. Brueggemann, *Genesis*, 356.

was in charge of the forced labor. Solomon had seventy thousand carriers and eighty thousand stonecutters in the hills, as well as thirty-three hundred foremen who supervised the project and directed the workers. At the king's command they removed from the quarry large blocks of high-grade stone to provide a foundation of dressed stone for the temple" (1 Kings 5:14–17). Adoniram had been given that position already at the end of David's reign (2 Sam 20:24). That means that this policy condemned by the Torah was already initiated by King David! It is thus not all that surprising that more and more people began to hate Adoniram. When he later became a negotiator for Solomon's successor, King Rehoboam, he was stoned by the people (1 Kings 12:18). Rehoboam wanted to make it worse for the people than his father had: "My father made your yoke heavy; I will make it even heavier. My father scourged you with whips; I will scourge you with scorpions" (1 Kings 12:14). He planned to continue the policies of King Solomon in a worse, even more severe form.

Joseph as the Interpreter of Dreams in the Qur'an

In addition to the dream that Abraham receives and in which he is commanded to sacrifice his son (Q 37:102), the Qur'an talks about dreams most extensively in the chapter called Yûsuf, which can justifiably be called a "dream narrative."[29] Joseph is presented as a dreamer and as an interpreter of dreams.[30] When he tells his father that he dreamed that eleven stars, the sun, and the moon bowed down to him, Jacob advises him against telling his brothers this dream because he knows that his brothers will become jealous. Then Jacob says: "Your Lord will thus choose you and you will learn to understand events[31] and to complete the grace given to you and the tribe of Jacob, as He did earlier to both your forefathers Abraham and Isaac" (Q 12:5–6). As soon as Joseph ends up in prison, he comes into contact with two other prisoners who have had dreams and ask him to interpret them (Q 12:36). "I will give you the interpretation before our meal is brought to us" (Q 12:37), and he does in fact do that (Q 12:41). The one dreamed that he saw himself pouring wine, and the other saw himself with bread on his head, which birds were eating. "Tell me your interpretation," he says. Joseph replies: "You, my fellow prisoners! Regarding the one, he will be soon be pouring wine for his lord. With respect to the other, he will be crucified and the birds will eat from his head. The matter you asked me about has

---

29. Cf. *E.Q.*, s.v. "Dreams and Sleep."
30. Qurtubi argues that Joseph was the best interpreter of dreams on earth.
31. *tawîl.*

already been decided" (Q 12:41). Joseph does ask the one he expects to be saved: "Remember me to your Lord!" But satan has him forget Joseph, and consequently Joseph remains in prison for several years more (Q 12:42). And then the dream Pharaoh has follows immediately, causing Pharaoh to become worried. Strikingly enough, in this story this man is called "king" and not "Pharaoh!"[32] He says: "I saw seven fat cows being eaten by seven thin cows, and seven green ears of grain and seven shriveled ears." "O you important members of my court [that is how he addressed his ministers], tell me the meaning of my dreams if you know how to interpret them." But his councilors called them "confused dreams" and confessed that they did not have enough expertise to interpret his dreams (Q 12:44). Just at that moment, the fellow prisoner of Joseph who had been saved remembered Joseph. He told the king: "I will give you the interpretation. Send me to Joseph." Arriving at the prison, the butler addressed Joseph as follows: "Joseph, the truthful" (Q 12:46).[33]

We should look at how the butler addresses Joseph. In interpreting the Qur'an one should always be aware of the close connection that exists between the *Tawra* and the *Injîl*, as well as with other Jewish sources, such as the Pseudepigrapha, the *haggada*, and the *midrash*. This address is an illustration of this. The rabbinic and pseudepigraphical sources often give Joseph the title the "righteous."[34] This is what Joseph is constantly called in the *haggada* and in the Jewish liturgy.[35] He was given this title undoubtedly because of his virtuous victory over the wiles of the wife of his master Potiphar,[36] as that is described in 4 Maccabees 2:2.[37] In the cabbalistic literature Joseph is hardly mentioned without this title. In the *midrash* the title *tsaddîq* refers to someone who shows charity. In addition, only Joseph and Noah have been given this distinction because they provided food for humans and animals in a time of hunger and need.

Following Jewish custom, Muslim writers also give Joseph the title *tsaddîq* but in the Arabic sense of the word: "the trustworthy."[38] The first successor to the prophet Muhammad, Abû Bakr, was also given this as an epithet: "the trustworthy."[39] Other figures in the salvation history of

32. *fir'awn*.
33. *siddîq*.
34. *Tsaddîq*; cf. Maimonides, 250, 364.
35. Paret, *Der Koran: Kommentar*, on Q 12:46.
36. In the Qur'an he is called *al-Azîz*.
37. Speyer, *Die biblischen Erzählungen*, 202–3.
38. Ginzberg, *Legends of the Jews*, 328–29, note 3.
39. *as-siddîq*.

the Qur'an who received the epithet are Abraham (Q 19:41) and Idrîs (Q 19:56).[40] Mary was also given this title, in its feminine form (Q 5:75).[41] So, the butler says to Joseph, who is still in prison: "Joseph the truthful, tell me about the seven fat cows that are eaten up by the seven thin ones and the seven green ears of grain and the seven shriveled ears" (Q 12:46). Then Joseph gives his interpretation: "You will have seven years in which you sow as usual. Whatever you harvest, leave it on the ears, except for a small amount that you will eat. Then there will seven hard years that will eat up what you have saved. Then there will be a year in which there will be rain and you will again press grapes" (Q 12:47-49).

At the end of this chapter it is said that Joseph's dream became reality: "Joseph seated his parents on the throne." That means that both his father and his mother Rachel were alive at this time in this story.[42] Joseph says, "O Father! This is the interpretation of my dream from earlier. My Lord has made it come true. He has always intended good with me."[43] The last sentence can be seen as a parallel of the core sentence from the Joseph narrative in Genesis: "You meant evil against me, but God meant it for good" (Gen 50:20; RSV). "God was gracious to me," Joseph says to his father at the conclusion of the story, "when He released me from prison and now brought you from the desert after satan brought discord between me and my brothers. My Lord finds ways and means to do what He wills. He is All-Knowing and All-Wise" (Q 12:100). And then he ends with the prayer: "Lord, You have given me dominion (in Egypt) and have taught me to understand events. You, Creator of heaven and earth! You are my protector in this world and the next. Let me die as someone who has surrendered [*muslim*] himself to God and include me among the righteous" (Q 12:101).

Jacob and his Two Sons Joseph and Benjamin in the Qur'an

The story of the life of Jacob is connected primarily with the role he plays in the story of Joseph. As is often the case in the Qur'an, many names of biblical individuals are not given. This is not because they are not known but precisely because it is assumed that they are known by the listeners. Of

---

40. Both times with the title "prophet," *al-nabî*.

41. *tsaddîqa*. A number of women in the Bible are given this title, according to Howovitz, cited by Paret, *Der Koran: Kommentar,* on Q 5:75.

42. The Bible says that she died after the birth of her second son, Benjamin (Gen 35:16-20).

43. *wa ahsana bî*.

the 16 *dramatatis personae* in this *sûra* only Joseph is mentioned by name. Thus, Jacob's name is not given either: he is constantly referred to as "father."

Another important person in this story about Joseph is Benjamin. The close relationship between the two brothers is a leitmotif in the Joseph narrative in the Qur'an. Each reference to Benjamin plays an important role in the development of the story, paradoxically enough not through what he says or does but through his relationship to his brother Joseph.

It is through Benjamin that Joseph gains a hold over and exercises power over his brothers. "When Joseph had provided his brothers with the ration, he said, 'Bring me a brother of yours [Benjamin] from your father the next time'" (Q 12:59). According to the Qur'an, it is the jealousy of the brothers with respect to both sons of Rachel—and thus not only Joseph—that directs events (Q 12:8). When the brothers return from Egypt to their father and tell him, "We will not be given any more grain until Benjamin comes with us to Egypt" (Q 12:63), there is a sense of *déjà vu* when the brothers then assure their father: "*We will look after him.*" That is, when they at the very beginning of the story ask their father if they can take Joseph with them, they say, "Father, why don't you trust us with Joseph? We are sincerely devoted to him. Send him with us tomorrow so he can enjoy himself and play" (Q 12:12). In that case, their promise was false and the harm that Joseph suffered was real. They throw him into the well and then sell him, and he is carried away into exile. When the brothers ask Jacob in the later scene if Benjamin can return with them to Egypt—because they will not be sold any grain otherwise—they give him the same kind of assurance: "*We will look after him.*" That gives Jacob the opportunity to reproach them: "Can I entrust him to you more than his brother years ago?" (Q 12:64). Jacob does not like it and will not let Benjamin go unless the brothers swear before God that they will bring his youngest son back to him (Q 12:66). There is double irony here. The first time the brothers lied but now they are speaking the truth. Jacob was prepared (though unwillingly) to believe them the first time, but it is different this time. The second irony is the following: when they first lied to Jacob, they said that Joseph had been killed by a wolf and they complained, hypocritically: "You don't believe us even when we speak the truth." Just as Jacob had to accept the lie *then*, so he cannot believe in the truth or sincerity of their words *now*. His fear of the evil that Joseph could meet was real in the first case, but the evil that Jacob now fears for Benjamin did not happen.[44]

Before the brothers return to Egypt Jacob commands his sons to not all enter the city via the same gate (Q 12:67), obviously with the idea that they

---

44. Johns, "Joseph in the Qurân," 34.

could otherwise be struck by the "evil eye."[45] The idea behind this comes from a Jewish *midrash* and does refer to entering the Egyptian capital, and not the country in general. After all, cities, and not countries, have gates.[46]

When the brothers arrive in Egypt with Benjamin, Joseph takes him aside and says to him: "Truly, I am your brother" (Q 12:69). When Joseph hides his cup in Benjamin's saddlebag (Q 12:70, 76), it is consequently "discovered" (Q 12:76), and the brothers say this: "That he has stolen something is no surprise, for his brother already stole something before" (Q 12:77). In a Jewish source as well we find a similar response by the indignant brothers: "And the brothers stood there and punched Benjamin on his shoulder, saying, 'Hey thief, son of a thief. You have shamed us; you are the son of your mother.'" The last statement is an allusion to Rachel, who stole the *teraphim*, the household gods that were to protect her father Laban's home (Gen 31:19). Because a man in the family had been mentioned, Jacob could also be in mind here. He did steal the blessing of his brother Esau (Gen 27:36).[47]

Jacob is again confronted with the loss of a son if Benjamin is detained in Egypt. When Jacob believed that he had lost Joseph, he cried out: "For me, patience is best" (Q 12:18). Despite this new pain after so many years of sorrow, Jacob is nevertheless able to respond in the same words as previously: "For me, patience is best,"[48] to which he immediately adds: "May God will bring them back to me together [i.e., both Benjamin and Joseph!]" (Q 12:83). Thus, Jacob hopes that Joseph is still alive. And then he turns away from his sons and says: "How sorrowful I am about Joseph!" His eyes are blinded by pure pain and weeping. The text states literally that his eyes turned white because of his weeping (Q 12:84). To that the brothers say, "You won't stop talking about Joseph until you finally get sick because of it and die" (Q 12:85). Jacob answers: "I make my complaint and my grief only to God. Because of God I know what you do not" (Q 12:86). According to the *haggada*, God revealed to Jacob that Joseph was still alive.[49] "Oh, my sons, go and search for Joseph and his brother. And do not despair of the solace of God. No one other than unbelievers despairs of the solace of God" (Q 12:87).[50]

When Judah, one of the brothers, speaks up and asks if one of the brothers can be detained in Benjamin's place because his father is a gray-haired old man, Joseph answers: "Far be it from us if anyone is detained

45. Speyer, *Die biblischen Erzählungen*, 214.
46. Paret, *Der Koran: Kommentar*, on Q 12:67.
47. Speyer, *Die biblischen Erzählungen*, 216.
48. Johns, "Joseph in the Qurân," 35–36.
49. Speyer, *Die biblischen Erzählungen*, 218.
50. Johns, "Joseph in the Qurân," 39–40.

other than the one with whom our property was found" (Q 12:79). Benjamin is the one who sees to it that something changes in his brothers' hearts. Jacob's command to seek Joseph and his brother (Q 12:87) leads to the climax of the story when Joseph reveals his identity. Before he lets them know who he is, Joseph asks his brothers the following question: "Do you no longer remember what you, in your foolishness, did with Joseph and his brother [Benjamin] in your ignorance?" (Q12:89). They then answered: "Are you really Joseph?" And Joseph replies, "Yes, I am Joseph" (Q 12:90).

Joseph's Shirt

At the beginning of the story, Joseph's brothers say that their father loves him *and his brother Benjamin* more than he loves them, even though there are so many of them. They call that a clear *error* on his part (Q 12:8). The word *error* is used again when Jacob becomes blind as a result of his grief at the loss of Joseph (Q 12:84). When Joseph makes himself known to his brothers (Q 12:90), he asks them to take his shirt back to Canaan with them to lay over his father's face so that he can regain his sight (Q 12:93). As soon as the caravan leaves Egypt with Joseph's shirt Jacob already declares: "I detect the smell of Joseph, but don't say that I'm not right in the head" (Q 12:94). According to tradition, Jacob says these words when the caravan is still eight days (nights) away.[51] Those living with Jacob responded: "By God, you are falling into your old *error* again!" (Q 12:95). But here Jacob's patience is justified. According to the commentators here, the bringer of good news[52] is Jacob's son Judah (*Yahûdha*),[53] who places the shirt over Jacob's face, and Jacob's sight is thus returned to him.

The smell[54] of Joseph's shirt was connected in Jacob's explanation with the spirit or breath of God.[55] He states: "Go, my sons . . . and do not despair of the solace of God. No one other than unbelievers despairs of the solace of God" (Q 12:87).

Certain exegetical traditions say that Joseph's shirt was brought by Gabriel from heaven. Joseph, it is also said, wore the shirt in a silver amulet around his neck and had it with him when he was thrown into the well. The scent of heaven that lingered in the shirt gave him the power to heal the sick.[56]

---

51. Van Ibn 'Abbâs († 686–688). *E.Q.* s.v. "Smell."
52. *al-bashîr*.
53. *E.Q.*, s.v. "Smell."
54. *rîh*.
55. *rawh Allâh*.
56. *E.Q.*, s.v. "Smell."

After his encouraging words to his sons, Jacob says: "Did I not say that, because of what God has revealed to me, I know what you do not?" (Q 12:96). Various forms of the word "know" occur in this chapter, in order to thus throw light on the "knowledge" of God, the knowledge God gives a prophet, in this case, the prophet Jacob. It is a knowledge that remains hidden to others.[57]

That the blind Joseph regains his sight is connected in a *midrash* with what Jacob says to his sons shortly before they depart together for Egypt; "I [God] will go down to Egypt with you, and I will surely bring you back. And Joseph's own hands will close your eyes" (Gen 46:4). It is said that the holy Spirit did not reveal himself during Joseph's absence. The rabbis also connect Jacob's blindness to his lack of spiritual enlightenment.

It is presupposed that Muhammad was well acquainted with the story of Tobias. That story tells of the return of a son who, on the command of an angel, has to rub gall from a fish into the eyes of his blind father, by which the father's sight returns.

> When they came close to Nineveh, Raphael said to Tobias, "You know what state your father was in when we left. Let's travel on and get your house ready before your wife arrives. See to it that you have the gall from the fish close at hand." They travelled on, followed by the dog. In the meantime Anna was sitting by the road on the lookout for her child. At a certain moment she saw him coming and reported to his father: "There comes your son, and with him is the man who went with him." Raphael said to Tobias: "I am certain that your father will regain his sight. Rub the gall on his eyes. As soon as it begins to sting, he has to rub his eyes until the white spots disappear, and then he will see you." In the meantime, Anna had rushed up, threw her arms around her neck and called out: "I see you, my child! Now I can die." And both of them wept. Tobit went to the door and fell. His son walked to him, picked his father up, rubbed the gall into his eyes, and said; "Courage, father." As soon as his eyes started to sting, Tobit rubbed them and the *white flecks/spots* fell like flakes of skin from the corners of his eyes. As soon as he saw his son, he threw his arms around him and said, weeping, "Blessed are you, God, and blessed is Your holy name forever and blessed are all your holy angels. You have tested me but you grant grace once again now I *see* my son Tobias. (Tob 11:1–8)[58]

---

57. Johns, "Joseph in the Qurân," 35; cf. *E.Q.*, s.v. "Face"; "Vision and Blindness"; "Clothing."

58. Speyer, *Die biblischen Erzählungen*, 219–20.

When Jacob arrives at Joseph's in Egypt together with his wife Rachel, Joseph says: "Go to Egypt in safety, God willing (*in shaʾ Allâh*)" (Q 12:99). There is a story of what someone once went through when a reciter of this passage gave an extraordinary tone to the recitation of the phrase *in shâʾ Allâh*. The recitation caused the pulse of the recitation to quicken at this point, as if the climax of the whole chapter is found here. That could be based on the fact that he was aware that there was a parallel phrase in another chapter of the Qur'an, namely, in *sûrat al Fath* (Q 48:27), the passage about the capture of the city of Mecca by Muhammad. Muhammad himself is assured: "You will enter the sacred mosque, *in shâʾ Allâhu âminîn* [if the Lord wills it in safety]." Thus, the command to Jacob to enter the gate of Egypt can be seen as a prefiguration of the command to Muhammad. For Muhammad, that was the assurance that he would also enter the city of Mecca in that way at some point.[59]

In the blessing that Jacob pronounces at the end of his life about his sons, preference is given to Judah and to the house of Joseph (both his sons, Ephraim and Manasseh) (Gen 49).[60] An echo of that blessing can be heard in the Qur'an when Jacob says to his sons: "Who will you serve when I am no longer here?" They said: "Your God and the God of your fathers, Abraham, Ishmael, and Isaac. *To him we surrender ourselves*" (Q 2:133).[61] This passage does not call the former and present brothers and readers to become "Muslims" in the contemporary sense of the word but to follow the religion of Abraham or to "surrender" themselves to God. "Say: 'We believe in God and what is given to us as revelation and what is sent to Abraham, Ishmael, Isaac, Jacob, and the tribes (of Israel) and what has been given to Moses and Jesus and the prophets from their Lord, without making any kind of distinction among them. To him we surrender ourselves'" (Q 2:136).

Human Guile and Divine Guile in the Story of Joseph

The twelfth chapter of the Qur'an is concerned from the prologue to the epilogue with guile: that of the brothers, that of the women, that of Joseph, and that of God.

At the beginning of the chapter, Father Jacob advises the young Joseph not to tell his dream of becoming a king to his brothers so that they would not plot against him, for "the Satan is a manifest enemy of humankind" (Q 12:5). Jacob refers to the Satan to focus attention on the source of guile, a temptation to which the brothers are inclined to succumb. All the brothers plot evil for

---

59. That is suggested by Johns, "Joseph in the Qurân," 38–39.
60. *KBS* on Genesis 49:1.
61. *E.Q.*, s.v. " Jacob"; cf. *E.Q.*, s.v. "Polytheism and Atheism"; "Monotheism."

Joseph, jealous as they are because of the love of their father for Joseph and his brother, just as Cain was jealous because God accepted Abel's sacrifice but not his own. The brothers want their father to think they mean well for Joseph. But their actual intention is to get rid of him, to do away with him. In the evening they come crying back and tell an outright lie: "A wolf devoured him," showing their father Joseph's shirt with "false blood" (Q 12:16–18).[62]

In the scene with Potiphar's wife, Joseph declares that she wanted him to submit to her, but he managed to escape, though he left his shirt behind that had been torn from behind (Q 12:25). Someone from the household staff testified by saying, "If his shirt was torn from the front, then she is telling the truth, but if it is torn from behind, then she is lying" (Q 12:26–28). When the latter proves to be the case, the husband declares: "This is one of your ruses, women! Your plottings are terrible. Joseph, let the matter drop! And you, woman, pray God for forgiveness for your guilt" (Q 12:28). Joseph states later, for that matter, that he is not free of weakness, for all souls are inclined to evil, except for those to whom God shows mercy: "Surely my Lord is Forgiving and Merciful" (Q 12:53).

The latter example is often cited to portray "women" as seducers, under the caption, "The Guile of Women." Certain Muslim exegetes also say that the guile of women is greater than that of men because women's guile is often more subtle and efficient. Some even go so far as to say that they see the guile of women as greater than that of the devil because the Qur'an says that the "plots of the devil are always weak" (Q 4:76). In comparison with that, the guile of women is disproportionately large. But this interpretation is correctly opposed by others as a obstinate prejudice. The Satan's guile is weak in comparison to God's power, not the wiles of women. The statement about the Satan is made by God, whereas that view of women comes out of the mouth of Potiphar, who does not speak in the name of God![63] At a certain point, there is talk in the city about the relationship between Joseph and Potiphar's wife. The women in the city say: "The governor's wife is trying to seduce her slave. He captured her heart. We see her openly going astray" (Q 12:30). And when Potiphar's wife hears about the women gossiping, she invites them for a meal and gives each of them a knife. Then she calls to Joseph: "Come out." When the women see him, they admire him so much that they cut themselves with the knives in their hands and say: "God be praised. This is not a human being, but an honorable angel" (Q 12:31). Zulaykha (Potifar's wife) then says: "Well, this is person you reproached me for. I did indeed try to seduce him, but he has kept his innocence. But if he does not do what I command him, he will be

---

62. *Dictionnaire*, s.v. "Ruse."
63. *Dictionnaire*, s.v. "Ruse féminine."

put into prison and become one of those who are considered the least of all" (Q 12:32). Joseph responded by saying: "O my Lord, to be placed in prison is more dear to me than what she invites me to. If you do not turn her plotting away from me, I will succumb and then I'll be a fool." God hears Joseph's prayer and turned her wiles away from him (Q 12:33–34).

After Joseph has been in prison for some time and has interpreted the dreams of the butler and the baker, the butler who has been restored to his position suddenly remembers Joseph again when the king needs someone to interpret his dreams. Joseph is called to the court by the king of Egypt, but when the messenger of the king comes to him, he says: "Go back to your lord and ask him how the women who cut themselves in their hands are. Surely my Lord knows her craftiness" (Q 12:50). And then the confession comes that releases Joseph of guilt:

> The king said to the women of the city: "What was going on then when you tried to seduce Joseph against his will?" They said: "God preserve us. We know of no evil he has done." The wife of the governor said: "Now the truth has come to light. I was the one who sought to seduce him. He was the one who told the truth." Joseph said: "This is so that he might know that I was not faithless in secret towards my master and that God does not let the guile of traitors succeed" (Q 12:51–52).

When Joseph's brothers come to Egypt because of the famine in Canaan, Joseph uses a trick to get his brother Benjamin into prison. It now appears that it is not only people who conceive of plots—God himself makes use of such. Joseph does think of the trick of putting his own cup in Benjamin's bag. And then he first searches the bags of the others before starting on his younger brother's. But when he finds the cup in Benjamin's bag, it is written in the Qur'an: "Thus We [God] used a trick for him." Just as the brothers conspired against Joseph at the beginning of the story, so Joseph now plots against them by putting his own cup in his younger brother's bag. But it turns out in the end that God is the one who thought up this trick (Q 12:76).[64] God uses a trick! Joseph's trick is ascribed to God. God is able to surpass the crafty designs people come up with.[65]

How will his brothers respond to this? It all started with the jealousy of the brothers about the love that their father had for Joseph, even though there were so many of them (Q 12:8). This jealousy became the reason behind their plots against Joseph. But the arrest of Benjamin has a dramatic

---

64. Paret, *Der Koran: Übersetzung*, uses the word überlisten (to outwit) in his translation.

65. Johns, "Joseph in the Qurân," 36.

effect on them. Again they find themselves caught between their father and a younger brother under their protection and whom the father loves deeply and dearly. But now they place the interests of their father above their own. They plead with Joseph to let Benjamin go and appeal to his pity: "Our little brother has an old gray-haired father. Therefore, take one of us in his place! We see you are an honorable man" (Q 12:78). But Joseph refuses. Then the brothers withdraw from the conversation and discuss in whispers how they can rescue their brother for their father's sake, just as they sought for a way to rid themselves of Joseph (Q 12:80). And instead of giving Benjamin up for lost—as they had done with Joseph—the eldest of them (Judah) refuses to leave Egypt and leaves it up to the other nine to bring the bad news to their father. This was the result of Joseph's trickery, the plot that God had made for Joseph (Q 12:76). And Joseph sees this deceit through to the end when he continues to refuse to take someone instead of Benjamin. What is going on there? Joseph wants to know if the brothers will leave Benjamin behind because they could think he is guilty. Will they abandon him and return to their father? Will they again tell their father about the loss of a son? Thus, the test was: Will they do the same thing they did with respect to Joseph at the time, or have they changed since then?[66]

The subject of tricks comes up again in the conclusion to the story: "This is one of the stories of the Hidden. We revealed it to you [Muhammad]. You [Muhammad] was not with them [Joseph's brothers] when they decided what they wanted to do and thought up a plot against him" (Q 12:102).

When, at the beginning of the story, the young Joseph at home dreams that the sun, the moon, and eleven stars bowed down to him, his father reproaches him as follows: "What is this dream you had? Will your mother and I and your brothers actually come and bow down to the ground before you?" (Gen 37:9–10). It is thus striking and suggestive for the changed disposition of Joseph that he places both his parents beside him on the throne and says: "Father, this is the interpretation of my dream from before. My Lord has made the dream come true and brought it to pass" (Q 12:100). And then Joseph ends with a prayer: "Lord, You have given me the kingship (in Egypt) and taught me to understand the outcome of events.[67] You, Creator of heaven and earth. In this and the future world you are my friend. Let me die as someone who has surrendered himself to God [*muslim*] and include me among the righteous" (Q 12:101).

---

66. Ibid., 36–38. Here Johns calls Gerhard von Rad's commentary on Genesis applicable on this point.

67. *Taʿwîl* is translated by Paret, *Der Koran: Kommentar,* as "outcome."

Joseph as a Role Model for the Prophet Muhammad

It is possible to see Joseph as a role model for the prophet Muhammad. There are parallels between what Joseph suffered at the hands of his brothers in Canaan and what Muhammad suffered from his fellow tribespeople in Mecca. Limitations were imposed on Muhammad regarding his activities in Mecca, right up the house of Arqam († 674). This man belonged to one of the most prominent families of the Quraysh and lived in the lowest part of the city of Mecca. The house of this young companion of Muhammad, on the hill of al-Safâ near the Ka'ba, was where the first meetings of the Muhammad's followers took place. It was the center of the young community until after the conversion of 'Umar ibn al-Khattâb, later the second caliph or successor of Muhammad. A well-known biographer, Ibn Sa'd, says that that house was the scene of many conversions.[68] There is also a parallel between the fact that Joseph was a viceregent in Egypt (thus in exile) of that country and the fact of Muhammad's leadership in Medina after his emigration[69] there. This connection between Joseph and Muhammad can also be deduced from what Joseph says to his two fellow prisoners who ask him to interpret their dreams: "Indeed, I abandoned the religion[70] of people who did not believe in God and rejected the future world" (Q 12:37). Abraham before him had done the same, and Muhammad would also do that by emigrating to Medina. 619/620 is given as the date of the revelation of this *sûra* about Joseph.[71] And it is seen as no coincidence that the Qur'anic verses that speak of prophetic rulers like David and Solomon are revealed in that same period.[72]

Just like Joseph, Muhammad is rejected by his fellow tribespeople and is exiled from his home country of Mecca. But what his enemies intend as evil God turns to good. Muhammad is vindicated and obtains the position of a wise and just ruler—just like Joseph.

Muhammad and Dreams

Muhammad's activities were accompanied by dreams, even though his opponents found them unbelievable. The Meccans who committed injustices whispered among themselves: "Is he not a man like us? Do you want to get involved with magic?" (Q 21:3). They found Muhammad's preaching

---

68. *E.I.*, s.v. "al-Arkam"; Glassé, *The Concise Encyclopaedia*, s.v. "Arqam."
69. *hijra*.
70. *milla*.
71. Bell *and* Watt, *Introduction to the Quran*, 110.
72. Johns, "Joseph in the Qurân," 44.

a "tangle of dreams" (Q 21:5) and used the expression here that the ministers of the king of Egypt also used in characterizing Pharaoh's dream of the fat and skinny cows and the green and shriveled ears of grain. And they did that while Joseph could indeed give a meaningful interpretation of the dream. The same applies thus to the preaching of the prophet Muhammad. What seems a tangled mess to the unbelieving Meccans proved in the end to indeed have a deep meaning. That is why we should take the time to look at a number of dreams Muhammad had. Let us first look at the dream that the prophet had a year before his emigration from Mecca to Medina: the dream of his nightly journey to Jerusalem (and his journey to heaven). Then we will look at the dream he had before the battle at Badr, the dream about concluding a treaty with his Meccan opponents, enemies on the borders of the sacred ground where Mecca lay, and finally the dream about the opening[73] of the city of Mecca for its "submission to God."

The Nightly Journey

Already a year before Muhammad's actual emigration[74] from Mecca to Medina in 622, he had a spiritual Exodus experience, a redemption experience, a vision[75] (Q 17:60). This vision alludes to a nightly journey,[76] a journey to heaven,[77] in which Muhammad is whisked away in the wink of an eye from Mecca to Jerusalem: "Praised be He who makes his servant travel by night from the sacred place of prayer [the Ka'ba in Mecca] to the most distant place of prayer,[78] whose precincts God has blessed" (Q 17:1). The latter is still a term for "Palestine," the holy or promised land in the Qur'an. The most well-known "nightly journey" in history is the Exodus from Egypt under Moses. But reference was made already earlier to a nightly journey, namely, that of Abraham's nephew Lot (Lût), who left the cities of injustice, Sodom and Gomorrah, at night before they were "overthrown."

The classic description of Muhammad's life tells the story of Muhammad's journey through the seven heavens in which he ascends to the divine presence. At the first level he meets Adam. Ascending even further, he

---

73. *fath.*
74. *hijra.*
75. *ru'yâ.*
76. *isrâ'.* Paret, *Der Koran: Kommentar,* on Q 17:60. Paret considers this improbable (302), referring to a relation to Q 8:43, the battle of Badr, and Q 48:27, the trip to al-Hudaybiyya.
77. *mi'râj.*
78. *al-masjdid al-aqsa.*

meets, respectively, Jesus together with John the Baptist, Yahyâ, his cousin on his mother's side, then Joseph, whose face shines like the full moon, then Enoch, Aaron and Moses, and finally, in the seventh heaven, Abraham.[79]

The Moment of Truth (The Battle of Badr)

In March 624, thus two years after the *hijra* or Exodus from Mecca to Medina, the first great battle of Muhammad's career took place near a small city, Badr. This city is 150 kilometers southwest of Medina, on the intersection of a road to Medina and the caravan route from Mecca to Syria.[80] This battle occurred shortly after Muhammad had broke with the Jewish tribes in Medina and the prayer direction[81] was changed from Jerusalem, the direction in which the Jews were to pray since the exile (Dan 6:11; Tob 3:11; cf. 1 Kings 8:44, 48; Ps 5:8; 28:2; 138:2; 55:18), to Mecca (Q 2:142–150). The battle took place in the month of Ramadan. Muhammad's followers numbered 305 in total, including 74 emigrants,[82] thus the people who emigrated to Medina with Muhammad. The rest were "helpers,"[83] as the followers of Muhammad in Medina were called. In contrast, the "troops" of the Meccans numbered about 1,000. The Muslims achieved a spectacular victory, which was understood and explained as God's confirmation of the case of the followers of Muhammad. The day on which the two armies met was thus viewed as a "kairos moment" (Q 3:13): the "moment of truth."[84] It is tempting to think here of Jewish influences because in a report of the victory of King Saul (Tâlût) over the Ammonites, the descendants of Lot (Lût), this victory is also called "the day of the *furqân*" (1 Sam 11:13).[85]

The word *furqân* is also used in reference to Scripture: the Qur'an (Q 25:1; 2:181), as well as the *Tawra* (Torah) (Q 21:49; 2:50) and the *Injîl* (Gospel) (Q 3:2).[86] With reference to the battle at Badr, "the day of the *furqân*" has to do with the distinction between the good and the bad parties. The battle is thus fought in the month of Ramadan, the month in which it is commemorated that the first revelation of the Qur'an was made to Muhammad! Viewed in that connection, the word then acquires the meaning:

---

79. Guillaume, *The Life of Muhammad*, 186.
80. *E.I.*, s.v. "Badr."
81. *qibla*.
82. *muhâjirûn*.
83. *ansâr*.
84. *yaum al-furqân*.
85. Jeffery, *The Foreign Vocabulary*, 226.
86. Ibid., 225–26.

rescue, liberation.[87] On that day God rescued the small group of Muslims from almost certain defeat, and thus what happened was not only a decisive break between good and evil but also a decisive separation of ways.[88]

Muhammad had a dream before the Battle of Badr in which he saw that his Meccan opponents were but few, which greatly encouraged the Muslims. It would turn that his opponents had three times the number of men; the Muslims were thus confronted with a great superior force: "But God has shown our opponents to be so numerous, you would have given up or argued among yourselves about it. But God liberated you. That happened so that God could fulfill what He had already determined (in His wisdom)" (Q 8:43–44). That should be read in conjunction with another verse: "God had already helped you in Badr when you were still insignificant. Thus fear God so that you will believe and be grateful" (Q 3:123).

The victory at Badr was possibly a sign[89] from God by which He gives the people a deceptive presentation of their opponents. We have thus to do here with a revelatory dream (Q 8:43) and a kind of apparition that occurred at the scene of the battle as the fulfillment of that dream: "There is a sign for you of two armies that meet in battle: one army that strives on the way of God (to do God's will) and another army that saw them as twice as large as they themselves while in reality they were much stronger with regard to numbers. God strengthens with his help whom He wills. That is a lesson for those who have understanding" (Q 3:13).[90] Exegetes differ on the question of who it was that saw the other as twice as great. However that may be, the victory is ascribed to a divine sign.[91] A similar "apparition" is given to Joseph as well when he was about to succumb to the seduction of Potiphar's wife. That would have happened if no sign[92] from God was present that turned the woman's wiles away from him (Q 12:24). Here exegetes think it was an apparition of his father.[93]

When Muhammad called on God for help before the battle, God heard him: "I will support you with a thousand angels standing behind you, ready to

---

87. Ibid., 228.

88. *E.Q.*, s.v. "Badr" and "Criterium"; cf. Glassé, *The Concise Encyclopaedia*, s.v. "Battle of Badr."

89. *âya*.

90. *E.Q.*, s.v. "Dreams and Sleep," 550–51.

91. *E.Q.*, s.v. "Apparition."

92. *burhân*.

93. *E.Q.*, s.v. "Apparition."

intervene in the battle." God announced this to support Muhammad and his allies. He gave them this good news[94] to set their hearts at ease (Q 8:9–10).[95]

It is striking in this connection to think of the story of the confrontation between Jesus and his opponents. When Jesus was in Gethsemane, Judas, one of his twelve disciples, approached him with a large group of people armed with swords and clubs. They had been sent by the high priests and elders of the people and arrested him. When one of Jesus' disciples drew his sword and cut off the ear of the servant of the high priest, Jesus said, "Put your sword back in its place . . . for all who draw the sword will die by the sword. Do you think I cannot call on my Father, and he will at once put at my disposal more than twelve legions of angels?" (Matt 26:52–54).

The Dream of Victory

The 48th chapter of the Qur'an is called *Al-Fath*. This refers to Muhammad's conquest of Mecca in January 630. It was "the opening," namely, for the "surrender" of the city Mecca to God.[96]

In March 628 Muhammad had a dream (cf. Q 48:27) in which he saw himself carrying out the rites of the small pilgrimage[97] in the still occupied Mecca. He decided then for that reason to go on an expedition to Mecca to show how much he respected the prestige of its shrine, the Ka'ba. He travelled with 1400 followers, most of whom had camels to sacrifice. The Meccans, however, thought that they would be viewed as weaklings if they let Muhammad into Mecca, even only as a pilgrim. Therefore, they sent a cavalry of 200 men to block his path. Muhammad evaded this blockade by travelling along an unusual and difficult route until he reached al-Hudaybiyya, a medium-sized village on the edge of the "sacred territory." Emissaries were exchanged, and they came to an agreement whereby it was agreed, among other things, that Muhammad would withdraw for the present but would return the following year to make the small pilgrimage. The city would then be evacuated for three days. After concluding this treaty, their camels were offered, and Muhammad's followers returned to Medina. A year later Muhammad carried out this rite together with a group of 2,000 men.

---

94. *bushrâ*.

95. Paret, *Der Koran: Übersetzung*; cf. Paret, *Der Koran: Kommentar*, 184 on Q 8:9, 10.

96. The first chapter of the Qur'an is called *sûrat al-fâtiha*, or "The Opening Chapter."

97. *'umra*.

The treaty that was intended for ten years only lasted ten months. That is when Muhammad's triumphal entry into Mecca occurred, in the month of Ramadan in 630.[98] Shortly after concluding the treaty on the pilgrimage to Mecca in the following year, this verse was revealed: "God has truly made the vision[99] He gave his messenger Muhammad come true. You will surely, God willing, enter the sacred house of prayer,[100] the Ka'ba" (Q 48:27).[101]

The Muslims were initially happy when they heard the dream because they believed that they would enter Mecca that same year. But this Treaty of al-Hudaybiyya was experienced as humiliating for the Muslims. Muhammad later explained to his followers that the treaty was, in fact, a victory. This was said after a clear success had occurred (Q 48:1) and God promised Muhammad a great victory (Q 48:3; cf. 110). "It is God who sent down the 'peace of God'[102] into the hearts of believers so that they would be strengthened even more in their faith. God alone has the hosts of heaven and earth at his disposal. He is all-knowing and wise" (Q 48:4).

After the conquest of Mecca, Muhammad let himself be inspired in his acts and behavior by the example of Joseph when he had acquired his position of power as the viceregent of Egypt and had met his brothers. Joseph said to them: "You will not be blamed today. God has forgiven you. There is no one as merciful as He is" (Q 12:92): "I am your brother Joseph" (Gen 45:5). It is said that on the day after Mecca was taken Muhammad took the two pillars from the doors of the Ka'ba and said to the leaders of the city: "What do you think I will do to you?" They answered: "Something good, noble brother and son of a noble brother, and you have the power." He said: "I will tell you what my brother Joseph said: 'You will not be blamed today.'" It is also said that Abû Sufyân, leader of the opposition to Muhammad, announced his "surrender" to God. "Abbas said to him: 'If you go to the messenger, recite this to him: "He has not blamed you today".' And Abû Sufyân did that. The messenger said: 'May God be merciful to you and to him that taught you that.'"[103]

---

98. *E.I.* s.v. "al-Hudaybîya."; Watt, *Companion to the Qur'ân*, 232; Watt, *Muhammad*, 46–52.

99. *ruyâ*.

100. *masjid al-harâm*.

101. *E.Q.* s.v. "Dreams and Sleep," 551.

102. *sakîna*; cf. Hebr. *schechina*.

103. According to al-Zamaksharî in his exegesis of this verse. Cited in Johns, "Joseph in the Qur'ân," 42.

VI

The Desert and the City

What I do claim is that the desert, which some poetry (which is probably early) regards as the local of YHWH's mountain home, functions in early prose as a symbol of freedom, which stands in opposition to the massive and burdensome regime of Egypt, where state and cult are presented as colluding in the perpetuation of slavery and degradation. The mountain of God is a beacon to the slaves of Egypt, a symbol of a new kind of master and a radically different relationship of people to state. Sinai is not the final goal of the Exodus, but lying between Egypt and Canaan, it does represent YHWH's unchallengeable mastery over both.[1]

Introduction

ISLAM IS AN IDEOLOGY that "comes out of the desert and can only produce deserts because it does not grant human beings any freedom"—so Geert Wilders.[2] Rabbi Raphael Evers responded to Wilders' statement by saying that Judaism was the very epitome of a desert religion: it had, after all, originated in the Sinai desert. And Evers is proud of that fact.[3]

---

1. Levenson, *Sinai and Zion*, 23.

2. Geert Wilders is the leader of a Dutch political party with an anti-Islam and anti-immigrant program. He said this at the end of a lawsuit against him in which he, as the defendant, was given the opportunity to speak last.
www.trouw.nl/tr/nl/4324/Nieuws/article/detail/1847306/2011/02/12/Woestijn-Islam-komt-uit-de-steden.dhtml.

3. See the article in *Trouw* mentioned in the preceding footnote.

In the historical evolution of humankind, deserts have been especially instrumental for developments that constitute an essential component in the so-called monotheistic religions: belief in the one God. In Judaism, Islam, and Christianity people speak of the mysticism of the desert. The (translated) title of an article published several decades ago was: "The Desert: The Geographical Framework of Religious Experience."[4] The desert is a place of personal religious experiences, inhabited by wild animals, evil spirits, demons of all kinds, and is the place of temptations and initiations. It is also the place that people are banished to. The desert is a school and can lead to self-knowledge. As a terrain of strife, the desert leads to the discovery of one's own nature or identity.[5]

In this chapter we will look at the question how the desert is related to the city of the human being. Cain, the first-born human child of Adam and Eve, the first human beings created by God, is called the founder of the first city (Gen 4:17). He is cursed and banished from the ground that opened its mouth to receive his brother's blood from his hand! That's why he went to live in the land of Nod, i.e., a "land of wandering or banishment." This land lies east of Eden, a phrase that also inspired the title of John Steinbeck's 1952 novel, *East of Eden*, which takes Genesis 4:11–16 as its starting point.

Hagar and Ishmael in the Desert and at the Wells (Beersheba and Mecca)

Hagar was Abraham's second wife (Gen 16:3). He married her at the instigation of his wife Sarah/Sarai because she herself could not bear children. Sarah gave him her Egyptian slave to conceive children for her that would be seen as her own (Gen 16:1–3). According to Jewish (and Islamic) exegesis, Pharaoh gave Hagar to Sarah when she left Egypt with Abraham. She might even have been Pharaoh's daughter.[6] Abraham's oldest son, Ishmael, was born out of that union (cf. Q 14:37). Sarah later gave birth to a son as well, Isaac.

This story has become very important because Jews, Christians, and Muslims trace their physical and spiritual roots to these two sons. Deserts, such as Sinai and Paran, play a major role in the various stories in this narrative.[7]

---

4. I.e., De Planhol, "Le désert, cadre géographique de l'expérience religieuse." Two of De Planhol's other works are his *Les nations du Prophète* and *Minorités en islam*.

5. Eliade, s.v. "Deserts and Retreats."

6. Genesis Rabbah 45:3; Noegel and Wheeler, *The A to Z of Prophets*, s.v. "Hagar."

7. A city called Paran lay in the vicinity of Mt. Sinai, where Moses was said to

As soon as Hagar found out she was pregnant, she treated Sarah with arrogance. After Sarah complained about her, Abraham gave her leave to do whatever she wanted with Hagar. From that point on, Sarah made Hagar's life so miserable that she fled into the desert. An angel found Hagar by a well and told her to return to Sarah and to her service. He assured her, however, that her descendants would be too numerous to count:

> "You are now with child
>   and you will give birth to a son.
> You shall name him Ishmael,
>   for the Lord has heard of your misery.
> He will be a wild donkey of a man;
>   his hand will be against everyone
>   and everyone's hand against him,
> and he will live in hostility
>   toward all his brothers."
>
> She gave this name to the Lord who spoke to her: "You are the God who sees me," for she said, "I have now seen the One who sees me." That is why the well was called Beer Lahai Roi; it is still there, between Kadesh and Bered. (Gen 16:7–14)

Although Hagar was an Egyptian, she lived with the first patriarch and matriarch of Israel, Abraham and Sarah. But neither Sarah nor Abraham ever called her by her name! They only spoke about and with her in her subordinate position of slave. The narrator and God's messenger did, however, call her by her name: "Hagar, servant of Sarai, where have you come from, and where are you going?" (Gen 16:8). She was not simply, as Sarah's slave, a *stranger* to God but a human being who needed divine protection. Although Sarah treated her cruelly, it was obvious that God was with her in the desert (Gen 16:7). The promise given to her is parallel to that given to Abraham: "I will confirm my covenant between me and you and will greatly increase your numbers" (Gen 17:2).

> Then the angel of the Lord called to Abraham from heaven a second time and said, "I swear by myself, declares the Lord, that because you have done this and have not withheld your son, your only son, I will surely bless you and make your descendants as numerous as the stars in the sky and as the sand on the

---

have fought the Amalekites; Wheeler, *Mecca and Eden*, 117.

seashore. Your descendants will take possession of the cities of their enemies." (Gen 22:15–17)[8]

The well that Hagar discovered is identified as the well of Beersheba, an oasis in southern Palestine that is connected in various ways with the patriarchs Abraham, Isaac, and Jacob. All three lived near the well (Gen 26:32–33). Abraham concluded a treaty at Beersheba with Abimelech, a king of the Canaanite city-state of Gerar. The latter had said to Abraham: "'Show to me and the country where you are living as an alien the same kindness I have shown to you.' Abraham said, 'I swear it.' Then Abraham complained to Abimelech about a well that Abimelech's servants had seized. But Abimelech said, 'I don't know who has done this. You did not tell, and I heard about it only today.' So Abraham brought sheep and cattle and gave them to Abimelech, and the two men made a treaty. Abraham set apart seven ewe lambs from the flock, and Abimelech asked Abraham, 'What is the meaning of these seven ewe lambs you have set apart by themselves?' He replied, 'Accept these seven lambs from my hand as a witness that I dug this well'" (Gen 21:23–31; cf. 26:32–33). This is why this place is called Beersheba, "seven wells."[9] Abraham was given water rights and called the well Sheba—thus the name Beersheba.[10] Without those water rights it was impossible to live in the desert: "Abraham planted a tamarisk tree in Beersheba, and there he called upon the name of the Lord, the Eternal God" (Gen 21:33).

When Sarah once saw Hagar's son Ishmael laughing about Isaac,[11] she demanded that Abraham send her and her son away, arguing that Ishmael should not share in her son's inheritance. Because Ishmael was also his son, Abraham thought the demand was inappropriate. But God showed him that he was not to view Sarah's demand that way: "Listen to whatever Sarah tells you because it is through Isaac that your offspring will be reckoned. I will make the son of the maidservant into a nation also, because he is your offspring" (Gen 21:8–13).

Then Abraham did what Sarah asked. The following day, he gave Hagar some bread and a skin of water, placing them on her shoulders, and sent her and Ishmael away. But Hagar wandered in the desert of Beersheba (Gen 21:14). Again the angel of the Lord followed Hagar into the desert.

---

8. Howard-Brook, *"Come Out, My People!"*, 269–70.

9. Arabic: *bi'r al-sab'a*.

10. The word is also translated as "oath." This translation is based on the fact that Abraham gave seven lambs to Abimelech as proof that he had dug the well, at which point both swore an oath (Gen 21:27–31).

11. A play on his name (Yitzhaq).

"With great irony, Genesis speaks of an Egyptian and her son who found themselves in the wilderness as a result of oppression at the hands of Israel's matriarch [Sarah], only to be rescued by God."[12] Four of the seven times the word "desert/wilderness" (Heb. *midbar*) is used in the book of Genesis involve Hagar and Ishmael (Gen 16:7 and 21:4, 20, 21; cf. Gen 14:6; 36:24; 27:22). This story is, in any case, at odds with the later story of the condemnation of strange women and their descendants by Ezra, the reformer from the period after the exile. And it is also directly contrary to what Nehemiah, the governor of Jerusalem at the time of Ezra, says about this. With Howard-Brook we could say, "Away from the eyes of the dominant people (here, Abraham and Sarah)—but not the eyes of readers—God is with those who would be expelled because of their foreignness, blessing them and their children."[13]

In Genesis 21:15–20 we read what happened to Hagar and Ishmael:

> When the water in the skin was gone, she put the boy under one of the bushes. Then she went off and sat down nearby, about a bowshot away, for she thought, "I cannot watch the boy die." And as she sat there nearby, she began to sob. God heard the boy crying, and the angel of God called to Hagar from heaven and said to her, "What is the matter, Hagar? Do not be afraid; God has heard the boy crying as he lies there. Lift the boy up and take him by the hand, for I will make him into a great nation." Then God opened her eyes and she saw a well of water. So she went and filled the skin with water and gave the boy a drink. And God was with the boy as he grew up.

Muslims also believe that Ishmael was still a child when he was driven into the desert (cf. Gen 21:14–15). But they think the place that is described here is Mecca. When they arrived there, Hagar and Ishmael were on the point of dying of thirst. Hagar then climbed the hill al-Safâ to seek water but found nothing. Then she went to al-Marwa but did not find any water there either. But when she returned to al-Safâ, she was unable to find Ishmael. After searching for him seven times without success, she said, "O Ishmael, you have died where I cannot see you." Then she found him, scratching at the ground with his feet—that's how thirsty he was. Then Gabriel called to her: "Who are you?" She answered, "Hagar, mother of the son of Abraham." Gabriel said: "To whom did he entrust you?" She said: "He entrusted us to God." He answered: "He has entrusted you to someone who is sufficient." The boy scratched the ground with his finger and the well of Zamzam bubbled

12. So Howard-Brook, *"Come Out, My People!"*, 270.
13. Ibid., 270.

up.¹⁴ The fact that Hagar was looking for water thus ended in the miraculous appearance of the well of Zamzam. It is clearly stated here that she ran seven times between al-Safâ and al-Marwa before the water appeared (and that act is re-enacted by the pilgrims performing the *hajj*). The angel told Hagar that she did not have to be afraid because Mecca would be the place where Abraham would build the house of God together with his son Ishmael—a reference to the Ka'ba.

The Islamic version of what happened in Genesis 21:22–34 thus shows great parallels with the tradition concerning Abraham's building of the Ka'ba in Mecca (Q 2:125, 127). Both versions refer to the well that saves the life of Ishmael (cf. Gen 21:17–21). Different sources added by the rabbis—that of the patriarchs and that of Moses and the Israelites—show parallels with how Abraham's well in Beersheba is described in Islamic exegesis. In such exegesis the episode in Beersheba occurs immediately after the departure of Abraham and Egypt from Egypt (Gen 12:10–20). By having this episode immediately follow the story of Pharaoh's inclusion of Sarah in his harem while unaware that she was married to Abraham, the Islamic exegesis emphasizes the connection between Abraham and Moses. Pharaoh's banishment of Abraham and Sarah is analogous to Moses' call to Pharaoh to let the people of God go in peace. In both cases, Pharaoh's "possession" of Israelites (Sarah/the people) resulted in plagues. And both Pharaohs give the departing party (Abraham and Sarah/the people Israel) expensive presents at their departure (Exodus) from Egypt.¹⁵

Ishmael in the Desert: Paran and Mecca

When Ishmael became a man, he lived in the Desert of Paran and his mother chose a wife for him from Egypt (Gen 21:21). The "Desert of Paran" is understood by the Muslim scholar and geographer Yâqût (1179–1229) as one of the names for Mecca in the Torah. He proposed the possibility that the area was south of Beersheba and was thus associated with the Idumeans.¹⁶ This area, the *Hijâz*, was associated with the desert of Beersheba, the location where Ishmael and Hagar were sent by Abraham and Sarah and where she became lost (Gen 21:14). Although the area was under the control of the tribe of Judah during the time of the kings of Israel, the region was called Idumea, a name for Edom that arose during the Hellenistic period. Idumea (the southern part of Palestine) was part of the kingdom of Herod, the Ro-

---

14. Brinner, *The History*, 70–71.
15. Wheeler, *Moses*, 74.
16. Ibid., 157, n. 70.

man province called Arabia. Ethnically, Idumea was Arabic, as was the state of Nabatea, which succeeded it. Nabatea included part of the area around Beersheba. The whole area south of Beersheba, including the area designated in the Bible as Paran, was considered to be Arabia from the second century onward. The association of both Paran (*Farân*, an Arabized Hebrew word) and Beersheba with Arabic peoples was part of the Jewish worldview during the centuries that led to the beginning of Islam in the seventh century.[17] It is said that Abraham met Ishmael in Mecca, where Ishmael was living on the spot of the future shrine, the Ka'ba.[18] "Abraham once went to visit the mother of his son, who lived in the land of Farân. He rode very fast on a magical horse, Buraq. But God knows best." Wahb b Munabbih understands the words *Tal Farân* here as "the outskirts of Mecca."[19]

Abraham and Ishmael built the Ka'ba during a later visit by Abraham (Q 2:125, 127). The descendants of Ishmael, including Muhammad himself, lived in the north of the Arab Peninsula. According to the tradition, Hagar and Ishmael were later buried in Hijr Ismâ'îl, in an enclosed area near the Ka'ba.

Abraham's Prayer for the Dedication of the Ka'ba

The book of Jubilees, a Jewish pseudepigraphical work, is a retelling of the book of Genesis and the first twelve chapters of the book Exodus. The history is divided into periods of 49 years, i.e., seven times seven so-called "year weeks." According to this book, Abraham often prayed for his sons: "My God, may Thy mercy and Thy peace be upon Thy servant, and upon the seed of his sons, that they may be to Thee a chosen nation and an inheritance from amongst all the nations of the earth from henceforth unto all the days of the generations of the earth, unto all the ages" (v. 9).[20]

The Qur'an tells how Abraham prayed as follows: "Make this area [i.e., Mecca] secure and keep me and my sons from serving idols" (Q 14:35). "Our Lord, I have made descendants of me, my son Ishmael and his mother Hagar live in a valley without crops near your sacred House" (Q 14:37). God wanted to make his house (the Ka'ba in Mecca) a place of penitence

---

17. Firestone, *Journeys*, 65, 205, n. 17.

18. Wheeler, *Moses*, 80.

19. According to Ibn Kathîr in his commentary, cited by Firestone, *Journeys*, 205, n. 18.

20. http://www.pseudepigrapha.com/jubilees/22.htm; Speyer, *Die biblischen Erzählungen*, 167; cf. Charles, *The Apocrypha*, 45.

for people and a place of safety or security. "Make the place[21] of Abraham a place of prayer!" (Q 2:125). Abraham and Ishmael were charged with purifying God's Ka'ba for those who carried out the circumambulation (*tawâf*), bowed down, or fell prostrate. And then Abraham said, "Lord, make this a safe place" (Q 2:126). And when Abraham and Ishmael were busy laying the foundations of the House, Abraham prayed, "Our Lord, accept it from us! You hear and know all. And grant, Lord, that we both are people who surrender to you and make the people who descend from us a community of people who surrender to you" (Q 2:127–28).

The holiness of this place is emphasized even more by the fact that it bears the footprints of Abraham that appeared here when he was building the Ka'ba. A tradition states that Abraham climbed this place to call the people to go on the pilgrimage to Mecca.[22] "Truly, the first house that is built for the people is the one in Bakkah,[23] for a blessing and right guidance for people in the whole world. It is the place of Abraham. Whoever enters is safe. People owe God the duty to go on the pilgrimage from the house insofar it is possible for them to do so" (Q 3:96–97; cf. 28:57; 29:67).[24]

The Theophanies on Three Mountains

At the end of the book of Deuteronomy ("second law" [Torah]), the blessing of Moses mentions three sacred mountains—Sinai, Seir, and Paran: "The Lord came from Sinai,/ and dawned over them from Seir;/ he shone forth from Mount Paran" (Deut 33:1–2). This is a poetic description of the revelation on Mount Sinai (Exod 19:18–20).[25]

The southern part of the Sinai Peninsula is called the "the land of the mountain"[26] (Q 52:1; 95:2).[27] *Tûr*, which means "mountain" is explicitly linked to Sinai in the Qur'an. *Sînîn* also refers to Mount Sinai. The term is almost always used in relation to the wanderings of the children of Israel in the wilderness of Sinai. Near the mountain was the wadi[28] where God spoke with Moses (Q 20:12; 79:16; Exod 3). On the north side of the mountain,

---

21. *maqâm*.
22. *E.I.*, s.v., "Makâm Ibrâhîm."
23. Bakkah is said to be Mecca.
24. Speyer, *Die biblischen Erzählungen*, 167–68.
25. *KBS* on Deuteronomy 33:2.
26. *bilâd al-Tûr*.
27. *E.I.*, s.v. "Sînâ."
28. *wâdî Tuwâ*.

now called the mountain of Moses,[29] is the wadi Shuʿayb, or the valley of Jethro, where the Holy Monastery of St. Catherine at Mount Sinai is located. The monks here claim to have a letter from Muhammad granting them protection. There is also a mosque within the walls of the monastery.[30] Mount Sinai is the mountain where God made a covenant with his people (Deut 5:2–3) and from where Israel continued on their journey to the promised land (Deut 1:6–7; Q 23:20; cf. 95:2).

Seir is primarily part of Edom's territory, west of Aqaba. The Edomites were the descendants of Esau, Jacob's brothers (Gen 36:11–15).[31] Just like Sinai, it is a place of divine revelation and of judgment. The prophet Ezekiel prophesied against Seir. Edom profited from the fall of Jerusalem by invading the land themselves:

> Because you harbored an ancient hostility and delivered the Israelites over to the sword at the time of their calamity, the time their punishment reached a climax, the word of the Lord came to me: "Son of man, set your face against Mount Seir; prophesy against it and say: 'This is what the Sovereign Lord says: I am against you, Mount Sier, and I will stretch out my hand against you and make you a desolate waste. I will turn your towns into ruins and you will be desolated. *Then you will know that I am the Lord*'" (Ezek 35:5, 1–4).[32]

"Know that God is the Lord," is one of the most characteristic expressions of the prophet Ezekiel. This knowledge will follow the stated punishment of individuals (Q 13:9; 14:8) or people (Q 6:7; 7:4; 12:16; 22:16) or the fulfillment of God's promises to the people or to foreign nations (Q 16:62; 20:42, 44; 34:27; 36:23; 37:14, 17; 39:7). Such knowledge entails the acceptance of God's sovereignty and holiness.[33]

Mount Paran is a specific mountain or mountainous region in the Desert of Paran, the most prominent desert in the eastern part of the center of the Sinai Peninsula. When Paran, Seir, and Sinai are cited together, it most likely concerns three individual mountainous regions in the southern desert that are all connected with theophanies.[34]

---

29. Jabal Mûsâ.
30. *E.I.*, s.v. "Al-Tûr."
31. Amalek is identified as Esau's grandson! (Gen 36:12).
32. *KBS* on Ezekiel 35:5.
33. *KBS* on Ezekiel 610.
34. Lundbom, *Deuteronomium*, 919–20.

According to Islamic traditions, Paran is the farthest desert, the wilderness in which Mecca would later be built. This is supported by the fact that Muhammad is connected with Ishmael by a direct link.

The Lessons of the Cities that Have Been Destroyed

A characteristic trait of the Qur'an is that it often refers to cities and cultures that have gone into decline and have been deserted by humans and animals. They have become "deserted places"[35] –deserts in fact. The decline could have occurred suddenly, as when the Mârib Dam broke. Mârib was the capital city of one of the kingdoms in old southern Arabia, close to the dam that collapsed.

The Bible mentions the kingdom of Sheba (1 Kings 10:1-4; Job 1:15; 6:19; Isa 60:6; Ezek 27:22), which was colonized after four centuries by Abyssinia. Sheba reached its high point in the sixth century B.C., and its last kings converted to Judaism. The reign of the last one, Dhû Nuwâs, whose name Yûsuf is known from inscriptions dating from that time, lasted 38 years. Strong nationalistic and anti-Abyssinian feelings played a role in the persecution of Christians that occurred under Dhû Nuwâs. After his first acts against them, the Abyssinians invaded and Dhû Nuwâs fled into the mountains. He nevertheless managed to regain power and engaged in a more intense persecution of Christians in the city of Najrân and three other places. Simeon of Beth Arasham wrote a letter in Syriac while that persecution was going on, to the abbot of Gabbûla, requesting him to tell the bishop of Alexandria in particular what was happening. He hoped that the bishop would urge the king of Ethiopia to intervene as quickly as possible. He also asked the abbot to take up contact with the rabbis in Tiberias so that they could exercise some influence on Dhû Nuwâs to help the Christians. Simeon took up the pen to shake people awake and to get them to do something for their fellow believers.

The basic theme of the *Book of the Himyarites* from that period, which deals with those persecutions, is that God rewards everyone according to his/her deeds and therefore punishes individuals for their sins. The latter refers to the invasion of the Abyssinians who liberated the Christians, rebuilt the churches, and killed Dhû Nuwâs and his sympathizers.[36] After the Abyssinian occupation, there was a short period of Persian rule prior to Islamic rule. The role of trade, which was the basis for their wealth (cf. 1

---

35. *uman khâiya*.
36. Attema, *Het Oudste Christendom*, 10-11; *E.I.*, s.v. "Dhû Nuwâs."

Kings 10:1), was important for the people. The most important trade route was the incense route, which ran from the southeast coast to the north.[37]

The Qur'an alludes to this history of Christian martyrs in the Qur'an.[38] Muhammad's biographer made this connection in any case. The passage in the Qur'an that has to do with this reads: "Cursed are the people of the trench, of the fire richly fueled, when they sit on the edge of the fire trench and witness what they have done to the believers. And they punished them simply because they believed in God the Almighty, the One Worthy of Praise" (Q 85:4–8). Here Muhammad cites an example from the past to demonstrate how unbelievers were punished for what they did to believers in the past. That is why this is preceded by: "Cursed were those who did this to others," and it is also said that God will intervene (Q 85:12; cf. 44:16), just as He intervened via the "storm wind" that struck Sodom, with the exception of Lot's family (Q 54:36).

The pronoun "they" in the sentence "And they punished them simply because they believed in God, the Mighty One, the One Worthy of Praise" refers to the Abyssinians who were called upon for aid (Q 85:8; cf. 5:59; 7:126). The *Book of the Himyarites* tells the story of how some people were found in a burning church and others were deliberately thrown into a sea of fire. A Greek source reports 427 men and women being killed in one massive burning at the stake. There is also the story of a mother and her child who were both thrown into a pit filled with fire. It is as if Muhammad is saying: "Watch out! This could also happen to you if you do anything to me and my followers. Look at this example." It is striking that Muhammad places Christians from the past and his own followers in one group. He was convinced that Jews and Christians and he himself stood for and proclaimed the same thing.[39]

The dam at Mârib was built for irrigation purposes. When it finally broke in 580, after a long period of neglect and lack of maintenance, an unimaginable and irreparable catastrophe occurred. The event made a deep impression on the Arab people of South Arabia and marked the end of a long period that went back to the time of the legendary queen of Sheba, who had been given the name Balqîs or Bilqîs in the Jewish and Islamic tradition (1 Kings 10:1–13). In the New Testament she is called the "Queen of the South" (Luke 11:31–32). She is also said to have married King Solomon,[40]

---

37. B.W., s.v. "Saba, Sabeeërs."

38. Paret, *Der Koran: Kommentar*, shows that there are also other interpretations; see 505-6 on Q 85:4-7.

39. Attema, *Het Oudste Christendom*, 10-13.

40. Glassé, *The Concise Encyclopaedia*, s.v. "Saba."

and the child that was born of this relationship is supposed to have founded the Ethiopian dynasty that would end with Negus Heile Salassie.

The Qur'an refers to this great catastrophe and also explains it. In the area they lived in, the Sabeans were given a sign[41] that they should have paid attention to. This sign is understood specifically to be the breaking of the dam. That was not all that long ago in Muhammad's time—he would have been about 10 years old when it happened! The word for "sign"[42] also means "verse" and is also used to refer to the verses of the Qur'an. The Qur'an consists of 114 chapters and about 6200 verses. The word âya itself appears about 383 times in the Qur'an. Examples of such a sign in the Bible is the fourth plague Egypt had to suffer. Moses had to go to the Pharaoh early in the morning, when the Pharaoh went to the river at his usual time to bathe.

Moses was to say to him:

> "This is what the Lord says: 'Let my people go, so that they may worship me. If you do not let my people go, I will send swarms of flies on you and your officials, on your people and into your houses. The houses of the Egyptians will be full of flies; even the ground will be covered with them.

'But on that day I will deal differently with the land of Goshen, where my people live; no swarms of flies will be there, so that you will know that I, the Lord, am in this land. I will make a distinction between my people and your people. *This sign will occur tomorrow.*'

> And the Lord did this. Dense swarms of flies poured into Pharaoh's palace and into the houses of his officials; throughout Egypt the land was ruined by the flies." (Exod 8:20–24; cf. Q 7:130–34; 27:12; 43:47–50)[43]

Âya means "sign," "warning," or "threat" as well as "miraculous sign." These are all signs that people should pay attention to. Qur'anic verses proclaim miracles that God gives to show his power, wisdom, and judgment. That can be, for example, miracles of nature, such as the rain that sustains life: "He causes rain to fall from heaven with which he revitalizes the earth that was dead. These are true signs for those who have understanding" (Q 30:24).[44] But these signs are not limited to nature. There are also the special acts done by the prophets or messengers by which God guides his creation. But if

---

41. âya.
42. Jeffery, *The Foreign Vocabulary*, 72–73; cf. Num 2:2.
43. Cf. Deut 4:34; Josh 4:6; Ps 78:43; 1 Sam 10:7.
44. Cf. Q 30:20–27 in its entirety; for further examples, see Q 16:67; 42:32.

these signs go unnoticed or, even worse, are rejected, these signs that are embedded in nature, the acts of the prophets, and revelation itself will entail terrible demonstrations of God's anger for those who fall short or do not succeed in explaining what these signs actually have to say. The Qur'an is full of stories of individuals and communities that have been punished and struck for their neglect or denial of the clear signs that the merciful God grants to his creation.[45]

The sign that the people of Sheba are given and do not pay any attention to was that there were two gardens[46] where they lived: one on the right side of the valley and one on the left. God granted human beings to understand this and asked them to make grateful use of the gifts they received. "It is a prosperous land and your Lord is forgiving." But the Sabeans turned away from obedience to God, whereby God caused an all-destroying flood. The two fertile gardens were replaced by two gardens that only produced bitter fruit. That is how God repaid their ingratitude. God does not visit retribution on anyone but the ungrateful (Q 34:15–17). An unbeliever is someone who is ungrateful.

In his *Antiquities of the Jews*, Flavius Josephus tells the story of Moses' Ethiopian campaign. In the end, the Ethiopians were all driven into Saba', the city where the king of Ethiopia then resided.

> The place was to be besieged with very great difficulty, since it was both encompassed by the Nile quite round, and the other rivers . . . made it a very difficult thing for such as attempted to pass over them; for the city was situated in a retired place, and was inhabited after the manner of an island, being encompassed with a strong wall, and having the rivers to guard them from their enemies, and having great ramparts between the wall and the rivers, insomuch, that when the waters come with the greatest violence, it can never be drowned; which ramparts make it next to impossible for even such as are gotten over the rivers to take the city.[47]

The Parable of the Arrogant Rich Man

A similar parable is told in the Qur'an of *two men and two gardens*: "Tell them the parable of two men. To the one we gave two gardens with vines,

---

45. *E.Q.*, s.v. "Portents."
46. Cf. Q 18:32–44.
47. Josephus, *The Complete Works*, Book II.

surrounded by palm trees. Fields were set up in between. Both gardens bore rich fruit. God made a river to flow between the two gardens." For Arabs living in the interior of Arab countries, nothing can be better than to have a garden with vines and palm trees and running water.[48]

> The owner had a good harvest from his garden. This fortunate individual, however, became greedy and began to brag, saying to his conversation partner, obviously a landless colleague: "I have more wealth and children and servants than you." He went into his garden and did an injustice against himself: "I don't believe that this garden of mine will ever deteriorate. Nor do I believe that the hour of judgment will come soon. And when I am brought before my Lord, I will receive something even better than this as a place of repentance." His companion answered: "Don't you believe in the one who created you out of dust, from a drop of sperm and then formed you as a man? But I confess: 'He is God, my Lord.' And I don't give him a partner alongside him. Why, then, didn't you say when you went into your garden: 'God's will be done. There is no other power than God.' And if you think I've less wealth and fewer children than you,[49] maybe God will give me something better than your garden and send judgment from heaven on yours and you wake up one morning to find it barren. Or maybe its water will flow away underground and you will no longer be able to water it." And, indeed, after the harvest, the rich man's garden was finished. He began to wring his hands in distress for everything he had spent on the garden and the fact that the garden looked so neglected, he said: "I should never have ascribed a partner to God." Now he had no people to help him and could not find anyone else. In this final stage he could do nothing more than pray for the one true God to help him. He rewards people the best, and He is best able to determine the end of things, according to the Qur'an. (Q 18:32–44)[50]

---

48. Paret, *Der Koran: Kommentar*, on Q 18:32 and on Q 17:91.

49. Having male children is one of the most desirable "goods" of this world (Paret, *Der Koran: Kommentar*, on Q 18:34, p. 313). "People are enamoured by what they desire: women, sons, large amounts of gold and silver, horses and cattle, and fields. Those are pleasures of life now. But the ultimate profit of them is with God" (Q 3:14; cf. 18:46; 17:6; 23:55–56; 26:88; 68:14; 74:12–13; 9:69; 57:20; 19:77; "Wealth, sons, gardens, and rivers" (Q 71:12); "Cattle, sons, gardens, wells" (Q 26:132–34; cf. 42:20).

50. *E.Q.*, s.v. "Parable," 10. The parable of the rich fool in Luke 12:13–21 can be seen as a parallel story.

There is a *midrash* that tells a parable of a king who owned a garden full of figs, grapes, and pomegranates. After a long absence, he found only thistles and scrub growing in it. Only a single rose remained, and in this rose he found comfort for his loss.

The motif of two gardens is also found in a Syriac source, which tells how a heartless man loses all his possessions, his gardens and fields as punishment.[51]

Muhammad's opponents refused to believe in him as long as he was unable to produce any well from the earth (or speed up growth in a garden, with dates and grapes, and rivers flowing through it) (Q 17:90–91; cf. 28:8; 2:266; 36:34; 23:19; 16:11; 13:4). Muhammad answered: "Do you think I'm more than just an ordinary, human messenger?" (Q 17:93).

The Unbelieving City

A parable in the Qur'an (Q 36:13–27) tells of the inhabitants of a city that two messengers were sent to. But they were thought to be liars. Then a third messenger was sent, and the citizens responded to him as follows: "You're just people like us, and the Merciful has not revealed anything to us. You're nothing more than liars." The city's inhabitants see a bad omen in the appearance of these messengers: "If you don't stop with your twaddle, we will certainly stone you." That happened to the apostle Paul as well after he preached in Lystra in Asia Minor. Then there was religious unrest when some people from Antioch managed to win over the city's inhabitants. "They stoned Paul and dragged him outside the city, thinking he was dead" (Acts 14:19; cf. 2 Cor 11:25; 2 Tim 3:11).

To return to the Qur'anic parable, then, a man came running from the other side of the city. He cried out, "O citizens, follow these messengers, follow those who don't ask you for any recompense and who are rightly guided. Why should I not serve Him who created me and to Whom we will be brought back in the end? Should I instead serve other gods whose intercession does not help, cannot save me, when the Merciful wishes to harm me? Then I would certainly be wrong. I believe in your Lord. Listen to me!" Apparently, this man was then killed because he was told after his speech: "Enter into paradise." He replied: "O, if only my fellow citizens knew that my Lord had forgiven my sins and included me among those who were honored to be allowed into his presence."[52]

---

51. Speyer, *Die biblischen Erzählungen*, 434 mentions the *Annecdota Syrica* here.
52. Translation following Paret's *Der Koran: Übersetzung*.

There are traditions that connect this parable to the city of Antioch and even give the three messengers names. One of them calls the messengers the disciples of Jesus: Simon, John, and Paul.[53] And the obedient citizen is called Habib. Indeed, it means that he was killed by being stoned.[54]

The city of Mecca, during the first period of Muhammad's activity (610–622) is an example of such an ungrateful and thus unbelieving city: "And God has given a parable of a city that rejoiced in security or safety and peace, whose provisions came from everywhere. When the city proved ungrateful for God's deeds of goodness, he caused it to suffer from hunger and fear as a punishment for what its inhabitants had done. And yet it was a messenger (Muhammad) who came to them from among them. But they saw him as a liar and were therefore punished because they had done wrong" (Q 16:112–13).

The Fate of the Cities

Such dramatic events like the Mârib Dam breaking and the parables cited above raise all kinds of questions. Pre-Islamic Arabic poetry already reflected on the ruins of cities and civilizations:[55] "Where are those who were before us?"[56] Such poetry answers that question by referring to the changes of the seasons and the need to abandon places like campsites when water grew scarce or when they were destroyed by natural disasters. In contrast to that Arabic poetry, however, the Qur'an gives a different explanation for the same question and a specific *historical* cause is given for such disasters. More than once the Qur'an invites its hearers to travel through countries and to become convinced of the tragic end that peoples encountered in the past: "Travel around the earth and see how wicked people end" (Q 27:69; cf. 30:42). "Travel on earth and see what the end is of those who were before them. Most of them were idolaters" (Q 30:42; cf. 3:137). The destruction of the places is thus ascribed to divine retribution for the ingratitude and unbelief of the previous inhabitants. They called it down upon themselves. If pagan poetry called for Stoic-like acceptance, becoming resigned to the overwhelming power of destiny or fate, the Qur'an, in contrast, is exhortative, proclaiming that even the strongest peoples will be destroyed if they ignore the warnings of the messengers sent to them. That message is urgent because the punishment is impending. At the same time, however, the

---

53. *E.Q.*, s.v. "Apostle."
54. *E.Q.*, s.v. "Parable," 10–11.
55. *athâl.*
56. *Ubi sunt qui ante nos fuerunt?*

Qur'an also emphasizes that there is still time to escape this fate by obeying the messengers![57]

The prophet Muhammad was commanded already very early to warn others about this: "Stand up and give warning" (Q 72:2), starting with his own close relatives (Q 26:214). That marks the beginning of his public activity, which is said to have lasted three years from the time he received his first revelation. "To him [Muhammad] We [God] have revealed an Arabic Qur'an to warn the inhabitants of the mother of cities, the metropolis Mecca, and those who live near it" (Q 42:7). And that is a proclamation of the judgment upon them: part of humankind will go to Paradise, and the other to hell. This proclamation is characteristic for the early messengers who had to warn their own communities of the specific fate that awaited them. Thus, the fate of the people 'Ad of the prophet Hud was the *lightning bolt* that struck the people. The same thing obtains for the people of Thamûd to whom Sâlih was sent as a messenger. One can also think here of the *storm wind* or sandstorm that struck the people of Lot (Q 54:34) or the *grievous punishment* (the Flood) that Noah warned his people about (Q 71:1).

Muhammad warned his fellow citizens of the catastrophe, the day of judgment (Q 40:14), and of the flaming fire (Q 92:14). It was said at least one time that that day of punishment was near. The prophet brought together a combination of vision, understanding of the scripture, and political action in himself.[58] Muhammad stood in a long tradition of warners. It was through God's mercy that Muhammad brought a warning to a people no one previously had come to warn (Q 28:46; cf. 32:3). And in the end there will no community[59] that has not been warned.

"Warning" is an essential part of the prophet's task (Q 6:19; cf. 7:2; 42:7; 46:12). But it is also very important to know that this warning cannot be separated from the good news the prophets bring (Q 6:48; cf. 18:56). What the prophets from Abraham up to and including Muhammad have experienced, received, and heard in the desert, they proclaimed in their time. They acted as *warners* who declared that God would come in judgment because God wanted the affairs of the world set right. At the same time, they were also *bringers of good news*. Those two tasks cannot be seen independently of each other. Thus, Muhammad also had to warn *the whole of humankind* and bring good news (Q 34:28).

---

57. *E.Q.*, s.v. "Geography."
58. *E.Q.*, s.v. "Warner."
59. *umma*.

Prophets pointed to the way that people had to travel; they talked about the "straight path" (Q 1:6–7),[60] as prayed in the opening chapter of the Qur'an. The Qur'an here confirms the *Tawra*, the Scriptures of Moses (Q 53:36), just as Jesus came to fulfill the law (Matt. 5:17) and confirmed the Torah (Q 61:6). By the way, as stated earlier, the Qur'an confirms both the *Tawra* and the *Injîl* (Q 3:50; 5:46).

The City

There is a beautiful illustration of the message that was received in the desert and has great relevance for the city. It can be found in the ninetieth chapter of the Qur'an, which was given the title, "The City,"[61] in reference to the city of Mecca. It is a chapter from the Meccan period of Muhammad's life (610–622). This message received in the desert has, in addition to Mecca, all other places where people live in mind, villages or cities, including our countries and cities. Here is an English translation of this chapter from the Qur'an:

The City (*al-Balad*)

I swear by this city.
And you, people, are free in this city.
And (I swear) by the father and his children.
Truly, We (God) have created humankind for drudgery.
Does man truly think that no one has power over him?
He says boastfully: "I have squandered a great deal of wealth (on one thing or another)."
Does he think that no one sees him?
Have We not given him two eyes?
A tongue and two lips?
And have We not shown him two ways?
He should have taken the steep road.
And how can you know what the steep road is?
(The steep road consists in) freeing a slave,
or giving food on the day of famine
to an orphan among your relatives,

---

60. *sîrat al-mustaqîm*.
61. *al-balad*.

to a poor needy person who has nothing to eat.
If he acts that way, then he one of those who believe and inspire one another to be patient and merciful.
They are the people of the right side.
But those who do not believe in Our revelations are people of the left side. An enveloping fire surrounds them.
(Q 90:1–20)

The Qur'an uses different words for "city." *Qarya* (pl. *Qurâ*, dual *al-qaryatan*) is used to refer to two cities, Mecca and Tā'if (Q 43:31).[62] The word is used for a place where people live, "a place where people meet each other." It derives most likely from the root *qr*, in Phoenician *qart*, as found in the name of the city of Carthage.[63] With respect to Hebrew, the place Kiriath Arba comes to mind, the older name for Hebron, or of Kiriath Jearim (Josh 18:15). When the word "city" is used in the singular, it refers to cities like Mecca (Q 47:14), Medina (Q 2:5), Sodom (Q 11:74–83; 21:74; 25:42; 29:28), Nineveh (Q 10:98) or a coastal city (Q 7:163).[64] The terms "mother of cities"[65] and the "metropolis" (Q 6:91; 42:5) refer to Mecca. The latter reference is probably pre-Islamic and points to the leading role that Mecca played in the religious and economic life in the *Hijâz*. Arabic philologists hold that the word also derives from a root that means "gathering people in hospitality."[66] Apart from one exception (Q 12:82), this is used both in the singular and in the plural for a city or cities that has/have been destroyed by God because the inhabitants rejected the messages of the prophet or his predecessors.[67]

The message to "the city" begins with an oath, with God swearing. Such a beginning is characteristic of the earliest revelations the prophet Muhammad received. The message is directed to every inhabitant of that place: "I swear by this place, this city Mecca, in which you may live." The word used in Arabic, *balad*, can mean "land," "region," "territory," or "place" (Q 2:120; 3:196; 7:55–56) and here refers to Mecca (Q 90:1). But at the same time one can also say that not stating the name explicitly means that it applies *pars pro toto* for *all* cities.

62. Ambros, *A Concise Dictionary*, 224.
63. *qart-hadasht*.
64. Speyer, *Die biblischen Erzählungen*, 313–14, 340–41.
65. *umm al-qurâ*.
66. *qarâ*.
67. *E.I.*, s.v. "karya"; cf. Jeffery, 236.

The name means a "place where someone lives."[68] God also swears by "a father and his children." It thus has to do with past, present, and future generations. The expression that humankind is created in stressful circumstances not only brings to mind associations with the "language of Canaan"[69] but also shows how the message is very close in both style and content to the Tanakh (*Tawra*) and the book of Psalms in particular. There are also parallels to the New Testament (*Injîl*). Here are some examples from the Old Testament: "Our days may come to seventy years,/ or eighty, if our strength endures;/ *yet the best of them are but trouble and sorrow,*/ for they quickly pass, and we fly away" (Ps 90:10). "Then the Lord said, 'My Spirit will not contend with humans forever, for they are mortal'" (Gen 6:3; Eccles 12:1–7).

"Does man truly think that no one has power over him?" That is certainly what Jonah (*Yûnus*) thought. He is called the "fishman," and he initially attempted to escape God's commission to bring a message to the city of Nineveh. And the same expressions are used: "When Jonah went away in anger and thought that *We [God] had no power over him*, he was swallowed by a fish, and he called to God in the darkness" (Q 21:87; cf. Jon 1). Jonah is held up by the prophet Muhammad as an example. "Be patient in the expectation of the decision of your Lord and do not be like Jonah the fishman when he was in the belly of the fish and called to God" (Q 68:48).

"Why was there no city that believed after the proclamation of the threatening punishment and that made good use of its faith, apart from the people of Jonah? When they believed, We removed the affliction of harm in this life from them and gave them life to enjoy it. And if You, Lord, will, all on earth will believe" (Q 10:98–99). God sent Jonah to a hundred thousand or even more (Q 37:147; cf. Jon 4:11) who then believed and enjoyed life for a certain time (Q 37:148).

When the topic is the squandering of possessions, then what is at issue is the "ethics" of the time before Muhammad appeared on the scene, when rich Arabs were known for their waste. They were prepared to go to all lengths in giving out wealth and money for the sake of their honor. The pre-Islamic poets describe how the rich could put on a show by squandering their fortunes, solely for the purpose of being seen by others. The Qur'an condemns such forms of boastful, proud extravagance in no uncertain terms: "Give your relatives what they are rightly owed, as well as the poor and traveler (son of the way), but do not be in any way *wasteful*" (Q 17:26; cf. 4:36–42; 7:31; 25:67).[70] In contrast, the Qur'an emphasizes something

---

68. Jeffery, *The Foreign Vocabulary*, 83–83.
69. Cf. above, the chapter on "The Language of Canaan."
70. *E.Q.*, s.v. "Honor"; see Paret, *Der Koran: Kommentar*, on Q 4:36.

completely different: public actions must be controlled by the fair, equal distribution of goods. That is how the ideal city as God intended it comes about. The right way of dealing with wealth is contrasted with the attitude of the squandering and wasteful hero.[71]

Then comes v. 7 in which the question is posed as to whether human beings actually think that no one sees them. Humans can ask God to protect them from the threats of their enemies, to hide them from criminal gangs, from the thugs who sharpen their tongues like knives and point their poisonous words like arrows, shooting at the innocent from concealed positions, by surprise, afraid of no one: "They encourage each other in evil plans,/ they talk about hiding their snares;/ they say, 'Who will see it?'" (Ps 64:1–5). "Does he who fashioned the ear not hear?/ Does he who formed the eye not see?" (Ps 94:9). In Proverbs 20:12, God states: "Ears that hear and eyes that see—/ the Lord has made them both." When it is said in Proverbs that God made both eye and ear, that means that human beings owe to God the fact that they can observe things and that they should therefore make use of that ability.[72]

When Muhammad had to deal with Jews (possibly Jewish rabbis) in Medina who resisted his message, he heard the words, "O you (my) messenger! Those who devote themselves to unbelief do not need to make you sad. They are included among those who say with their mouths, 'We believe,' but do not believe in their heart. They say something with their tongue that is not in their heart" (Q 5:41). The Qur'an condemns these people (Q 3:167; cf. 48:11).[73]

When the topic is the two ways, an echo of Jesus' last major discourse in the gospel of Matthew can be heard (Matt 25:31–46). Matthew's gospel contains five major discourses by Jesus, the first of which is the Sermon on the Mount (Matt 5–7) and the fifth the discourse on the final judgment (Matt 25:31–46). In the Sermon on the Mount, Jesus tells a parable about the broad and narrow gates/roads: "Enter through the narrow gate. For wide is the gate and broad is the road that leads to destruction, and many enter through it. But small is the gate and narrow is the road that leads to life, and only a few find it" (Matt 7:13–14).

In the fifth discourse, the discourse about the last judgment, the sheep are divided from the goats. Those who have acted righteously are placed on the right and those who have done wrong on the left. To those on the right, the "king" in the role of judge says that they are blessed and will inherit the kingdom:

71. Cf. Neuwirth, *De Koran*, 242.
72. *KBS* on Proverbs 20:12.
73. Paret, *Der Koran: Kommentar*, on Q 5:41.

> "For I was hungry and you gave me something to eat, I was thirsty and you gave me something to drink, I was a stranger and you invited me in, I needed clothes and you clothed me, I was sick and you looked after me, I was in prison and you came to visit me."

Then the righteous will answer him, "Lord, when did we see you hungry and feed you, or thirsty and give you something to drink? When did we see you a stranger and invite you in, or needing clothes and clothe you? When did we see you sick or in prison and go to visit you?"

The King will reply, "Truly I tell you, whatever you did for one of the least of these brothers and sisters of mine, you did for me."

Then he will say to those on his left, "Depart from me, you who are cursed, into the eternal fire prepared for the devil and his angels. For I was hungry and you gave me nothing to eat, I was thirsty and you gave me nothing to drink, I was a stranger and you did not invite me in, I needed clothes and you did not clothe me, I was sick and in prison and you did not look after me."

They also will answer, "Lord, when did we see you hungry or thirsty or a stranger or needing clothes or sick or in prison, and did not help you?"

> He will reply, "Truly I tell you, whatever you did not do for one of the least of these, you did not do for me." (Matt 25:35–45)

In the end it appears that those who have done nothing have in fact called their own judgment over themselves: "We have not served You." They do not want to be a "servant" of God (*'ebed YHWH*, *'Abd Allâh*).

One of the accounts of the last judgment in the Qur'an refers to the right and left hands:

> On that day you will be brought before the judge and nothing you have done is hid from Him. When the record of people, with the list of their deeds, is placed in his *right hand* [Q 17:71; 84:7], he says, "Read my record. I have nothing to fear. I knew I would be held accountable." He is then rewarded with a pleasant life in a garden at an elevated location, with fruit hanging low to the ground [so that it can be easily plucked]. [And the inhabitants of the garden are told]: "Eat and drink and enjoy it.[74] You are being given all of this as a reward for what you did before, in days past [of your life on earth]. But those who are given the record [with the list of their deeds] in their *left hand*[75]

---

74. *Hani'n*: an expression still used in Arabic for "good health" after enjoying a meal.
75. In Q 84:10 it says: "Whoever, in contrast, is given a record behind his back. . . ."

say: "Would that my record were not given to me and that I did not know what the judgment over me will be. Would that it be over and done with now that I am dead![76] What has my wealth brought me? I have now lost all my power." (Q 69:18-29)

"Truly, he did not believe [during his life] in the almighty God, and he did not urge people to feed the poor or to give food to the destitute. That is why he has no friend now" (Q 69:33-35).[77]

After the resurrection of the dead on the last day, people will be divided into three categories in accordance with what they have done on earth. The first consists of those on the right[78] and the second of those on the left.[79] The third group includes the "pioneers" who find themselves at the forefront (Q 56:7-10). The same word[80] is used elsewhere for the first pioneers, namely the emigrants from Mecca and the helpers from Medina (Q 9:100).[81]

Each individual is accountable for what he or she does during his or her life on earth, for what his or her record contains, with the exception of those on the right side. They will ask each other in the garden what became of the sinners: "What brought you to the heat (of hell)?" The others (the sinners) will say: "We were not among those who prayed. We did not give the poor anything to eat. We hung around with those who engaged in idle talk and declared the day of judgment to be a lie until what is certain for everyone (death or truth) arrived" (Q 74:38-47).[82]

---

76. Muhammad's unbelieving contemporaries believed that life ended definitively with physical death and that there was no last judgment.

77. Cf. the translation by Paret, *Der Koran: Übersetzung*.

78. Cf. Q 56:27, 90:18; 74:39.

79. Cf. Q 56:41.

80. *sâbiqûn*.

81. Cf. Paret, *Der Koran: Kommentar*, 467.

82. Cf.: "What do you think of those who say the judgment is a lie? They are those who cast off the orphan and do not urge others to give food to the poor (the destitute). Woe to those who perform *salât* but do not pay any attention to the commands, those who want to be seen by people and refuse to help others in their basic needs" (Q 107). "You are not generous to orphans and do not urge each other to give food to the poor. You sooner devour entirely the inheritance (of your wards) and love wealth above everything else" (Q 89:15b-20).

The Macrocosm of the City and the Microcosm of the Human Being

Q 90 tells the story of two cities. The city God wills is contrasted with the city that the unbelievers, the ungrateful, the unjust would like to have, a city like the one Cain founded. What is striking here is the reflection of the urban structure in the concept of the human being: the macrocosm of the city and the microcosm of the human being. The topographical features of the city—the two paths, the two ways, the steep road—are connected with the traits of the human body. The physical structure of the human body is characterized by the organs, of which some are even formed doubly—two lips, two eyes, two ears—to enable the human being to discover the right path for responsible moral behavior. Both urban and physical structures are thus divine signs that are translated into ethical commands. The topographical features of the difficult paths and the steep road that structure the public space of the city should also be read as moral tasks and commands. That is why the individual also has to climb the steep road on behalf on others.

Travelling the road that God indicates can be difficult. The city has many steep byways, and travelling along steep roads is comprised of social achievements. First is the freeing of slaves. The noose tied around the neck of the slave must be literally and figuratively untied. The idea of feeding the poor and the hungry clearly reflects this: "Is not this the kind of fasting I have chosen:/ to loose the chains of injustice/ and untie the cords of the yoke,/ to set the oppressed free/ and break every yoke?/ Is it not to share your food with the hungry/ and to provide the poor wanderer with shelter—/ when you see the naked, to clothe them,/ and not to turn away from your own flesh and blood?" (Isa 58:6–7; cf. Matt 25:31–46).[83] Liberation, feeding, and care for the poor are thus cited as three important actions. The social system of the city rests on the fear of God.[84]

Living Together in the One Community

When social unrest arose in ancient Rome about 500 B.C. through a difference of opinion between patricians and plebians, Consul Menenius Agrippa—so Livy, the famous historian during the time of Caesar Augustus, tells us—was sent to the conflicting parties as a mediator. He tells the following story:

---

83. Neuwirth, *De Koran*, 244.
84. Ibid., 245.

In the days when all the parts of the human body were not as now agreeing together, but each member took its own course and spoke its own speech, the other members, indignant at seeing that everything acquired by their care and labour and ministry went to the stomach, whilst it, undisturbed in the middle of them all, did nothing but enjoy the pleasures provided for it, entered into a conspiracy; the hands were not to bring food to the mouth, the mouth was not to accept it when offered, the teeth were not to masticate it. Whilst, in their resentment, they were anxious to coerce the stomach by starving it, the members themselves wasted away, and the whole body was reduced to the last stage of exhaustion. Then it became evident that the stomach rendered no idle service, and the nourishment it received was no greater than that which it bestowed by returning to all parts of the body this blood by which we live and are strong, equally distributed into the veins, after being matured by the digestion of the food.[85]

This allegory has become a classic story, and the classically educated Paul of Tarsus was probably familiar with it as well, even though it did not have to be Livy's version he knew. The metaphor is also used by Xenophon and Cicero.[86] Paul himself used it for the community in Corinth: despite the diversity of gifts in the community (1 Cor 12:13–30), they were all members of one body. In his letter to the members of the community in Corinth, Paul speaks of how there must be unity among the various groups in this community. He speaks about the body of the Messiah (*Masîh* ["the anointed"]), the expected just king:[87] Paul writes:

> Just as a body, though one, has many parts, but all its many parts form one body. . . .

Now if the foot should say, "Because I am not a hand, I do not belong to the body," it would not for that reason stop being part of the body. And if the ear should say, "Because I am not an eye, I do not belong to the body," it would not for that reason stop being part of the body. If the whole body were an eye, where would the sense of hearing be? If the whole body were an ear, where would the sense of smell be? But in fact God has placed the parts in the body, every one of them, just as he wanted them to be. If they were all one part, where would the body be? As it is, there are many parts, but one body.

---

85. *Ab Urbe condita*, II, 16, 32, 33.
86. Xenophon, *Memorabilia* (2.III.18) and Cicero, *De Officiis* (III.v 22).
87. Cf. Meuzelaar, *Der Leib des Messias*.

The eye cannot say to the hand, "I don't need you!" And the head cannot say to the feet, "I don't need you!" On the contrary, those parts of the body that seem to be weaker are indispensable, and the parts that we think are less honorable we treat with special honor. And the parts that are unpresentable are treated with special modesty, while our presentable parts need no special treatment. But God has put the body together, giving greater honor to the parts that lacked it, so that there should be no division in the body, but that its parts should have equal concern for each other. If one part suffers, every part suffers with it; if one part is honored, every part rejoices with it.

> Now you are the body of [the Messiah], and each one of you is a part of it. And God has placed in the [community] first of all apostles, second prophets, third teachers, then miracles, then gifts of healing, of helping, of guidance, and of different kinds of tongues. Are all apostles? Are all prophets? Are all teachers? Do all work miracles? Do all have gifts of healing? Do all speak in tongues? Do all interpret? Now eagerly desire the greater gifts. And yet I will show you the most excellent way. (1 Cor 12:12–31)

This way is the way of love (1 Cor 13).

VII

Humankind's Journey in the Wilderness

> Liberation theology is a tautology
> *(EDWARD SCHILLEBEECKX)*

> Crucial, at the end of the day, however . . . what the movement ultimately drew its power from was the stark and awe-inspiring relationship between one man and his God, the solitary soul cut adrift amid the barren landscape of the desert, who then called his brethren to piety.[1]

The Beginning of History: Cain and Abel

THE HISTORY OF HUMANKIND begins with a fratricide: Cain (Qâbîl) kills his brother Abel (Hâbil) (Gen 4:8; Q 5:27–31). The farmer kills the shepherd because he does not want to be his brother's "shepherd," his brother's "keeper," even though being a shepherd or keeper is what every human being is called to be.

The Qur'an tells the story of the first human children without mentioning their names: "Tell them truthfully the message of the two sons of Adam when they brought offerings. The offering of the one was accepted, and that of the other not. The latter said, 'I will certainly kill you.' The other said, 'God accepts only that which comes from the righteous. If you stretch out your hand to kill me, I will not stretch out my hand to kill you. I fear God, the Lord of Worlds'" (Q 5:27–28). "But Cain's evil inclination drove him to kill his brother Abel, so he killed him. Then God sent a raven that scratched in the dirt. Cain said, 'Would I were like the raven so that I could bury my

---

1. Sarris, *Empires of Faith*, 267.

brother.' And then he felt remorse. That is why We wrote that whoever kills one person, apart from retribution or for sowing corruption on the earth, it is like he has killed all of humankind" (Q 5:30-32). This last statement especially accords with the Jewish exegesis of this story.[2]

The history of humankind has remained bloody since Cain killed Abel. Matthew 23:35 emphasizes this by pointing to "all the righteous blood that has been shed on earth, from the blood of righteous Abel to the blood of Zechariah son of Berekiah" (cf. 2 Chron 24:20-22), who was killed in the court of the temple. Abel and Zechariah were the first and last "righteous people" whose murders are related in the Old Testament. There is, for that matter, still another later Zechariah († 67/68 A.D.) from the first century of the Christian calendar who was killed by Zealots—the jihadists of that time.[3]

The (proto)evangelium of James, an early Christian work dating from after 150 A.D., describes how Zechariah, the father of John the Baptist (Yahyâ) was killed by King Herod in the court of the temple because he refused to tell the king where his son John was staying. Herod was, namely, afraid that John wanted to be king. Angry, Herod said: "His son will certainly become king over Israel!" Zechariah responded by saying "If you shed my blood, I am a witness of God. God will receive my spirit if you shed innocent blood in the temple of the Lord." Zechariah was indeed murdered at first light.[4]

Nevertheless, God protected Cain against blood vengeance. He was not killed because of his murder of Abel, which he was afraid would happen. He did receive a "sign" that has become known as "the sign of Cain." This was not a kind of "scarlet letter," as found in Nathaniel Hawthorne's 1850 novel of that name, a sign that allows one to recognize the guilty person at a distance. It is, rather, a sign of protection by God (Gen 4:15).

It has not been very different for the descendants of "Cain" and "Abel" throughout history. Cain's descendants went and go the same way as Cain (Jude 11; cf. Gen 4:6). Balaam (Bal'am) and Korah (Qârûn) (Num 16:22-24; Q 28:76-80) are mentioned in this context as well. Balaam was a seer from Mesopotamia who was hired by Balak, the king of Moab, to curse the children of Israel. Korah unleashed a rebellion against Moses' leadership during the Israelites' wanderings in the desert. "Woe to them! They have taken the way of Cain; they have rushed for profit into Balaam's error; they have been destroyed in Korah's rebellion" (Jude 11). The way of Cain is thus the way in which one does not want to be his brother's keeper, his brother's shepherd

---

2. Mishnâ Sanhedrîn IV, 5. Cf. Paret, *Der Koran: Kommentar*, 120. E.I., s.v. "Hâbîl wa Kâbîl."

3. *KBS* on Matthew 23:35.

4. Protoevangelium of James 23:1-3; Oussoren and Dekker, *Buiten de vesting*, 389.

(Gen 4:8). People who go that way wander off the straight path and choose the road followed by Balaam "who loved the ways of wickedness" (2 Pet 2:15–16).

The descendants of Cain were the rulers of the orphaned children of Abel. Cain founded the first city, which he named not after himself but after his oldest son Enoch (Gen 4:17). That was not what Romulus did. Like Cain, he killed his brother Remus, but he did give his own name to the city he founded, Rome, which was the most important city in European history for centuries.

Cainites or Kenites?

The name of the tribe of Kenites, to which Jethro (Shu'ayb), Moses's father-in-law belonged (Judg 1:16), was derived from the name Cain. Cain is thus the father of the Kenites, a nomadic people who were part of the Midianites (Num 10:29; cf. 1 Sam 15:4–6). In the oracle that Balaam proclaims over the Kenites he calls them "Cain" (Num 24:22). The Kenites were a subgroup of the Midianites and indirectly related to Israel (Num 10:29; Judg 4:11).[5]

The Kenites were one of the nomadic shepherd peoples inhabiting the southern part of the mountainous area west of the Jordan river and the Negev desert. They did not separate from the Amalekites, who did not have any fixed territory, until the beginning of the monarchy in Israel. King Saul (Tâlût) had said to the Kenites: "Go away, leave the Amalekites so that I do not destroy you along with them; for you showed kindness to all the Israelites when they came up out of Egypt." Then the Kenites separated from the Amalekites (1 Sam 15:6), assimilated into the tribe of Judah and turned to farming. But there were groups of Kenites who continued their nomadic existence as tent-dwellers outside cultivated areas (Judg 4:17; 5:24). The explanation for the name Cain as "smith"[6] leads to the idea that Kenites worked as nomadic or itinerant smiths (Gen 4:22). They were worshippers of the Lord (YHWH) (Judg 4:11) and were thought to be related to Moses.[7] Just as Cain was protected by God, so Moses, who was also a murderer (Exod 2:12), was protected by the Lord as well. After he killed a man, Moses fled into the desert to Midian, where he lived among the Kenites.

The worship of God as the Lord (YHWH) can indeed be traced back to the Kenites and the Midianites. Both peoples were nomadic tribes living in the Sinai Peninsula, in the Negev, and in the Arab Peninsula south of the

---

5. Olson, *Numbers*, 150.
6. An Arabic term.
7. *B.W.*, s.v. "Kenieten"; *Bijbelse Encyclopaedie*, s.v. "Kenieten."

Gulf of Aqaba. Jethro was a priest in Midian (Madyan) (Exod 3:1; 18:1). He is sometimes called a Midianite (Num 10:29) and sometimes a Kenite (Judg 1:16). Jethro is said to have introduced Moses to belief in YHWH. After the children of Israel had been liberated from the Egypt, Jethro rejoiced with Moses about that liberation. He confessed at that time that God (YHWH) was greater than all gods and brought a burnt offering and other sacrifices to him. Aaron and all the elders of Israel came and shared a communal meal with Moses' father-in-law (Exod 18:10–12). "In the person of Jethro, the first of the 'heathen,' namely, this 'heathen' who seeks the living God, enters the religious community with the people of God."[8] He prepares a great feast for God, and the participation of Aaron and the elders as representatives of this people in the meal for God, eating and drinking, is to be seen as a prelude to the covenant meal on Mount Sinai (Exod 24:9–11).[9]

On their journey to the Promised Land, the Kenites joined the children of Israel and settled there (Judg 1:16; 1 Sam 15:6), maintaining good relations with Israel (1 Sam 15:6).[10] Moses lived with the Midianites (people of Madyan) (Q 20:40; 28:22–29), to whom Shu'ayb had been sent as a prophet (Q 7:85–93; 11:84–95; 29:36–37),[11] but they declared their prophet to be a liar (Q 22:44; 29:37). The "people of the scrubland" (Q 26:176–91) were indeed identified as Midianites.[12] The people of Midian were, namely, accused of highway robbery.

The stories about Shu'ayb are grouped in the Qur'an with those of four other prophets: Noah, Hûd, Sâlîh, and Lot. Shu'ayb's prophethood is reported at the end of this list, just before Job, Dhu al-Kifl,[13] and Jonah. He transferred the mantle of prophethood to Moses, symbolized by his staff, which had been passed on to him from Adam via all previous prophets.

It is said that the people of Midian were descended from a son of Abraham and Ketura (Gen 25:4; 1 Chron 1:32). Wahb ibn Munabbih, one of Muhammad's Jewish sources, said that Shu'ayb came from the people of Babylon and believed in Abraham. Descriptions of the land of Midian

---

8. So C.F. Keil, cited in Fischer and Markl, *Das Buch Exodus*, 202.

9. Fischer and Markl, *Das Buch Exodus*, 202.

10. Lundbom, *Deuteronomium*, 920. Others are mentioned later, such as Heber the Kenite (Judg 4:11–22), Jehonadab, the son of Recab (2 Kings 10:15–24), and the Recabites who lived during the time of the prophet Jeremiah (Jer 35), all descendants of nomadic peoples.

11. Wansbrough, *Quranic Studies*, 21–25, analyzes three versions of the story in the Qur'an; cf. *E.I.*, s.v. "Shu'ayb."

12. Noegel and Wheeler, *The A to Z of Prophets*, s.v. "Shu'ayb," 303.

13. He is seen by Muslim exegetes as the son of Job and, like Job himself, as a prophet.

report that it was located on the edge of Syria, on the border of the Hijâz, close to the lake of the people of Lot (the Dead Sea).[14] All the prophets, according to Muslim exegetes, are descended from Abraham: the prophet Muhammad via Ishmael, the Israelite prophets via Isaac and the prophet Shuʿayb via Midian, the son of Abraham and his wife/concubine.[15]

According to some exegetes, the name of God, YHWH, which He revealed to Moses (Exod 3:12), is connected with the story of Cain. "A legend of all YHWH experiences in which the Kenites living in Midian trace back their faith, their cult, and their destiny to Cain."[16] "Outlawed nomads managed, just like Cain, to be protected by YHWH. . . . Moses owed his deepest religious experience . . . to their faith, cult, and law: YHWH is a God who reigns in revenge because only God has the right to decide over life and death, good and evil."[17]

Moses in the Desert

> One day, after Moses had grown up [according to Acts 7:23 he was forty years old], he went out to where his own people were and watched them at their hard labor. He saw an Egyptian beating a Hebrew, one of his own people. Looking this way and that and seeing no one, he killed the Egyptian and hid him in the sand. The next day he went out and saw two Hebrews fighting. He asked the one in the wrong, "Why are you hitting your fellow Hebrew?"

> The man said, "Who made you ruler and judge over us? Are you thinking of killing me as you killed the Egyptian?" Then Moses was afraid and thought, "What I did must have become known."

> When Pharaoh heard of this, he tried to kill Moses, but Moses fled from Pharaoh and went to live in Midian [an area south of Edom and east of the Gulf of Eilat], where he sat down by a well. (Exod 2:11–15)

Moses ended up at the house of a priest of Midian and was invited to eat there. In the end, he decided to live there, marrying the daughter of this priest, Zipporah, who gave birth to Gershom (Exod 18:2–3). This name is

---

14. Noegel and Wheeler, *The A to Z of Prophets*, s.v. "Shuʿayb."
15. Noegel and Wheeler, *The A to Z of Prophets*, s.v. "Keturah."
16. Heyde, *Kain*, 33.
17. Houtepen, *Geloven in gerechtigheid*, 140, to whom I also owe the reference to Heyde above.

connected with the word *ger*, which means "stranger," someone who stays for a longer period of time in another country and enjoys certain rights there.[18] Moses' sister Miriam and his brother Aaron would later object to the fact that he assumed leadership during the journey in the desert because he had married a foreign woman, a Cushite, throwing the question back at him: "Hasn't [the Lord] also spoken through us?" (Num 12:1–2).

The Journey in the Desert as a Life Journey

The book Numbers—"In the Desert" is its title in Hebrew—tells the story of the forty-year journey of the children of Israel through the desert (cf. also Deut 2:7; 8:2, 4; 29:4–5; Josh 5:6; Neh 9:21; Ps 95:10). That story is symbolic of the life journey or pilgrimage of humankind during a human life. The theme of the "pilgrimage" was taken up countless times in the Bible throughout the centuries. The journey in the desert begins with the Exodus from Egypt (Exod 15:22), the Desert of Sin (Exod 16:1; 17:1; Num 33:11–12), and Paran.

Crises in the relationship between God and his people erupted during the journey in the wilderness: difficulties that made the road hard. The low point was the worship of the golden calf (Exod 32; cf. Q 7:150–51; 20:92–94). At these moments Moses and/or Aaron are faced again and again with the question: How can Israel be given rest, despite the resistance and the grumbling and murmuring of the people (Exod 15:24; 16:2; 17:3; Num 14:2, 36; 16:41)? The final and greatest danger the people encounter appears just before the conquest of the land: Balaam, at the instigation of King Balak, the king of Moab, attempts to drive the people away (Num 22–24), and the people engage in sexual immorality with Moabite women during the "idolatrous worship of Baal of Peor" (Num 25).[19]

In the New Testament Paul provides a typological exegesis in one of his letters of this journey through the wilderness. Everything that happened on this journey is a lesson to us to not, as "our fathers" did, set our hearts on evil things (1 Cor 10:6, 11).[20] It thus has to do with the journey the children of Israel make after they are liberated from the oppressive, imperialistic power of Pharaoh of Egypt. It has to do with their journey to the promised city, the land, the city, or the earth where justice will reign. This journey is characterized as follows: "First, that wherever you live, it is probably Egypt; second,

---

18. *KBS* on Exodus 2:21.
19. Cf. Hos 2:13; *B.W.*, s.v. "woestijnreis."
20. The message that the prophet Muhammad (and the other prophets) brings is often presented in a twofold way as "warning" (*nadîr*) and "good news" (*bashîr*).

that there is a better place, a world more attractive, a promised land and third, that the way to the land is through the wilderness. There is no way to get from here to there by joining together and marching."[21]

The Three Masks of Cain

In the time that preceded the Iranian Revolution of 1979, there was a well-known Iranian thinker, the sociologist 'Ali Sharî'atî (1933–1977), who is seen as the spiritual father of the Persian "spring." He studied in Meshed and was given a scholarship to pursue a doctorate at the Sorbonne in Paris, returning to Iran in 1964, where he was arrested on suspicion of political activities against the Shah. He died shortly before the Iranian Revolution broke out. Many held the Iranian secret service, the Savak, to blame for his premature death in England.[22] The Iranian Revolution claimed 'Ali Sharî'atî for itself. This was completely out of place because Sharî'atî stood for something completely different than the founding of the Iranian republic, which was the purpose of the revolution under the leadership of Ayatollah Khomeini. Sharî'atî can be characterized as an Islamic "liberation theologian."[23]

In a speech that was published as a book, he discussed the pilgrim journey of humankind and referred in that context to the pilgrimage (*hajj*) to Mecca that every Muslim should perform at least once (if possible) in his or her life. In this speech he examines the story of Cain and Abel and argues that, in the history of humankind, the descendants of Cain appear to the descendants of Abel in three different masks: the mask of Pharaoh (*fir'awn*), that of Korah (Qârûn), and that of Balaam (Bal'am).

The Mask of Pharaoh: The Arrogance of Power

The title of the ancient ruler of Egypt, Pharaoh, literally means "the large house," part of the palace complex[24] in Memphis. That became the term for the king of Egypt himself, just as "porte" 3,000 years later would refer to the

---

21. Michael Walzer, cited by Brueggemann (2010), 169, note 17.

22. He was buried in Damascus by the (Lebanese Shiite) imam Musa Sadr. Sadr himself "disappeared" during a trip to Rome via Libya in August 1978. Khadafi, the Libyan president, is said to be responsible for his "disappearance." It is typically Shi'i to speak not of the death of an imam but of his "disappearance."

23. Examples in Sunni Islam are Mahmud Taha (Sudan), Abdallahi al-Na'im (Sudan), and Farid Esack (South Africa).

24. Kemp, *The City of Ekhnaten and Nefertiti*, chapter 4: "The Apartments of Pharaoh."

Ottoman sultan. The term appears 74 times in the Qur'an, but—strikingly enough—not in sura Yûsuf, where the ruler of Egypt is called "king" (Q 12:43, 50, 54). "Pharaoh" occurs repeatedly with references to Moses and Aaron.[25] The Arabic form of his title, *fir'awn* (cf. Q 2:46–49), was explained as a permanent title for the Amalekite kings, analogous to Kisrâ, the title of the sovereign of Persia, and Qaysar (Caesar) for the emperors of Byzantium/Rome (Rûm).[26] According to the Qur'an, a pharaoh was a cruel, arrogant ruler who transgressed all boundaries (Q 20:24, 43). Analogous to the title Pharaoh (*fir 'awn*) as a typical term for the proud tyrant, there is a verb (*tafar'ana*) which means "to act like a hardened tyrant." The Pharaoh who is mentioned in the Qur'an and the Bible is actually always the Pharaoh of the Exodus and the story of the oppression of the children of Israel (*Banû Isra'îl*), as recorded in the book Exodus (Exod 1–14). The Hebrews were strangers who had been settled in Egypt for a long time but were assured by a divine promise that they would return to the country of their forefathers.

This history of the children of Israel in Egypt is briefly recalled by the Qur'an (Q 2:49–50; 14:6; 17:101–3) and sometimes further elaborated to a certain extent: "This is the story [*hadith*] of Moses" (Q 20:9–98), "the true story of Moses and Pharaoh" (Q 28:2–50), "This is the history of one unbelieving city among many others," is the beginning of the story (Q 7:101–2) that continues with "Moses and the children of Israel" (Q 7:103–55) and "Moses and Aaron" (Q 10:75–92).

In the Qur'an Pharaoh is accompanied by two advisers who are missing from the book of Exodus in the Bible: Korah and Haman (Q 29:39; 40:24). In the *midrash*, however, Korah, who led a revolt against Moses after the Exodus (Num 16) was, however, called "a rich partisan of Pharaoh." Haman does not make an appearance until much later and in a different place as a minister of the Persian king Ahasueros (Xerxes), and advocated the liquidation of the Jews in the kingdom (see the book of Esther in the Bible). Haman was commissioned by Pharaoh to build a tower (of Babel) so that Pharaoh could see and inspect God (Q 28:38; 40:36).[27] The latter refers to Pharaoh's divine aspirations: "I know no other God than myself" (Q 28:38), "I am your Lord, the highest of all" (Q 79:24). These aspirations can also be found in the *haggada*.

It is often suggested that the Qur'an mixes different Bible stories with each other: the story of the tower of Babel (Gen 11) and the figure Haman, who only appears much later in history, in the story of Esther in Persia,

---

25. *E.Q.*, s.v. "Pharaoh."
26. Chapter 30 of the Qur'an bears the title Rûm.
27. *Dictionnaire*, s.v. "Pharaoh," 670.

plays an important role.[28] But the Qur'an makes theological connections that indicate the intrinsic bond that exists between all proud rulers, whether it be those of Babel, Persia, or Egypt.

There are striking parallels everywhere in this story with the story of the mission of the prophet Muhammad: for example, the rejection of the message by the unbelievers will be punished in the end whereas the believer will be saved.[29] The lesson for Muhammad's contemporaries is that they—just like the people of Pharaoh and the people of ʿĀd or Thamûd, Noah, Lot, Midian, and others—will be destroyed by God if they continue to refuse to believe in the prophet.[30]

A believer in Pharaoh's household who had kept his faith hidden for the sake of his own countrymen once asked Pharaoh: "Would you really kill a man because he says, 'My Lord is God,' while he has come to you with clear proof from your Lord? If he is a liar, then that will be to his own disadvantage. But if he speaks the truth, then you will experience something of what he is threatening? God surely does not lead someone who is a liar and knows no bounds" (Q 40:28). Haman is the only advisor of the Pharaoh who is mentioned by name (Q 28:8, 38). Moses comes to Pharaoh, Korah, and Haman with divine signs and proofs, but all three became arrogant (Q 29:39; 40:23, 24).[31]

"The Pharaoh of every prophet is the king of his own time." This definition in *Lisân al ʿArab* (a dictionary from the 13th century) shows that the figure of Pharaoh in more than 25 chapters of the Qur'an "does not concern a historical person but a role that is played in a permanent theological drama."[32]

Human Arrogance

When a person thinks he is great and superior to others, he is in effect claiming one of the attributes of God whereas He alone is great. That is why arrogance is a serious sin. To be arrogant and act without shame means, therefore, claiming to be like God (Q 59:23).[33]

Satan was the first to be arrogant, to act contrary to God's command, and refused to bow before Adam. That is why he was declared an unbeliever (Q 7:13; 38:74–75). Pharaoh became the human mirror image of Satan

28. *E.I.*, s.v. "Firʿawn."
29. *E.I.*, s.v. "Firʿawn."
30. *E.Q.*, s.v. "Pharaoh."
31. Ibid.
32. *Dictionnaire*, s.v. "Pharaoh."
33. God is the "truly great one" (*mutakabbir*).

when he rejected the message God had revealed to Moses (Q 28:39) and deceived his people by being arrogant toward them (Q 10:75; 23:46; 29:39). For that matter, Pharaoh and his people claimed the opposite—that Moses and Aaron wanted to lead the people of Pharaoh away from their traditions so that they themselves could obtain supremacy in Egypt (Q 10:78). In contrast, Moses prayed that God would protect him and his people from all arrogant people (Q 40:27).

There are many communities, groups, and individuals who are depicted as arrogantly rejecting the word of God. Every time God called them to follow the straight path, so that he can forgive them, the people of Noah stuck their fingers in their ears (Q 71:7) and the people of ʿĀd responded with: "Who is stronger than us?" (Q 41:15). The people of Thamûd said, "We don't believe in what you believe in" (Q 7:75-76), and the people of Midian said: "We will drive you, O Shuʿayb and those who believe like you do, out of our city unless you return to our faith" (Q 7:88). Over against the arrogant are the humble people who are unconditionally obedient to God and are willing to accept his revelation. The Christians[34] are cited as those who are closest to the believing "Muslims" with regard to love. This is explained by stating that the priests and monks among them are not arrogant (Q 5:82). Namely, they do not consider it beneath their dignity to serve God. This obtains only for the followers of Jesus as well as for the angels and the whole creation: the trees "bowing down," the animals (Q 16:48[35]-49; 21:19) and those who constantly believe in God's "signs" without becoming arrogant (Q 32:15).

In opposition to the arrogant disobedience of Satan and Pharaoh, Jesus is described as a servant of God who is neither arrogant nor rebellious (Q 19:30-32). Jesus never considered it beneath him nor felt himself too inferior to be a servant of God (Q 4:172; cf. Phil 2:6-7).

The ideal behavior that can be expected from "Muslims" is to be called worthy servants of the Most Merciful so that they live among others on earth in humility (Q 25:63; cf. 17:37; 31:18; 40:75; 57:23). The advice of Lukmân, known for his wisdom (Q 31:12, 13, 16-19) is that people should not walk around haughtily on the earth for God does not love conceited braggarts and boasters (Q 31:18).[36]

---

34. nasâra.
35. Cf. Kramers' note in *De taal van den Koran* on Q 16:48.
36. Nasr Abu Zayd in: *E.Q.*, s.v. "Arrogance."

The Mask of Korah (Qârûn): "Money Rules the World"

One of the contrasts between a true prophet and a "seer" or a "soothsayer"[37] is that a prophet does not ask for any recompense (Q 10:72; 12:104; 25:57; 26:109, 27, 145, 164, 180; 34:47; 38:86; 6:90; 11:1; 42:23; 52:40; 68:46; 11:29). The latter is seen as proof of a true priestly office. It is said about the soothsayers before the advent of Islam that they were paid for the information they provided. They judged in exchange for gifts.

The prophet Micah thus reproached the priests of Jerusalem for asking for payment for teaching and the prophets for telling fortunes for money (Mic 3:11). "Your rulers are rebels, companions of thieves; they all love bribes and chase after gifts. They do not defend the cause of the fatherless; the widow's case does not come before them" (Isa 1:23).[38]

The true prophets answer that they do not receive any payment in return for the prophecies they tell so that they can make money in the name of God. To the contrary, it was God who gave them their reward and provided for their needs. That is said by, among others, Noah (Q 10:72; 26:109; 11:29), Hûd (Q 26:127; 11:51), Sâlih (Q 26:145), Shuʿayb (Q 26:180), Lot (Q 26:164), and Muhammad (Q 12:104; 25:57; 34:47; 20:132; 51:57; 23:72; 38:86; 6:90; 42:23; 52:40; 68:46)—indeed, by messengers (Q 36:21). The criteria for judging the genuineness of prophets was that they lived modestly and did not desire anything for themselves.[39]

During the journey of the children of Israel through the wilderness, Korah, Moses' nephew, rebelled against the leadership of Moses and Aaron. Together with Dathan and Abiram, he went to them and said, "You have gone too far! The whole community is holy, every one of them, and the Lord is with them. Why then do you set yourselves above the Lord's assembly?" (Num 16:3). From the beginning he wanted to sabotage the leadership of Moses during the journey through the wilderness (Num 16:32). According to a Jewish legend, Korah was the treasurer, the minister of finance, for Pharaoh. Apparently, the total amount of the funds he stole was so great that three hundred mules were needed just to carry the keys of the treasury rooms.[40]

In the Qur'an Korah is called Qârûn (Q 28:76–82; 29:38; 40:24). While the biblical story emphasizes the rebellion of Korah, Dathan, and Abiram against the prophetic and priestly authority of Moses and Aaron, the Qur'an

---

37. kâhin.

38. Radscheit, *Die koranische Herausforderung*, 41.

39. Radscheit, *Die koranische Herausforderung*, 73, 74; Eric R. Dodds, cited by Radscheit, *Die koranische Herausforderung*.

40. Ginzberg, *Legends of the Jews*, 718.

stresses his wealth.[41] He is a kind of Croesus figure, known from the expression, "as rich as Croesus." The enormous wealth of this Lydian king from the sixth century B.C. is the stuff of legend. When Solon—an Athenian merchant, poet, and statesman—met him (which was, by the way, historically impossible), he was not impressed with his fortune. Solon declared: "Call [a person who has led a happy, prosperous, peaceful life] however, until he die, not happy but fortunate."[42]

Qârûn is mentioned in one breath with Haman, Pharaoh's treasurer. Both are examples of extraordinary pride and arrogance. All three act arrogantly toward Moses and stigmatize him as a magician and deceiver. Qârûn acts in a presumptuous way because of the immense wealth given to him on account of the knowledge he possesses. He gives a grandiose display of his wealth and, together with his palace and all his possessions, is swallowed up by the earth. He is thus an example for those who prefer the fleeting wealth of this world above the reward God gives in the hereafter and for those who believe and do good works.[43]

The Islamic "stories of the prophets,"[44] borrowed partly from rabbinic literature, cite even more particularities. God says to Moses: "O Moses, I command you to decorate the ark of the Torah with gold. Teach Korah the art of alchemy." So Moses gave him all the gold he needed to cover the ark in which the Torah was preserved. Moses' sister was Korah's wife, and she had learned the art of alchemy. Korah learned it from her and put it into practice. When his wealth increased, he built a palace with walls of gold and silver. It was his custom to go riding every Sabbath dressed in clothes that were more beautiful than those anybody had ever worn before.

Korah attempted to discredit Moses and said: "Moses, how exactly are you better than me? I read the Torah as well as you do, and, just like you, I'm a descendant of Levi." "You're right," Moses answered, "except that I am God's messenger." He then attempted to compromise Moses by sending a prostitute to him to whom he said: "If you do something for me, I will make you rich: when the children of Israel are assembled, I will be there. Mingle in the crowd and call out: 'Moses commanded me to come and then made me a dishonorable proposition, but I don't want to subject myself to him.'"

The following day, however, God made her remorseful, so she went to Korah's gate and said: "O children of Israel, Korah called me yesterday

---

41. *Dictionnaire*, s.v. "Qârûn."

42. https://nl.wikipedia.org/wiki/Croesus; https://legacy.fordham.edu/Halsall/ancient/herodotus-creususandsolon.asp.

43. *E.I.*, s.v. "Kârûn."

44. *Qisâs al-anbiyâ*.

and said this." When Moses heard about it, he was furious and said: "May the Lord make me victorious over Korah." He went to Korah and declared: "Enemy of God, you seduced the woman to compromise me, but God prevented it." He then called upon the earth to seize him, and Korah's palace sunk a yard into the earth and swallowed him up to his knees. "Moses," Korah screamed, "Don't do this!" "O earth," Moses said, "take him." The earth swallowed him up to his waist, and he was unable to speak. If he had sought God's help, God would have saved him. Instead, his palace and everything in it, including him, sank into the earth. This was just as God had said: "And We made the earth split and swallow his palace" (Q 28:81).[45]

The exegetical traditions do say that he wanted to be rid of Moses' leadership when the obligation to give alms was instituted.[46] This obligation, the *zakât* (which would become one of the five pillars of Islam), was a matter of conflict between Muhammad and the Jews in Medina.

The story of Qârûn functions as a warning.[47] Here Korah represents the mask of wealth and money.

The Mask of Balaam: The Spin Doctor

The story of Balaam can be found in the biblical book Numbers (Hebr.: "In the Desert") (Num 22–25). To understand this story properly, one needs—as is the case, by the way, with all other stories in the Qur'an and the Bible—to see that it is not a historical report. It is not as if one can, on the basis of these stories, precisely trace the Israelites' journey through the desert: an enemy here, hunger and thirst there, a mountain here, an oasis there. The point is not what happened thousands of years ago in that Sinai Peninsula. The stories are told and written down so that we can hear and see what happens all the time—today as well. The readers of this story or, one could say, the "spectators" before whom this story was acted out, receive more insight by this. It is revealed to them how they are to understand their own time and how they are to find a way through the desert of their own time and world. Balak is the king of the Moabites, a hostile people, even though the Moabites were descended from Lot, Abraham's brother or nephew. This king sent men to a soothsayer called Balaam, who lived in Peor on the Euphrates in northern Mesopotamia. He wanted him to curse the people of Israel because he felt threatened by these tribes traveling past. The name

---

45. Al-Kisâ'î, *Tales of the Prophets*, 245–46.
46. *E.Q.*, s.v. "Korah."
47. *Dictionnaire*, s.v. "Qârûn."

"Balak" means "destroyer," a very appropriate name for a king who wanted to have Israel cursed.[48]

For Judaism, Balaam is the example of someone who wanted to bring ruin upon Israel, a notion that is also taken over in the New Testament. He was said to have been commanded by a heathen ruler to turn the people into idolaters, something that his imitators still do (2 Pet 2:15; Jude 11; Rev 2:14).[49]

The elders of Moab and the elders of Midian visit Balaam and have the payment with them for his services. They come to him and give him King Balak's message. Balaam invites them to spend the night and says that he will let them know then what the Lord will tell him (Num 22:8).[50] And God does come to Balaam and speaks to him (Num 22:9–14). The procedure is repeated: the men sent by the king have to spend the night again to hear what God has to say (Num 22:19). Balaam is commanded by God to accompany the men sent but to say only the words that God inspires him to say (Num 22:20).

Political Satire

Part of the three long chapters devoted to this story can be called a biting political satire.

> That night God came to Balaam and said, "Since these men have come to summon you, go with them, but do only what I tell you."

Balaam got up in the morning, saddled his donkey and went with the Moabite officials. But God was very angry when he went, and the angel of the Lord stood in the road to oppose him. Balaam was riding on his donkey, and his two servants were with him. When the donkey saw the angel of the Lord standing in the road with a drawn sword in his hand, it turned off the road into a field. Balaam beat it to get it back on the road. Then the angel of the Lord stood in a narrow path through the vineyards, with walls on both sides. When the donkey saw the angel of the Lord, it pressed close to the wall, crushing Balaam's foot against it. So he beat the donkey again. Then the angel of the Lord moved on ahead and stood in a narrow place where there was no room to turn, either to the right or to the left. When the donkey saw

---

48. *B.W.*, s.v. "Balak."
49. *B.W.*, s.v. "Bileam"; "Peor."
50. *B.W.*, s.v. "Bileam."

the angel of the Lord, it lay down under Balaam, and he was angry and beat it with his staff.

Then the Lord opened the donkey's mouth, and it said to Balaam, "What have I done to you to make you beat me these three times?" Balaam answered the donkey, "You have made a fool of me! If only I had a sword in my hand, I would kill you right now." The donkey said to Balaam, "Am I not your own donkey, which you have always ridden, to this day? Have I been in the habit of doing this to you?" "No," he said.

Then the Lord opened Balaam's eyes, and he saw the angel of the Lord standing in the road with his sword drawn. So he bowed low and fell facedown. The angel of the Lord asked him, "Why have you beaten your donkey these three times? I have come here to oppose you because your path is a reckless one before me. The donkey saw me and turned away from me these three times. If it had not turned away, I would certainly have killed you by now, but I would have spared it."

Balaam said to the angel of the Lord, "I have sinned. I did not realize you were standing in the road to oppose me. Now if you are displeased, I will go back."

> The angel of the Lord said to Balaam, "Go with the men, but speak only what I tell you." So Balaam went with Balak's officials. (Num 22:20–35)

It is very significant that the eyes of a "seer" need to be opened.

Two Talking Animals: The Serpent and the Donkey

There are only two animals in the Bible that talk: the serpent in the Garden of Eden (Gen 3:1–8; 2 Cor 11:3) and this donkey. The religious, mythical significance of the serpent is that it is "a cunning animal." No animal was as crafty as the serpent; it was the embodiment of evil seduction (Gen 3:1), and it managed to deceive Eve (2 Cor 11:3). This animal is thus a symbol of the evil that besieges human beings.[51] Its venom and its tongue symbolize the craftiness of the wicked (Ps 58:4). The discourse of enemies is as deadly as the venom of snakes with their darting tongues (Ps 140:3).[52] The parables of Jesus also use the serpent as a symbol of cunning (Matt 10:16), hypocrisy, and malevolence (cf. "brood of vipers" in Matt 12:34). Jesus promises immunity to his disciples (cf. Q 3:52): "they will pick up snakes with their

---

51. *KBS* on Genesis 3:1.
52. Hossfeld and Zenger, *Psalms 3*, 551.

hands; and when they drink deadly poison, it will not hurt them at all" (Mark 16:10; Luke 10:19).[53]

Where Genesis talks about the serpent, the Qur'an talks about the satan, who makes human beings slip up (Q 3:155): he whispered evil thoughts into their ears (Q 7:20; cf. 20:120). And it is Moses who can change his staff into a serpent in the sight of Pharaoh and his ministers (Q 7:107, 117; 20:7–21; 20:69; 26:32; 27:10; 28:31).

Craftiness, wisdom, and cunning are mentioned as the characteristics of the serpent (Job 5:12; 15:5). The craftiness of the serpent is proverbial (Matt. 10:16) and is connected with its ability to produce venom and/or to shed skin: through shedding its skin, it is reborn. Fairy tales and fables also draw connections between specific animals and certain characteristic.[54]

How a serpent moves, i.e., by slithering on its belly, is seen as a danger for human beings. The same also obtains for the idea that the serpent eats dust (Mic 7:17; Isa 65:25). These characteristics are ascribed to the fact that God has cursed serpents (Gen 3:14-15). The mysterious and creepy sides of the serpent—its connection to the earth and shedding its skin—showed a very suggestive relation between death and life. Because of that, the snake was seen as a numen with ambivalent power.

In the story of the talking *donkey*, the point is of course not whether animals can talk but *what* these talking "stories" have to say. What is put in the mouth of this "dumb" beast in this case? The blindness of the so-called seer is exposed: "a donkey—a beast without speech . . . spoke with a man's voice and restrained the prophet's madness" (2 Pet 2:15-16).

The story of Balaam can be read as a comic satire that critiques both society and religion. Satires are sharp because they are intended to provoke and urge others to act. And throughout history humorless people in power have found that especially irritating. That is why satirists have been persecuted by governments. Balaam mistreats his faithful donkey by beating her three times and even threatening her with a sword. The donkey, in turn, makes her rider look ridiculous. Her sensible behavior turns Balaam into a comical figure. It is, of course, literally a comedown to sit on a donkey that simply lays down, just plops down under her rider.[55] But when she also turns around, opens her mouth, and reprimands her rider in human language, only then does the rough humor strike home.

---

53. *B.W.*, s.v. "Slang."

54. Westermann, *Genesis 1-11*, 325-26.

55. There are depictions of a scene in which a donkey on which St. Antony of Padua is riding kneels before the consecrated host and thus recalls the donkey of Balaam, which does bow before the holy one. Cf. Biedermann, 123.

That the donkey speaks functions as a warning for Balaam: he has to watch *what* he says and not curse Israel. He can only speak the words God puts in his mouth. The fact that the donkey speaks should teach him that the mouth and tongue are in God's hand: "You can't kill me with your *hand*, how can you destroy a whole nation with your *mouth*?"[56] It is striking to remember that the person who was hired because of his "mouth" is put in his place by a talking donkey.

Thus, this story is not recorded as a report of something that happened in the *past* but is intended to provide more insight into the *present*, into the time it was written down—possibly the fourth century B.C. The question is then who is meant by "Balak," "Balaam," and the "donkey." Should we think here of King Nebuchadnezzar, the ruler who had the temple destroyed in 585 B.C.? Or is the Persian king a better candidate? Or does Balak refer to both? If this story should be read as always pertaining to the time in which it is read, then we should look at the issue of what kind of king is intended here: one who wants to sow corruption on the earth.

And who is the representative of "the one who came afar," Balaam? His name can be translated as "master of the people." Quite possibly, he was the governor of Judah who travelled the long road from the royal court of Persia—the ruler of that time—to Palestine, which was under the authority of that same Persia. The book of Numbers is not only about a story from the 13th century B.C., the journey through the Sinai desert. It also concerns what happened in the fourth century before Christ, at the time of the foreign Persian domination and the repercussions this had for Palestine (which was called Yehud) at the time.

Finally, who is *the female animal* that carries this comical figure on her back without complaining, allows herself to be beaten and threatened with the sword? Is that not then the patient, exploited, and oppressed people of Israel? That seems likely if one remembers the prophetic words God puts in Balaam's mouth.[57]

Balaam in the Time of the Roman Empire

The last book of the Bible, Revelation, contains letters John wrote to the seven churches in the Roman province of Asia (Asia Minor, today's Turkey). One is addressed to the community (*ecclesia*) in Pergamum, where a world-famous library was located that contained more than 200,000 parchment

---

56. Douglas, *The Doctrine of Defilement*, 216–21; Ginzberg, *Legends of the Jews*, 766.

57. So Douglas, *The Doctrine of Defilement*, 221.

scrolls. Our word "parchment" is derived from the name of this city. Countless people went to the city to seek help and primarily healing in the temples of Zeus Soter ("Zeus the Healer") and especially that of Asclepius Soter, the god of medicine. Doctors still use the so-called staff of Aesculapius—a serpent coiled around a staff—as the symbol of their profession. There was also a well with curative powers there that drew many pilgrims yearly to Pergamum, a kind of Lourdes in antiquity.[58]

The "seer" John provides revelations, disclosures, about what was happening in his time, what was still going to happen, and constantly happens. He reveals (*apocalypsis*: "uncovering") what was happening in the Roman empire under the Caesars: the violence against the small, weak human being. The economic exploitation of the outlying provinces of the large Roman Empire, like Palestine and Asia Minor, was unmasked as theft. He exposes the lying propaganda of the empire.

But one could also ask why there is no concrete language in John's letter to the community in Pergamum. Why does he not call a spade a spade? Why does John only speak about "where Satan has his throne"? And why does he write "Babylon" in the book of Revelation when he clearly means "Rome"? To answer that question, one needs to understand that a book like Revelation is resistance literature, addressed to a resistance community. The writer of such a letter has to be careful with respect to word use since the letter can be intercepted or fall into the wrong hands. That is why there is a deliberate choice for disguised terms. It is therefore no coincidence that there is no overt reference anywhere in the book of Revelation to Rome or Caesar. Does this then mean that it is not about Rome or the Caesars? Not at all—to the contrary! Rome is designated "the whore of Babylon" (Rev 17). The woman is seated on the seven heads, the seven hills on which Rome is built. And the seven kings of Rome are discussed, of whom five have already fallen and one, the last, still has to come (Rev 17:9–10) The five who have died refer to the Caesars who have already died: Caligula (†41), Claudius (†54), Nero (†68), Vespasian (†79), and Titus (†81). The sixth who was ruling at that time was Dominitian (Caesar from 81–96).[59] The book of Revelation was probably written during his rule.

The "whore of Babylon" is thus not a reference to the red-light district of Rome. Here we must keep in mind the "language of Canaan." The language used here is disguised, symbolic language, intended for the proper readership. "He who has an ear, let him hear"—yes, indeed, "hear." One

---

58. *B.W.*, s.v. "Pergamum."
59. *KBS* on Revelation 17:10–11.

should not forget that this letter would primarily be read aloud! For the community at Pergamum it was plain talk.

"Whore" symbolizes infidelity. The prophet Hosea depicted the marriage relationship between God and his people. He had to marry an adulterous wife and father bastards through her—literally or figuratively, who can say? The adulterous woman symbolizes unfaithful Israel who chased after foreign gods, which symbolizes the rejection of God (Hos 1:2-3; 2:7; 3:3; 4:12-15; 9:1; cf. Jer 2:2; Ezek 16, 23).[60] Thus, in the letter to Pergamum, Rome is condemned as the "great whore." Such a judgment was earlier proclaimed over the city of Nineveh because of the sexual immorality that had been committed by that prostitute (Nah 3:4). The "woe" addressed to this "city of blood" that exploited the socially defenseless people in the city (Nah 3:1; Jer 2:34; Mic 3:9-11; Hab 2:12).[61] And the city of Tyre will suffer the same fate as the prostitute in the song: "Take up a harp, walk through the city,/ O prostitute forgotten;/ play the harp well, sing many a song,/so that you will be remembered" (Isa 23:16). This oracle by Isaiah uses the image of an old and forgotten prostitute, an image that refers to the economic system in the world in which people are prepared to do everything for money, just like a prostitute. But when she becomes older, she is forgotten, neglected, and no longer needed or desired, the prophet remarks sarcastically.[62]

But even Jerusalem does not escape this verdict. Jerusalem offers her desirability for sale to everyone who passes by (Ezek 16:15), throws her beauty away and spreads her legs for everyone. Her desire is insatiable. She commits sexual immorality with the Egyptians, with her lustful neighbors; time and again she engages in sexual immorality to provoke God (Ezek 16:25-26).

It is in line with that "tradition" that Rome is called a whore: the "whore of Babylon," "Babylon, the great," or even "the mother of prostitutes" (Rev 17:1, 5).[63] Thus, Rome is characterized as the focus of idolatry and sexual immorality. One should think here—just as with the temple prostitution in Peor in Balaam's time—not of sex primarily (although that played a role). Rather, what is at issue is the fact that Rome, through its political and economic power, like a public prostitute, seduced the kings and inhabitants of the earth—the kings allied with her and the peoples subject to her—to

60. *B.W.*, s.v. "Hoer"; *KBS* on Isaiah 1:21.

61. *KBS*.

62. Brueggemann, *Isaiah 1-39*, 186.

63. Expressions of this kind are also used in Arabic. That was clear when Saddam Hussein spoke during the Gulf War of the "mother of all battles." The Qur'an speaks of "the mother of the book" (i.e., the essence of the book) to "which the holy books" can be traced back (Q 13:39; 43:4).

commit fornication with her and to commit idolatry: the imperial cult and everything that that entailed with respect to injustice.[64] Thus, that image of the prostitute refers to prostitution in Babylon or Rome in the sense of the misuse of power and money, which leads to "corruption and the shedding of blood." It thus concerns a charge against the political and economic policy of the emperor in the city and the empire, with the horrible way in which people were subjected, oppressed, exploited, and sucked dry. The rape of justice can also indeed lead to young girls being driven to prostitution to survive and to care for relatives.

Balaam is mentioned in the letter to the community in Pergamum as follows:

> These are the words of him who has the sharp, double-edged sword. I know where you live—where Satan has his throne. Yet you remain true to my name. You did not renounce your faith in me, not even in the days of Antipas, my faithful witness, who was put to death in your city—where Satan lives.

Nevertheless, I have a few things against you: There are some among you who hold to the teaching of Balaam, who taught Balak to entice the Israelites to sin so that they ate food sacrificed to idols and committed sexual immorality. Likewise, you also have those who hold to the teaching of the Nicolaitans. Repent therefore! Otherwise, I will soon come to you and will fight against them with the sword of my mouth.

> Whoever has ears, let them hear what the Spirit says to the churches. To the one who is victorious, I will give some of the hidden manna. I will also give that person a white stone with a new name written on it, known only to the one who receives it. (Rev 2:12–17)

This letter gives us a good example of a new application of this story. It no longer refers to the Babylonian Nebuchadnezzar or the prince of Persia but to the Roman Caesar, whose grasping tentacles reached all the way to the province of Asia. Jesus had been born during the rule of Caesar Augustus and began his public ministry under the latter's successor. Paul appealed, by his rights as a Roman citizen, to Nero (Acts 25:11), and Nero had him killed with the sword. It was because Paul was a Roman citizen that he was not crucified like Peter, who, according to legend, was crucified upside down. The destruction of Jerusalem in the year 70 was carried out by Titus, who then became Caesar. The book of Revelation was thus written during the rule of Domitian (81–96). "Babylon" is thus a pseudonym for Rome and

---

64. *KBS* on Revelation 17:1–2.

was referred to that way both by Jews as well as the disciples of Jesus (1 Pet 5:13). A large part of the world was infected by its immorality—its idolatry—in the form of the imperial cult (Rev 14:8).[65] The historical Babylon had destroyed Jerusalem under Nebuchadnezzar and led the people away into exile. Thus, Babylon could serve as a model of a political power that was the enemy of God and his people.[66]

Pergamum was where the official seat of the governor of Caesar was located, just as Pilate was the governor in Jerusalem at the time of Jesus. On a hill 300 meters high the beautiful, large altar of the supreme Zeus towered above the city. It was also the center of the divine worship of the god Roma, the personification of the city of Rome, "mother Rome." That city was also where the first temple for Caesar Augustus "the Exalted" was built. Almost immediately after coming to power, Augustus began working on the imperial cult in all seriousness. Barely four years after being conquered by Octavian (later Augustus), the local elite of the city humbly asked him for permission to honor him in this way.

The imperial cult was the "religion" that connected the inhabitants of the city and the cities of the empire with each other: palace, cult, temple, and gods. All social activities were embedded in that system. All inhabitants of the city were expected to participate in the imperial cult and thus demonstrate their "faith" in the dominant imperial system. Temples also played a major economic role. Large-scale business transactions were not possible without the temples functioning as banks. They were the key to the economic life of the city and empire. The lives of the subjects were ruled from the cradle to the (usually early) grave by the totalitarian state power. Thus, the imperial cult was not an innocent way to pass the time. As the exalted human being, the Son of Man (cf. Dan 7:13), who wields "the sharp, double-edged sword" (Rev 2:12), addresses the wicked city in this letter. The sword is a sign of judgment (Isa 17:1; 34:5; Hebr 4:12; Rev 1:16; 19:15). The letter calls the community to change its ways and to stop worshipping idols. If they do not, the Son of Man will not hesitate to take the double-edged sword out of his mouth and use it against them. As Isaiah had long ago prophesied: "He will strike the earth with the rod of his mouth;/with the breath of his lips he will slay the wicked" (Isa 11:4; cf. Rev 11:15; 2 Thess 2:8). The Son of Man himself enters into the controversy taking place in the community at Pergamum with the sword in his mouth—his tongue.

---

65. *KBS*.
66. *KBS* on Revelation 17:5.

Serving the Beast

The letter uses hard, direct language: "I know where you live—where Satan has his throne." The throne of the emperor represents the commercial and power center, the economic and military might of the Roman empire. It is the center of the destructive power that sows corruption and engages in financial exploitation. The biblical terms for those activities are respectively "Moloch (or Molech/Molek)" and "Mammon."

"Moloch" is a bastardization of the Hebrew word for "king" and the name of the false god to whom children were sacrificed. The peoples who lived in Canaan before the arrival of the Israelites engaged in this practice. It was, we should note, the great king of peace, Solomon, who first erected an altar to Moloch in Jerusalem, for which he was also judged (1 Kings 11:7–13). Children were sacrificed in fire in the Ben-Hinnom valley near Jerusalem in honor of Moloch (Lev 18:21). The name is reflected in the Hebrew *gehinnom*, which was translated into biblical Greek as *gehenna* and became a term for hell. The Arabic translation is *jahannam* (Q 2:206; 3:12, etc.).

Different kings in Judah were guilty of worshipping Moloch (2 Kings 16:3; 2 Chron 28:3). These included Ahaz (735–727 B.C.) and Manasseh (2 Kings 21:6; 2 Chron 33:6). King Josiah put an end to this practice by desecrating the altars there so that no one could sacrifice his son or daughter anymore to Moloch (2 Kings 23:10). This terrible custom was forbidden in the Torah (Lev 18:21; cf. 20:2–5) and also by the prophets (Jer 32:34–35; cf. Jer 19:5; Ezek 16:20). Psalm 106 looks back on this practice with horror:

> They sacrificed their sons
>   and their daughters to false gods.
> They shed innocent blood,
>   the blood of their sons and daughters,
> whom they sacrificed to the idols of Canaan,
>   and the land was desecrated by their blood.
> They defiled themselves by what they did;
>   by their deeds they prostituted themselves.
> Therefore the Lord was angry with his people
>   and abhorred his inheritance.
> He gave them into the hands of the nations,
>   and their foes ruled over them.
> (Ps 106:37–41)[67]

---

67. Lundbom, *Deuteronomium*, 439–40.

"Mammon" is the word that personifies cupidity (Matt 6:24; Luke 16:9, 11, 13). The "World Trade Center" of Rome sucked the empire dry and provinces like Israel/Palestine were bowed down by the consequences of that.

The Qur'an also points to the dangers of wealth and possessions. The gathering of wealth is repeatedly described as useless (Q 15:84). It will not help in the last judgment (Q 69:28; cf. 92:11; 111:2). The people of the prophet Shu'ayb asked him if he wanted them to give up what their fathers had worshipped and stop doing what they wanted with their possessions (Q 11:87). The Qur'an also says that God had given Pharaoh and his most prominent ministers a great deal of luxury and wealth to lead their people away from God (Q 10:88). And that was also done by the unbelievers in Muhammad's own time (Q 8:36).

Hoarding, greed, and arrogance go together (Q 57:23-24; 4:36-38). A "woe" is declared to those who amass wealth and think that their wealth will stay with them forever (Q 104:1-3; cf. 3:157; 10:58; 43:32; 28:78; 70:18). It will appear at the last judgment that what was gathered is of no use, and the same holds for arrogance (Q 7:48; cf. 15:84; 39:50; 40:82; 45:10; 111:2; 69:28; 92:11; 3:10, 116; 58:17; 2:264). The fundamental problem of greed is thus also the claim to self-sufficiency (Q 92:8). The price one pays for greed is oneself: "Whoever is miserly works against himself. God is the one who is rich; you are the poor" (Q 47:38). It will go well with those who are free of selfish miserliness (Q 64:16).[68]

Those who first read or heard John's letter to the community at Pergamum understood very well what the throne of Satan was intended to mean, where the throne was located, and who sat on it. They knew where the altar of the emperor was. "The throne of Satan" represented the demonically inspired worship of "the beast." The beast became the symbol of the Roman Empire that, because of its imperial cult, represented an unacceptable type of state power for believers.[69]

The seer speaks of two beasts (Rev 13), inspired by the dream vision of four animals in Daniel (Dan 7). The first beast rises *out of the sea*, the place where mythological monsters live, and resembles the dragon, Satan (Rev 12:3), from whom it also receives dominion over the world (Rev 13:2). The second beast rises *out of the earth* and speaks like a dragon (Rev 13:11). The apocalyptic appearance of the dragon is linked to the creation myth (Ps

---

68. *E.Q.*, s.v. "Wealth."
69. *KBS* on Revelation 13:1.

74:13), where the mythological sea monster represents the old serpent or Satan, God's enemy (Rev 12:3, 9).[70]

This beast is also called a *false prophet* (Rev 16:13; 19:20; 20:10). The one beast thus rises from the sea and represents the Roman Empire. The other appears in Asia Minor (the province of Asia, where Pergamum lies) and is the false prophet, the propagandist of the imperial cult. The second beast serves the first and propagates the worship of the emperor. Together, the two beasts personify the political and religious power of the Roman Empire.[71] The number of the beast is given as 666 (Rev 13:18), for which the most probable explanation is that the number represents the numerical value of the name Nero Caesar.[72]

The *ecclesia*, the church or community in Pergamum, which is attempting to persevere in that city with its cult of the "beast," is called to resist the *beastly* practices of the Roman Empire. The believers are not to place their trust in the "Exalted" (Augustus), who is called the savior, the redeemer[73] of the world.

Over against the throne of the emperor is, namely, the *throne of God*. "Righteousness and justice are the foundation of his throne" (Ps 97:2). Justice is the foundation, the platform on which the throne of the divine or earthly king sits (Pss 2 and 96). The community is called to believe in the Messianic king, to trust that justice and righteousness will triumph despite all. One of the members of the Pergamum community, Antipas, a faithful witness to God's righteousness and justice, was probably lynched. He was a martyr where the accomplices of the beast, of Satan, live. Nevertheless, the bloody persecution that claimed one of their own members as a victim, did not lead the whole community to deny or give up that hope and that faith.

Other sounds could be heard in the community, however: "You have people there who hold to the teaching [in contemporary language it is probably better to say: ideology] of Balaam, who taught Balak to entice the Israelites to sin" (Rev 2:14). "I have that against you," John writes. People are tolerated within the community who make compromises with the idols, the false gods of the beastly power, the wealth and propaganda of the other beast: the false prophet who provides propaganda for the first two false gods.

Balaam advised King Balak on how he could coax his opponents along by idolatrous practices: with a bit of uncoerced gaiety, some intoxication through drink and some sex, everything turns out fine. Just as the Israelites

---

70. *KBS*; *B.W.*, s.v. "Draak."
71. *KBS* on Revelation 13:11.
72. *KBS* on Revelation 13:18.
73. *soter*.

engaged in sexual immorality with Moabite women during their journey through the desert, so some members of the community in Pergamum are also guilty of sexual immorality. This is not, however, a question of some members of the community visiting the red light district in Pergamum. No, here it was a question of the symbolic language of the Scripture. It is not a question of too many visits to Midtown in Manhattan but a question of what goes on on Wall Street, in the New York Stock Exchange. It is not sexual immorality as usually understood but as in the whole of Scripture, "the rape of justice and love." The relationship between God and his people was, after all, one of marital fidelity: "I will betroth you to me forever;/ I will betroth you in righteousness and justice,/ in love and compassion./ I will betroth you in faithfulness" (Hos 2:21–22).[74]

The Qur'an is also acquainted with the apocalyptic language of the last book of the Bible. That obtains, in particular, for the places where "the beast" is mentioned: "Then I saw another beast, coming out of the earth. He had two horns like a lamb, but he spoke like a dragon" (Rev 13:11). "A messenger from God has emerged out of the demonic being in the book of Revelation!"[75]

"And when the word concerns them, We will cause a beast[76] to come up out of the earth that will speak to them like a messenger because they were not convinced of Our signs or revelations in their earthly lives. And on the day we gather all those from the community who called Our sign a lie, they will be brought together in separate groups. When they finally come then, He will say 'You have declared my signs to be a lie without understanding anything of them. Or what else have you done?' And the judgment will be pronounced upon them because they have engaged in injustice. And they nothing to say that can justify them" (Q 27:82–85; cf. Matt 25:31–48).[77]

Food for On the Way

"He who has an ear, let him hear what the Spirit says to the churches [communities]." That is what Revelation 2:17 says, following it with: "To the one who is victorious, I will give some of the hidden manna." i.e., provision, food for on the way. "Manna" is the bread that God has rained down from heaven and that the Israelites ate during their journey through the wilderness (Exod 16:6–9; cf. Ps 78:25, 105:40). God took care of the children of

---

74. Nieuwenhuis, *Johannes de ziener*, 707–10; cf. Naastepad, *Geen vrede*, 16–23.
75. Paret, *Der Koran: Kommentar*, on Q 27:82.
76. *dâbba*.
77. Cf. Cook, *Studies in Muslim Apocalyptic*, 120–22, section 1.

Israel during this journey: "God carried you, as a father carries his son" (Deut 1:31).[78]

Manna is their food for on the way—whatever is needed for daily sustenance, no less but also no more. The pilgrims in the desert went out daily to gather what they needed for one day (Exod 16:17–18). The one gathered more; the other less. But the one who gathered much never had too much and the one who gathered little did not have too little. Everyone had precisely what he needed. They did not live off hoarded supplies but from day to day. Only before the Sabbath did they gather a double amount to last two days. They did not store it in barns, not for the next day, not for the whole week, not for the future. The petition in the Lord's prayer is very striking in that respect: "Give us today our daily bread": our food for today, our ration for on our way.[79]

God wanted to teach the children Israel through the manna that people did not live by bread alone but by everything that comes from the mouth of God (Deut 8:3–4). Daily food is only one of the gifts God gives to sustain life. Everything that comes from God sustains life. What Moses says in his major discourse on the evening of the entrance into the promised land is that the Israelites have to follow the commands that lead to life: "Now, Israel, hear the decrees and laws I am about to teach you. Follow them so that you may live and may go in and take possession of the land the Lord, the God of your ancestors, is giving you" (Deut 4:1).[80] Hearing and doing are the constantly recurring themes in the book of Deuteronomy ("the second law"!), the foundation of the Tanakh, the New Testament, and the Qur'an as well!—especially the words: "not by bread alone." Indeed, everything that comes from God supports and shores up life. Observing the commandments leads to life.

When Jesus is tempted by Satan in the desert, he also quotes these words (Matt 4:4; Luke 4:4). Satan wanted Him to turn stones into bread. That was a strong temptation because Jesus had already been fasting for forty days. On the basis of Deuteronomy 8:3–4, the rabbis make a connection between bread and the Torah.[81] "In the desert the children of Israel received the Torah as the bread that gives people life. The Torah teaches: if people share with one another, there is bread enough for everyone and

---

78. *KBS* on Deuteronomy 1:31.

79. "The greedy bring ruin to their households,/ but the one who hates bribes will live" (Prov 15:27).

80. Lundbom, *Deuteronomium*, 234.

81. Ibid., 349–50.

no one needs to suffer from want."[82] There would be enough for everyone's need, though not for everyone's greed, Mahatma Gandhi would say later.

The Promised City, the Promised Land, the Promised World

The Bible and the Qur'an are not concerned with history in the modern sense of history, of finding out what exactly happened. That entails, for example, that the firstborn of Egypt were not killed and that Korah's gang was not swallowed up by the earth, even though that does get depicted in Christian and Islamic art. The Israelites who left Egypt with Moses as the "first generation" did not undergo a divine punishment. That is all story, all narrative, and needs to be read/heard as such and that have to be heard as a message in narrative form. What can be made of all these stories? What should we "hear" in them? That God is completely on the side of the weak and those who suffer. At the same time, He wants to continue to warn people and keep them from living among each other like Pharaoh and wearing the masks of Pharaoh, Korah, and/or Balaam. The latter is what happened under King Solomon, for example, who acted like Pharaoh and was therefore judged. The language used here make one think of a new Exodus (1 Kings 11).

It was Stefan Heym who, with his *King David Report*, first opened my eyes to such a reading of the history of David and Solomon. Already when I first read that book I thought: But that's actually how the books of Samuel and Kings present it! Against the background of these stories is the depiction of an ordering of life determined and willed by God and to which He binds Himself as the God of justice and righteousness. He obligates himself in particular to the protection of those who are denied their human rights. That is what he uses his "power" (*potentas*)[83] for, without violence (*violentia*)! There is nothing here of an irrational vengeance that wants to destroy but simply the continuance and restoration of the fundamental ordering of life by means of "legitimate violence," which cannot be denied the state today either. These biblical stories speak of God acting, "with a raised hand," by which He fights against his enemies and those of His people. What is said here obtains just as much for the God who speaks in the Qur'an. I think here of a text often cited and misused by extremists that states that they must "strike terror" into the hearts of God's enemies (Q 8:60) and thus legitimize "terrorism" and terroristic violence. But these "terrorists" neglect to quote

---

82. Oosterhuis and Van Heusden, *Het evangelie van Lukas*, 44.

83. The word *potestas* can also be interpreted as *sacra potestas* ("sacred violence"), a sanction in the name of God, so (correctly) Houtepen, *Geloven in gerechtigheid*, 143.

the verse that immediately follows, which states that they are to cease from such violence against those who are inclined to peace (Q 8:61).[84]

That obtains for other voices in the Bible that should also be heard, such as that of Jonah (Yûnus). Nineveh can repent. From the dispute between Jonah and God, it turns out that the prophet wanted to flee because he knew that God was a good and merciful God who forgives sin. He prayed to God: "Isn't this what I said, Lord, when I was still at home? That is what I tried to forestall by fleeing to Tarshish. I knew that you are a gracious and compassionate God, slow to anger and abounding in love, a God who relents from sending calamity" (Jon 4:2). But God makes it clear to the prophet: "And should I not have concern for the great city of Nineveh, in which there are more than a hundred and twenty thousand people who cannot tell their right hand from their left—and also many animals?" (Jon 4:11). That is the message that is to be communicated to the peoples of the world.[85] The Qur'an proclaims that God has prescribed mercy to himself (Q 6:12, 54).

The story of the journey through the wilderness, a guide for all people who are traveling, retains its continuing relevance for today: the prototype for the pilgrimage of humankind, a ymbol of the lifelong journey of the human being to the promised city, the promised land, and the promised world where justice and righteousness reign.

---

84. That is also true, by the way, of the movie *Submission*. Cf. Wessels, *The Torah*, 169.

85. Zenger, *Das erste Testament*, 66–67.

Bibliography

Agten, Jean, et al. *Bibliodrama begeleiden: Wegwijzers voor de praktijk*. Antwerp: Garant, 2007.
Akveld, Leo M., and Els M. Jacobs, eds. *Nationaal Jubileumboek VOC 1602–2002: De kleurrijke wereld van de VOC*. Bussum: Thoth, 2002.
Alexander-Knotter, Mirjam, et al. *De 'Joodse' Rembrandt: De mythe ontrafeld*. Amsterdam: Waanders/Zwolle: Joods Historisch Museum, 2007.
Ambros, Arne A. *A Concise Dictionary of Koranic Arabic*. Wiesbaden: Reichert, 2004.
Armstrong, Karen. *The Bible. The Biography*. London: Atlantic Books, 2007.
Assmann, Jan. *Thomas Mann und Ägypten. Mythos und Monotheismus in den Josephsromanen*. Munich: C.H. Beck, 2006.
Attema, Dirk Sijbolt. *Arabië en de Bijbel*. Den Haag: Van Keulen N.V., 1961.
———. *Het Oudste Christendom in Zuid-Arabië*. Amsterdam: Noord-Hollandse Uitgeverij Maatschappij, 1949.
Attridge, Harold W. *The Epistle to the Hebrews: A Commentary the Epistle to the Hebrews*. Minneapolis: Fortress, 1989.
Ayoub, Mahmoud M. *The Qur'an and Its Interpreters*. Volume I. Albany: State University of New York Press, 1984.
Barakat, Ahmad. *Muhammad and the Jews*. New Delhi: Vikas PublishingHouse, 1979.
Barnard, Willem. *Een winter met Leviticus*. Zoetermeer: Meinema, 200).
Bauer, Walter. "Politeuma." *Griechisch-Deutsches Würterbuch zum Neuen Testament*. Berlin: Alfred Töpelmann, 1958.
Bauer, Walter. *Wörterbuch zum Neuen Testament*. Berlin: Alfred Töpelmann, 1958.
Bauschke, Martin. *Der Spiegel des Propheten. Abraham im Koran und im Islam*. Frankfurt: Lembeck, 2008.
Becker, Adam H., and Annette Koshiko Reed, eds. *The Ways that Never Parted: Jews and Christians in Late Antiquity*. Minneapolis: Fortress, 2007.
Behm, Johannes. *Die Offenbarung des Johannes*. Göttingen: Von den Hoeck and Ruprecht, 1949.
Bell, Richard, and William Montgomery Watt. *Introduction to the Quran*. Edinburgh: Edinburgh University Press, 1970.
Beuken, Willem André Maria. *Jesaja deel II A*. Nijkerk: Callenbach, 1986.
Biedermann, Hans. *Prisma van de symbolen* (reprint). Utrecht: Het Spectrum, 1993.
Bijbel met werken van Marc Chagall. Haarlem: Nederlands Bijbelgenootschap/Beernem: Vlaams Bijbelgenootschap, 2000.

Bijbel. Willibrord vertaling. 's-Hertogenbosch: Katholieke Bijbelstichting, 1995.
Bikker, Jonathan, and Gregor J.M. Weber. *Late Rembrandt*. Brussel: Mercatorfonds, 2014.
Blachère, Régis. *Le Coran: Traduction selon un essai de reclassement des sourates*. Paris: Editions G.P. Maisonneuve, 1951.
Boyarin, Daniel. *Border Lines: The Partition of Judaeo-Christianity*. Philadelphia: University of Pennsylvania Press, 2007. Paperback edition.
Braverman, Mark. *Fatal Embrace: Christians, Jews, and the Search for Peace in the Holy Land*. Austin: Synergy Books, 2010.
Brinner, William M. *The History of al-Tabarî*. Volume II: *Prophets and Patriarchs*. Albany: State University of New York Press, 1987.
Brosse, Jacques. *Mythologie der Bäume*. Olten: Walter, 1989.
Brueggemann, Walter. *1 and 2 Kings*. Georgia: Smith and Helwys Macon, 2000.
———. *Biblical Perspectives on Evangelism: Living in a Three-Storied Universe*. Nashville: Abingdon, 1993.
———. *The Collected Sermons of Walter Brueggemann*. Louisville, Kentucky: Westminster John Knox, 2011.
———. *A Commentary on Jeremiah: Exile and Homecoming*. Grand Rapids: Eerdmans, 1998.
———. *Genesis. Interpretation: A Bible Commentary for Teaching and Preaching*. Atlanta, Georgia: John Knox, 1983.
———. *Isaiah 1–39*. Louisville, Kentucky: WJK, 1998.
———. *Isaiah 40–66*. Louisville, Kentucky: WJK, 1998.
———. *Like Fire in the Bones: Listening for the Prophetic Word in Jeremiah*. Minneapolis: Fortress, 2006.
———. *Out of Babylon*. Nashville: Abingdon, 2010.
———. *The Prophetic Imagination*. Minneapolis: Fortress, 2001. Reprint.
———. *Sabbath as Resistance: Saying No to the Culture of Now*. Louisville, Kentucky: WJK, 2014.
———. *The Word Militant: Preaching a Decentering Word*. Minneapolis: Fortress, 2010.
Brueggemann, Walter, and William H. Bellinger, Jr , *Psalms*. New York: Cambridge University Press, 2014.
Buhl, Frants. *Das Leben Muhammeds*. Darmstadt: Wissenschaftliche Buchgesellschaft, 1961.
Burgmer, Christoph. *Streit um den Koran: Die Luxenberg-Debatte: Standpunkte und Hintergründe*. Berlin: Hans Schiler, 2007. Reprint.
Callaway, Mary. *Sing, O Barren One: A Study in Comparative Midrash*. Atlanta, Georgia: Scholars, 1986.
Cameron, Averil, and Lawrence I. Conrad, eds. *The Byzantine and Early Islamic Near East*. Princeton, New Jersey: Darwin, 1992.
Campenhausen, Hans Baron von, and Erich Dinkler. *Die Religion in Geschich te und Gegenwart*. Tubingen: J.B.C. Mohr, 1957.
Charles, Robert Henry, ed. *The Apocrypha and Pseudepigrapha of the Old Testament*. Volume Two: *Pseudepigrapha*. Berkeley: Apocryphile, 2004.
Cicero. *On Obligations*. Walsh, P.G., ed. Oxford, Oxford University Press, 2010.
Collins, John J., and Daniel C. Harlow. *The Eerdmans Dictionary of Early Judaism*. Grand Rapids: Eerdmans, 2010.
Cook, David. *Studies in Muslim Apocalyptic*. Princeton, New Jersey: Darwin, 2002.

Cuypers, Michel. *The Banquet: A Reading of the Fifth Sura of the Qur'an*. Series Rhetorica Semitica. Miami: Convivium, 2009.
Van Dale Groot woordenboek der Nederlandse Taal. 's-Gravenhage: Martinus Nijhoff, 1961. Reprint.
Davies, Philip R. *Scribes and Schools: The Canonization of the Hebrew Scriptures*. Louisville: Westminster John Knox, 1998.
Deurloo, Karel. *Exodus en Exil. Kleine Bijbelse Theologie*. Deel I. Kampen: Kok, 2003.
———, et al. *Koning en tempel*. Kleien Bijbelse Theologie. Deel II. Kampen: Kok, 2004.
Dickens, Charles. *Litte Dorrit*. Edited by Stephen Wall and Helen Small. London: Penguin Books, 2003.
Dictionnaire du Coran. Sous la direction de Mohammad Ali Amir-Moezzi. Paris: Robert Laffont, 2007.
Dodds, Eric R. *Heiden und Christen in einem Zeitalter der Angst: Aspecte religiöser Erfahrung von Mark Aurel bis Konstantin*. Frankfurt a.M 1992.
Douglas, Mary. *The Doctrine of Defilement in the Book of Numbers*. Oxford: Oxford University Press, 1993.
Drewermann, Eugen. *Das Markus Evangelium*. Zweiter Teil: *Bilder von Erlösung*. Olten: Walter, 1988.
Drijvers, Han J.W. "The Gospel of the Twelve Apostles: A Syria Apocalypse from the Early Islamic Period." In *The Byzantine and Early Islamic Near East*, edited by Averil Cameron and Lawrence I. Conrad, 189–213. Princeton, New Jersey: Darwin, 1992.
Dungan, David L. *Constantine's Bible: Politics and the Making of the New Testament*. Minneapolis: Fortress, 2007.
Eisenbaum, Pamela. "Paul as The New Abraham." In Richard A. Horsley, *Paul and Politics: Ekklesia, Israel, Imperium, Interpretation*, 130–45. Harrisburg, Pennsylvania: Trinity Press International, 2000.
Eliade, Mircea, ed. *The Encyclopedia of Religion*. New York: Macmillan, 1987.
Elliott, Neil. *The Arrogance of Nations: Reading Romans in the Shadow of Empire*. Minneapolis: Fortress, 2010.
———. *Liberating Paul: The Justice of God and the Politics of the Apostle*. Minneapolis: Fortress, 2006.
The Encyclopaedia of Islam. New Edition. Leiden: Brill/London: Luzac and Co, 1960–.
Esack, Farid. *Qur'an, Liberation and Pluralism*. Oxford: One Word, 1988.
Firestone, Reuven. *Journeys in Holy Lands: The Evolution of the Abraham-Ishmael Legend in Islamic Exegesis*. New York: State University of New York Press, 1990.
Fischer, Georg, and Dominik Markl. *Das Buch Exodus*, Neuer Stuttgarter Kommentar Altes Testament. Stuttgart: Katholisches Bibelwerk, 2009.
Flavius Josephus. *The Complete Works of Flavius Josephus*. Translated by William Whiston 1737. http://www.ultimatebiblereferencelibrary.com/Complete_Works_of_Josephus.pdf.
Gairdner, Willaim Henry Temple. *al-Ghazzali's Miskat al-anwar*. London: The Royal Asiatic Society, 1924.
Geiger, Abraham. *Judaism and Islam: A Prize Essay*. Madras: M.D.C.S.P.C.K, 1898.
Gelder, Geert Jan van. *Een Arabische tuin: Klassieke Arabische poëzie*. Amsterdam: Bulaaq/Leuven: Halewyck, 2000.
Gilet, Lev. *Communion in the Messiah: Studies in Relationship between Judaism and Christianity*. London: Lutterworth, 1942.

Gerstenberger, Erhard S. *Psalms, Part 1 with an Introduction to Cultic Poetry.* Grand Rapids: Eerdmans, 1991. Reprint.

Ginzberg, Louis. *Legends of the Jews: Bible Times and Characters, From the Creation to Moses in the Wilderness.* Volume One. Philadelphia: The Jewish Publication Society, 2003.

Glassé, Cyril, ed. *The Concise Encyclopaedia of Islam* Rev. London: Stavey International, 2001.

Goedegebuure, Jaap. *Nederlandse schrijvers en religie 1960–2010.* 's-Gravenhage: Vantilt, 2010.

Goldman, Shalom. *The Wiles of Women. The Wiles of Men. Joseph and Potifar's Wife in Ancient Near Eastern Jewish and Islamic Folklore.* Albany: State University of New York Press, 1995.

Golziher, Ignaz. *Vorlesungen über den Islam* (Wissenschaftlichen Buchgesellschaft). Darmstad. Mit Genehmigung des Univeritätsverlages Carl Winter (Heidelberg), herausgegebene Sonderausgabe. Unveränderte fotomechanischer Nachdruck, 1963.

Grosheide, Frederik Willem ed. *Bijbelse Encyclopaedie.* Kampen: Kok, 1950.

Grosz, Markus, and Karl-Heinz Ohlig, eds. *Schlaglichter: Die beiden ersten islamischen Jahrhunderte.* Berlin: Hans Schiler, 2008.

———, and ———, eds. *Vom Koran zum Islam.* Berlin: Hans Schiler, 2009.

Guillaume, Alfred. *The Life of Muhammad: A Translation of Ishâq's Sîrat Rasûl Allâh.* Lahore: Oxford University Press, 1955/1967. Reprint.

Haenchen, Ernst. *Die Apostelgeschichte.* Göttingen: Vandenhoeck and Ruprecht, 1965.

Hamblin, William J., and David Rolph Seely. *De tempel van Salomo: Mythe en geschiedenis.* Haarlem: Altamira Becht, 2007.

Hammarskjöld, Dag. *Markings.* London: Faber and Faber, 1997.

Hartwig, Dirk, et al. *"Im vollen Licht der Geschichte": Die Wissenschaft des Judentums und die Anfänge der kritischen Koranforschung.* Würzburg: Ergon, 2008.

Hayek, Michel. *Le Mystère d'Ismaël.* Paris: Mame, 1964.

Hekster, Oliver, and Corjo Jansen, eds. *Constantijn de Grote: Traditie en verandering.* Nijmegen: Vantilt, 2012.

Herodotus. *The Histories.* Translated by Aubrey de Sélincourt. Penguin Classics. Harmondsworth, etc.: Penguin Books, 1954.

Heyde, Henning. *Kain, der erste Jahwe-Verehrer. Die ursprüngliche Bedeutung der Sage vom Kain und ihre Auswirkung.* Stuttgart: Calwer, 1965.

Heym, Stephan. *The King David Report.* Evanston: Northwestern University Press, 1998.

Homer. *The Odyssey.* Translated by E.V. Rieu. Harmondsworth, etc.: Penguin, 1946.

Horsley, Richard A. *Jesus and Empire: The Kingdom of God and the New World Disorder.* Minneapolis: Fortress, 2003.

———. *Paul and Politics: Ekklesia, Israel, Imperium, Interpretation.* Harrisburg, Pennsylvania: Trinity Press International, 2000.

Hossfeld, Frank-Lothar, and Eric Zenger. *Die Psalmen: Psalm 1–50, Die Neue Echter Bibel, Kommentar zum Alten Testament.* Würzburg: Echter, 1993.

———, and ———. *Psalmen 51–100, Herders Theologischer Kommentar zum Alten Testament.* Freiburg: Herder, 2007.

———, and ———. *Psalms 3: A Commentary on Psalms 101–150.* Minneapolis: Fortress, 2011.

Houtepen, Anton. *Geloven in gerechtigheid: Bijdragen tot een oecumenische sociale ethiek.* Zoetermeer: Meinema, 2005.
Howard-Brook, Wes. *"Come Out, My People!" God's Call out of Empire in the Bible and Beyond.* Maryknoll, New York: Orbis Books, 2010.
———, and Anthony Gwyther. *Unveiling Empire: Reading Revelation Then and Now.* Maryknoll, New York: Orbis Books, 1999.
Hutgren, Arland J. *Paul's Letter to the Romans. A Commentary.* Grand Rapids: Eerdmans, 2011.
Ibn Hazm. *De ring van de duif: Een Moorse verhandeling over minnaars en liefde.* Introduced and translated by Remke Kruk and Jan Just Witkam. Amsterdam: Bulaaq, 2008.
Ibn Warraq, ed. *The Origins of the Koran. Classic Essays on Islam's Holy Book.* Amherst, New York: Prometheus Books, 1998.
Isaac, Jules. *L'enseignement du mépris.* Paris: Fasquelle, 1962.
Izutsu, Toshikiko. *Ethico-Religious Concepts in the Qur'ân.* Montreal: McGill University Press, 1966.
———. *God and Man in the Koran: Semantics of the Koranic Weltanschauung.* Tokyo: The Keio Institute of Cultural and Linguistic Studies, 1964.
Jeffery, Arthur. *The Foreign Vocabulary of the Quran.* Baroda: Oriental Institute, 1938.
Jenni, Ernst, and Claus Westermann. *Theologisches Handwörterbuch zum Alten Testament.* Parts I and II. Munich: Chr. Kaiser/Zurich: Theologischer Verlag, 1984.
Jestice, Phyllis G. *Encyclopedia of Irish Spirituality.* Santa Barbara: ABC-Clio, 2000.
Jewett, Robert. *Romans. A Commentary.* Minneapolis: Fortress, 2007.
Johns, Anthony H. "Joseph in the Qurân: Dramatic Dialogue, Human Emotion and Prophetics Wisdom." In: *Islamo Christiana* 7 (1981) 22–55.
Keilson, Hans. *Liever Holland dan heimwee. Gedachten en herinneringen.* Amsterdam: Van Gennep, 2012.
Kemp, Barry. *The City of Ekhnaten and Nefertiti: Amnarna and Its People.* London: Thames and Hudson, 2012.
Ketterij, Cornelis van de. *De weg in woorden: Een systematische beschrijving van piëtistisch woordgebruik na 1900.* Dissertation VU University. Assen: Van Gorcum, 1972.
Khalidi, Tarif. *The Qur'an. A New Translation.* London: Penguin Classics, 2008.
Al-Kisâ'î, Muhammad ibn 'Abd Allâh. *Tales of the Prophets (Qisâs al-anbiyâ').* Chicago: Kazi Publications, 1997.
Kittel, Gerhard, ed. *Theologisches Wörterbuch zum Neuen Testament* (In Verbindung mit zahlreichen Fachgenossen hrsg. und forgesetzt von Gerh. Friedrich). Stuttgart: Kohlhammer, 1950.
Koehler, Ludwig, and Walter Baumgärtner, eds. *Lexicon Veteris Testamenti Libros.* Leiden: E.J. Brill, 1953.
Koenen, Mieke. *Dwars tegen de keer: Leven en werk van Ida Gerhardt.* Amsterdam: Athenaeum-Polak and Van Gennep, 2014.
Koningsveld, Sjoerd van. *Revisionisme en Moderne islamitische Theologie.* Leiden: Leiden University, 2009. https://openaccess.leidenuniv.nl/bitstream/handle/1887/19713/afscheidsrede%20Van%20Koningsveld.pdf?sequence=2.
Kraemer, Joel L. *Maimonides: The Life and World of One of Civilization's Greatest Minds.* New York etc.: Doubleday, 2008.
Kramers, Johannes Hendrik. *De taal van den Koran.* Leiden: Brill, 1940.

Krantz, Reinhard G., and Herman Spieckermann. *Zeit und Ewigkeit als Raum göttlichen Handelns: Religionsgeschichtliche, theologische und philosophische Perspektiven.* Berlin: De Gruyter, 2009.

Leaman, Oliver, ed. *The Quran: An Encyplopedia.* London: Routledge, 2006.

Leene, Henk. *Newness in Old Testament Prophecy. An Intertextual Study.* Leiden: Brill, 2014.

Levenson, Jon D. *Sinai and Zion: An Entry Into the Jewish Bible.* San Francisco: Harper Collings Publishers, 1985.

Liedboek, Zingen en bidden in huis en kerk. Zoetermeer: BV Liedboek, 2013.

Livy. *From the Founding of the City.* Translated by Rev. Canon Roberts. https://en.wikisource.org/wiki/From_the_Founding_of_the_City/Book_2.

Lüling, Günter. *Über den Urkoran: Ansätze zur Rekonstruktion der vorislamisch-christlichen Strophenlieder im Koran.* Erlangen: Lüling 2004. Reprint.

Lundbom, Jack R. *Deuteronomium. A Commentary.* Grand Rapids: Eerdmans, 2013.

Luxenberg, Christoph. *Die Syro-Aramäische Lesart des Koran. Ein Beitrag zur Entschlüselung der Koransprache.* Berlin: Hans Schiler, 2004. Reprint.

Maimonides, Moses. *The Guide of the Perplexed.* New York: Dover Publications, 1956.

Massignon, Louis. *L'hospitalité Sacrée.* Unpublished text presented by Jacques Keryell. Preface by René Voillaume. Paris: Nouvelle cité, 1987.

Mann, Thomas. *Joseph und seine Brüder* (I *Die Geschichten Jakobs* [Berlin: S. Fischer, 1933]; II *Der junge Joseph* [Berlin: S. Fischer Verlag, 1934]; III *Joseph in Ägypten* [Vienna: Berman-Fischer, 1936]; IV *Joseph der Ernährer* [Stockholm: Bermann-Fischer, 1943]).

———. *The Theme of the Joseph Novels.* Washington: [n. p.], 1942. http://babel.hathitrust.org/cgi/pt?id=uc1.b3442043;view=1up;seq=25

Mayer, Klaus. *De Gott der Väter: Die Chagalll-Fenster zu St. Stephan in Mainz.* Band I. Würzburg: Echter, 1999.

Mawdûdî, Abul A'lâ. *Towards Understanding the Qur' ân: Abridged Version of Tafhîm al-Qurân.* Translated and edited by Zafar Ishaq Ansari. Leicester: The Islamic Foundations, 2007.

McAuliffe, Jane Dammen. *The Cambridge Companion to the Qur' ân.* Cambridge: Cambridge University Press, 2006.

———, ed. *Encyclopaedia of the Qur'ân.* Leiden: Brill, 2001–2006.

Meuzelaar, Johannes Jacobus. *Der Leib des Messias: Einer Exegetischer Studie über den Gedanken vom Leib Christi in den Paulusbriefen.* Kampen: Kok, 1979. Xerox copy of the 1961 edition.

Miskotte, Kornelis Heiko. *Bijbels ABC.* Baarn: Ten Have, 1992.

Moor Westermann, Eric M., and Wilfried Uitterhoeve. *Van Achilles tot Zeus: Thema's uit de klassieke literatuur, muziek, beeldende kunst en theater.* Nijmegen: SUN, 1987.

Mulder, Eildert, and Thomas Milo. *De omstreden bronnen van de Islam.* Zoetermeer: Meinema, 2009.

Naastepad, Thomas Johannes Marie. *Geen vrede met het bestaande. Uitleg van het boek Openbaring.* Baarn: Ten Have, 1999.

Nagel, Tilman. *Der Koran und sein religiöses und kulturelles Umfeld.* Munich: Oldenbourg, 2010.

Neuwirth, Angelika. *Der Koran als Text der Spätantike: Ein europäischer Zugang.* Berlin: Verlag der Weltreligionen im Insel, 2010.

———. *De Koran*. Band I: *Frühmekkanische Suren*. Berlin: Verlag der Weltreligionen, 2011.

———, et al. *The Qurân in Context: Historical and Literary Investigations into the Qurânic Milieu*. Leiden: Brill, 2010.

———. *Scripture, Poetry and the Making of a Community: Reading the Qur'an as a Literary Text*. London: Oxford University Press, 2014.

———. "The Spiritual Meaning of Jerusalem in Islam." In *City of the Great King: Jerusalem from David to the Present*, edited by Nitza Rosovsky, 93–116. Cambridge MA: Havard University Press, 1996.

———. "Structural, Linguistic and Literary Features." In McAuliffe, Jane Dammen, ed. *Encyclopaedia of the Qur'ân*, 97–113. Leiden: Brill, 2001–2006.

Newby, Gordon Darnell. *A History of the Jews of Arabia: From Ancient Times to Their Eclipse under Islam*. South Carolina: South Carolina Press, 2009.

———. *Making of the Last Prophet: A Reconstruction of the Earliest Biography of Muhammad*. Columbia: University of South Carolina Press, 1989.

Nieuwenhuis, Jan. *Johannes de ziener: Het Evangelie, de brieven en de openbaring*. Kampen: Kok, 2004.

Noegel, Scott B., and Brannon M. Wheeler. *The A to Z of Prophets in Islam and Judaism*. Lanham: Scarecrow, 2010.

Ohlig, Karl-Heinz, and Gerd-Rüdiger Puin, eds. *Die dunklen Anfänge: Neue Forschungen zur Enstehung und frühen Geschichte des Islam*. Berlin: Hans Schiler, 2005.

Olson, Dennis T. *Numbers*. Louisville, Kentucky: University of Chicago Press, 1996.

Oosterhuis, Huub. *In het voorbijgaan*. Bilthoven: Amboboeken, 1968.

———, and Alex van Heusden. *Het evangelie van Lukas. Vertaald en van aantekeningen voorzien*. Vught: Skandalon, 2007.

Oussoren, Pieter, and Renate Dekker. *Buiten de vesting: Een woord-voor-woord vertaling van alle deuterocanonieke en vele apocriefe Bijbelboeken*. Vught: Skandalon and Plantin, 2009. Reprint.

Ovid. *Metamorphoses*. Translated by and with an introduction by Mary M. Innes. Harmondsworth, etc.: Penguin, 1961.

Paret, Rudi. *Der Koran. Kommentar und Konkordanz*. Stuttgart: Kohlhammer, 1971.

———. *Der Koran. Übersetzung*. Stuttgart: W. Kohlhammer, 1962.

———. *Mohammed und der Koran*. Stuttgart: Kohlhammer, 1957.

Pascal, Blaise. *Pensées*. Translated by A.J. Krailsheimer. London, etc.: Penguin, 1966. Amsterdam: Boom, 1997.

Paumgartner, Bernard. *Mozart*. Utrecht: Spectrum [n.y.].

Planhol, Xavier de. "Le désert, cadre géographique de l'expérience religieuse." In: *Les Mystiques du désert dans l' islam, le judaïsme, et le christianisme*. Papers delivered at a conference of the Association des Amis de Sénanque, 28 July–3 August 1974.

———. *Minorités en islam: Géographie, politique et sociale*. Paris: Flammarion, 1997.

———. *Les nations du Prophète: Manuel géographique de politique musulmane*. Paris: Fayard, 1993.

Pietersma, Albert, and Benjamin G. Wright, eds. *A New English Translation of the Septuaginta*. New York: Oxford University Press, 2007.

Radscheit, Matthias. *Die koranische Herausforderung. Die tahaddî-Verse im Rahmen der Polemikpassagen des Korans*. Berlin: Klaus, 1996.

Reicke, Bo, and Leonhard Rost. *Bijbels historisch woordenboek*, Parts I–VI. Utrecht: Het Spectrum, 1970.

Reinink, Gerrit Jan. "Ps.—Methodius: A Concept of History in Response to the Rise of Islam," In *The Byzantine and Early Islamic Near East*, edited by Averil Cameron and Lawrence I. Conrad, 149–87. Princeton, New Jersey: Darwin, 1992.

Rippin, Andrew, ed. *The Blackwell Companion to the Qur' ân*. Oxford: Blackwell Publishing, 2006.

Romein, Jan, and Annie Romein. *Erflaters van onze beschaving: Nederlandse gestalten uit zes eeuwen*. The Hague: Querido's, 1971. Reprint.

Rosenberg, Alfred. *Der Mythus des 20. Jahrhunderts: Eine Wertung der seelischgeistigen Gestaltenkämfe unserer Zeit*. Munich: Hoheneichen, 1930.

Sacks, Jonathan. *Covenant and Conversation: A Weekly Reading of the Jewish Bible*. Jerusalem: Maggid Book and The Orthodox Union, 2010.

Sarris, Peter. *Empires of Faith*. 1. Oxford: Oxford University Press, 2011.

Schama, Simon. *De ogen van Rembrandt*. Amsterdam: Contact, 1999.

———. *The Story of the Jews. Finding the Words 1000 BCE—1492*. London: The Bodley Head, 2013.

Schleiermacher, Friedrich. *Over de religie: Betogen voor de ontwikkelden onder haar verachters*. Amsterdam: Boom, 2007.

Schmitz, Bertram. *Der Koran: Sure 2 'Die Kuh'. Ein religionshistorischer Kommentar*. Stuttgart: Kohlhammer, 2009.

Schuman, Nicholas Abraham. *Gelijk om gelijk: Verslag en balans van een discussie over goddelijke vergelding in het Oude Testament*. Amsterdam: VU Uitgeverij, 1993.

Serafin, Steven R., ed. *The Continuum Encyclopedia of American Literature*. New York: Continuum, 2003.

Shapiro, Israel. *Die haggadischen Elemente im erzählenden Teil des Korans*. Berlin: Gesellschaft zur Förderung der Wissenschaft des Judentums, 1907.

Speyer, Heinrich. *Die biblischen Erzählungen im Qoran*. Darmstadt: WBG, 1962.

Spijkerboer, Anne Marijke. *Rembrandts engel*. Vught: Skandalon, 2006.

Stählin, Gustav. *Die Apostelgeschichte*. Göttingen: Van den Hoeck and Ruprecht, 1968.

Stanley, Christopher D. *The Colonized Apostle: Paul Through Postcolonial Eyes*. Minneapolis: Fortress, 2011.

Steiner, George. *Real Presences*. London: Faber and Faber, 1989.

Sterman Sabbath, Roberta, ed. *Sacred Tropes: Tanakh, New Testament and Qur'an as Literature and Culture*. Leiden: Brill, 2009.

Stillman, Norman. *The Jews of Arab Lands: A History and Source Book*. Philadelphia: The Jewish Publication Society of America, 1979.

Strack, Hermann Leberecht, and Paul Billerbeck. *Kommentar zum Neuen Testament aus Talmud und Midrasch*. Vol. 2. Munich: Beck, 2014.

Stroumsa, Sarah. *Maimonides in His World. Portrait of a Mediterranean Thinker*. Princeton, Oxford: Princeton University Press, 2009.

Sweeney, Marvin A. *The Twelve Prophets*. Vols. 1 and 2. *Berit Olam: Studies in Hebrew Narrative and Poetry*. Edited by David W. Coter. Collegeville, Minnesota: The Liturgical Press, 2000.

Tümpel, Christian, et al. *Rembrandt en de Bijbel: Alle etsen*. Zwolle: Waanders Uitgevers/ Amsterdam: Bijbels Museum, 2006.

Visser 't Hooft, Willem Adolp. *Rembrandts weg tot het Evangelie*. Amsterdam: W. ten Have, 1956.

Voolen, Edward, et al. *De 'Joodse' Rembrandt. De mythe ontrafeld*. Zwolle: Waanders, 2007. In cooperation with Amsterdam: Joods Historisch Museum.

Waaijman, Kees. *De profeet Elia*. Nijmegen: B. Gottmer, 1985.
Wansbrough, J. *Quranic Studies. Sources and Methods of Scriptural Interpretation*. Oxford: Oxford University Press, 1977.
Watt, William Montgomery. *Companion to the Qur'ān*. London: George Allen and Unwin Ltd., 1967.
———. *Muhammad at Medina*. Oxford: Clarendon Press, 1953.
Wehr, Hans. *A Dictionary of Modern Written Arabic*. Wiesbaden: Otto Harrassowitz, 1961.
Weitzman, Solomo. *The Lure of Wisdom*. New Haven: Yale University Press, 2011.
Welch, Alford T. "Formulaic Features of the Punishment Stories." In *Literary Structures of Religious Meaning in the Qur'an*, edited by Issa Boullata, 77–116. Richmond, Surrey: Curzon, 2000.
Wessels, Anton. *Europe: Was it Ever Really Christian?* London: SCM Press, 1994.
———. *Islam in Stories*. Peeters Leuven, Paris Dudley, MA 2002.
———. *Islam verhalenderwijs*. Amsterdam: Nieuwezijds, 2002. Reprint.
———. *De moslimse naaste*. Kampen: Kok, 1978.
———. *The Torah, the Gospel, and the Qur'an. Three Books, Two Cities, One Tale*. Grand Rapids: Eerdmans, 2013.
Westermann, Claus. *Genesis 1–11*. Neukirchen-Vluyn: Neukirchener Verlag Der Erziehungsvereins, 1976. Reprint.
———. *Genesis 3. Teilband (Genesis 37–50)*. Neukirchen-Vluyn: Neukirchener, 1982.
———. *Genesis 12–36: A Continental Commentary*. Minneapolis: Fortress, 1995.
———. *Gottes Engel brauchen keine Flügel*. Munich: Siebenstern, 1957.
Wheeler, Brannon M. *Mecca and Eden. Ritual, Relic, and Territory in Islam*. Chicago: The University of Chicago Press, 2006.
———. *Moses in the Quran and Islamic Exegesis*. London: Routledge, 2002.
———. *Prophets in the Quran: An Introduction to the Quran and Muslim Exegesis*. London: Continuum, 2002.
Wimmer, Stefan Jakob, and Stephan Leimgruber. *Von Adam bis Muhammad: Bibel und Koran im Vergleich*. Stuttgart: Katholisches Bibelwerk, 2007. Reprint.
Wright, Nicholas Thomas. *Jesus and the Victory of God*. London: SPCK, 1996.
Wullschlager, Jackie. *Chagall: A Biography*. New York: Alfred A. Knop, 2008.
Xenophon. *Memorabilia*. Translated by Amy Bonnette with an Introduction by Christopher Bruell. Ithaca: Cornell University Press, The Agora Editions, 1994.
Zakovitch, Yair. *"And You shall tell your son . . . ": The Concept of the Exodus in the Bible*. Jerusalem: The Magnes Press/The Hebrew University, 1991.
Zenger, Erich. *Das Erste Testament: Die jüdische Bibel und die Christen*. Kevelaer: Topos Taschenbücher, 2011.
———. *Psalmen: Auslegung in zwei Bänden*. Band I: *Mit meinem Gott überspringe ich Mauern*. Band II: *Ich will die Morgenröte wecken*. Freiburg: Herder, 2011.
———. *Stuttgarter Psalter: Mit Einleitungen und Kurzkommentaren*. Stuttgart: Katholisches Bibelwerk, 1980.
Zuurmond, Rochus. *God noch gebod: Bijbels-theologische notities over de brief van Paulus aan de Galaten*. Baarn: Ten Have, 1990.
———. *Niet te geloven: Apostolische geloofsbelijdenis en Bijbel*. Vught: Skandalon, 2010.

Subject Index

Aaron, 18–19, 31, 44, 87, 108, 153, 186, 188, 190, 192–93. *See* Härûn.
'Abdallah, father of the prophet Muhammad, 15
Abel, 83, 148, 183–85, 189. *See* Hâbil.
Abimelech, 160
Abraham, xi, 1–2, 10–12, 23, 26, 29–30, 35, 43, 47–49, 51–53, 55, 57, 58–71, 73–75, 86, 88, 93–96, 104, 108, 123–27, 130–31, 133, 140, 142, 147, 151–53, 158–64, 173, 186–87, 195, 211, 213. *See* Ibrâhîm.
Adam, 17n17, 99, 152, 158, 183, 186, 191
Abu Bakr, first caliph, 55, 96, 141
Abu Bakr al-Baghdâdî, 112
Achaemenid Empire, 19
Aesculius, 200
Ahab, 29, 36. *See* Jezebel, Elijah.
Ahasueros, 190. *See* Xerxes.
Akiba, rabbi, 94
Alexander the Great, 80, 109, 117
Alexandria, 5, 72, 80, 166
Al-Hamra, Alhambra, 92
Allah, 14–16, 23, 45
alms, 58, 110, 195. *See* zakât.
Ammonites, 64, 153. *See* Lot, Lût.
Antioch, 5, 171–72
anti-Semitism, 2, 11, 129
Apocalypse, apocalyptic, 39, 46, 109, 200, 205, 207. *See* revelation.

Aqaba, Gulf, 165, 186
Araba Deserta, 93
Arabia, 9–10, 93–97, 103–4, 163, 166–67
Arabia Felix, 93
Arab Peninsula, 93, 101, 163, 185
Aramean, 23n43, 75
ark of Noah, 24, 94
arrogant, arrogance, 45, 71, 73, 87, 103, 159, 169, 189–92, 194, 205
Asclepius Soter, 200
Asia (Minor), ix, 91, 171, 199, 200, 202, 206
Asshur, 77, 79–82, 84–85, 123
Assyria, Assyrians, 47, 79, 84–85, 87
Asterix and Obelix, 113
asylum, 1, 56
atheism, atheist, 107, 111

Baal, 29–31, 33, 35–37, 188
Baalbek, 33, 37
Babel, 61, 91, 106, 123, 190–91. *See* Babylon.
Babylon, 20, 38–40, 44, 70, 77, 86–90, 96, 102–3, 106, 132, 186, 200–203. *See* Babel.
Badr, Battle of, 152n76, 152–54
Baghdad, 12
Baghdâdî, Abu Bakr al-, 112
bahr, 24. *See* sea, *yamm*.
Balaam, 64, 184–85, 188–89, 195–99, 201–2, 206, 209
balad, 174, 175. *See* city.

SUBJECT INDEX

Barnabas, 49. *See* Paul.
bashîr, 188n20. *See* 'Good News', Gospel.
Beast, 198, 204–7
Beersheba, 158, 160, 162–63
Benjamin, 131, 136, 142–45, 149–50
blessing, 25, 28–29, 85, 112, 125n70, 144, 147, 161, 164
bushrâ, 62, 63, 77n2, 81, 98, 79, 101n95, 103, 133n15, 195n94. *See* Gospel.
Byzantium, Byzantine, 10, 77, 96–97, 190. *See* Rûm.
Byzantine Empire, 96

Caesar, xi, 97, 111–20, 130, 190, 200, 202–3, 206
Cain, 148, 158, 180, 183–85, 187, 189. *See* Abel.
Caligula, Emperor, 200
caliph, caliphate, 3, 94, 96, 108–9, 112–13, 151
camel, 10, 38–39, 47, 61, 155
Canaan, Canaanites, 47, 64, 74, 135, 137, 139, 145, 157
Cappadocia, 91
caravan(s), 9, 95, 145, 153
Chagall, Marc, 61, 134n22
church and state, xi, 113, 116, 119
circumambulation, 164. *See tawâf*.
city, xi, 5, 9, 19, 24, 29–30, 39, 41, 48, 56, 61, 64–66, 68–73, 75, 79, 82, 90, 94–97, 103, 114–15, 117, 125, 132, 138, 143, 147–49, 151–53, 155–61, 163, 165–67, 169, 171–77, 179–80, 185, 188–90, 192, 200, 201–3, 206, 209–10. *See balad*.
city gate, 65
city, holy, 9, 90
City, promised, xi, 188, 209–10
Claudius, Emperor, 57, 200
Claudius Lysias, 6
community, ix, 8, 10–11, 24, 57, 59, 75, 80, 85, 88, 91, 100, 114, 124–27, 130, 151, 164, 173, 180–82, 186, 193, 199–203, 205–7. *See qahal, ecclesia, umma*.

Creator, creation, creature, 5, 17–18, 20–21, 24, 31, 33, 40, 58, 66, 69–70, 90, 92–93, 95, 99, 108–9, 123, 142, 150, 168–71, 174, 176, 192, 205
Croesus, 194. *See* Qârûn.
Cyrus, the Great, King of Persia, 19, 39. *See* Kores.

Dan, city of, 48
darkness, 5, 17, 24, 44, 65, 70, 176. *See* light.
David, King, 27, 41, 65, 105–6, 140, 151, 209. *See* Dâwûd.
Dâwûd, 27
Dedan, Dedanites, 95–96
desert, xi, 2, 4, 8, 24–26, 29, 35, 48, 56–58, 60, 64, 68, 88, 90, 93–95, 115, 121, 142, 157–63, 165–67, 169, 171, 173–75, 177, 179, 181, 183–85, 187–88, 195, 199, 207–8. *See* wilderness.
deus absconditus, 19
deus otiosus, 69
Dhu al-Kilf 186
Dhû Nuwâs, 9, 166
dîn, 110, 112–13, 122–23, 125–27
dîn Allah, 123
dîn wa dawla, religion and state, 112–13
Dome of the Rock, 3
donkey, 38–42, 47, 159, 196–99
dragon, 20, 205, 207
dream(s), 26, 42–43, 59, 129–30, 134–35, 137–38, 140–42, 147, 149–52, 154–56, 205. *See* Joseph.
Dumah, 48n4, 101–2

earth, 16–17, 23–27, 29, 34, 41, 46, 58–59, 69, 75, 78–79, 84–85, 88–89, 107, 109–11, 121, 123, 126, 134, 136, 140, 142, 150, 156, 163, 168, 171–72, 176, 178–79, 184, 188, 192, 194–95, 198–99, 201, 203, 205–7, 209
ecclesia, 8, 12, 57, 72, 199, 206
Ecclesiastes, 72

Edom, Edomites, 54, 96, 101n96, 162, 165, 187. See Idumea, Seir.
Egypt, 6, 18, 23–24, 26, 36, 40, 44, 53–54, 58, 64, 66, 68–70, 73–75, 77, 79–91, 94–96, 109, 120, 123, 128, 130–32, 134–39, 142–47, 149–52, 156–59, 161–62, 169, 185–92, 201, 209
Elijah, the prophet, 29–37, 73, 96, 110. See Ilyâs.
Elisha, 37, See al-Yasa'.
emigrant(s), 69, 94, 153, 179. See muhâjir, hijra.
empire, 39, 132, 202–3
empire of justice and love, 121
Ethiopia(n), 9, 25n50, 95, 97, 166, 168–69
Exodus, 58, 64, 68–70, 81, 86–91, 95–96, 96n62, 134, 138, 152–53, 157, 162–63, 188, 190, 209. See hijra.

faith, faithful, faithfulness, 6, 9, 12, 15, 29–31, 45–46, 69, 75, 87, 109–10, 112, 123–24, 156, 176, 187, 191–92, 198, 202–3, 206–7. See dîn.
Farewell Pilgrimage, 121–23
fath, 147, 152n73
"father of all believers", 1, 11, 47, 86, 104. See Abraham, Ibrâhîm.
fâtir, 95. See Creator.
Flavius Josephus, 115, 169
flood, 173. See Noah.
fool, foolish, foolishness, 20, 106, 108, 111, 121, 145, 149, 170, 197
foreigners, 53, 66, 77, 85
furqân, 153

The Gallic Wars, 113. See France.
garden, 26, 45–46, 64, 103, 169–71, 178–79, 197. See parable.
gehenna, 204, See jahannam, hell.
Gentiles, 6, 8, 118
Gerasa, 114
ger, 73. See stranger, Gershom.
Gershom, 73, 187. See ger.
Gethsemane, 155

Ghassanids, 96
ghayb, 21, See hidden.
Ghazâlî, Abû Hamîd, al, 26–27
Gibeah, 56
Golden Calf, 19, 108, 188
Gomorrah, 62, 64, 67–73, 96, 152. See Sodom.
Good News, xi, 2, 4, 11, 41, 77, 98, 101–3, 138, 145, 155, 173, 188n20. See Gospel, bashîr.
Gospel, 2, 4, 8, 11–12, 72, 99, 101, 103, 114, 119, 128, 153, 177. See Injîl.
Granada, 92. See Hamra.
greed, greedy, 170, 205, 208n79, 209
guide, guidance, 5, 7–8, 21, 24, 26, 44, 57, 92, 98, 100, 133, 164, 168, 171, 182, 210. See Torah, Tawra.
Guide for the Perplexed, 92. See Maimonides.

Hâbil, 183. See Abel.
hadîth, 3, 190. See tradition.
Hagar, the mother of Ishmael, 43, 158–63. See Ishmael.
haggada, 31, 141, 144, 190
hajj, 97n68, 121n48, 162, 189. See pilgrimage.
Ham, 95
Haman, 190–91, 194
Hammarskjöld, Dag, 13
al-Hamra (Alhambra), 92
Hanukkah, 117
Hârûn, 31. See Aaron.
Hârûn al-Rashîd, 97n70
heal(ing) health, 49, 79, 82–84, 100, 114, 145, 178, 182, 200
Hebron, 1, 61, 74, 175. See Kiriath Arba.
Heliopolis, 138
hell, 95, 173, 179, 204. See gehenna, jahannam.
Hellenistic, Hellenism, 24, 72, 129, 162
Heraclius, 97
Hermes, 49, 50. See Mercury, Pau.
Herod, King, 6, 25, 111, 115, 130, 162, 184

SUBJECT INDEX

Herodians, 111, 114–16
Herodotus, historian, 39, 194
hidden, hiddenness, xi, 19, 20–22, 24, 27–28, 46, 99, 120, 129, 137–38, 146, 150, 191, 202
Hijâz, 96, 124, 162, 175, 187
hijra, 7, 68, 69, 96, 151n69, 152n74, 153. *See* nightly journey.
Hitler, 4, 117, 128
holy book(s), 95, 201n63. *See mishaf.*
holy city, 9, 90
holy dwelling, 16
holy ground, 35
holy land, 58, 69, 88, 152. *See* promised land.
holy olive tree, 26
Holy One, 34, 198n55
holy scripture, 22, 78
Holy Spirit, 91, 92, 146
holy task, 139
holy temple, 17
holy texts, 77
holy valley, 25, 123. *See* Tuwâ, Moses.
holy war(s), 12, 117
Horeb, 29, 34, 108
horse(s), 37–41, 105, 163, 170
Hosea, prophet, 201
hospitality, xi, 1, 47–50, 55–58, 63–67, 71, 95, 175
host(s), hosting, 29n63, 43, 54, 56–58, 156, 198n55
hostage, 106
hostile, hostility, x, 48, 63, 70, 87, 89, 158, 165, 195
Hûd, Arab prophet, 68, 94, 186, 193. *See* 'Âdites.
Hugo the Great, 59
humankind, 1, 10, 34, 52, 99, 108–9, 158, 173–74, 176, 183–85, 187–89, 191, 193, 195, 197, 199, 201, 203, 205, 207, 209–10
hypocrisy, hypocritical, hypocrites, 77, 95 , 108 , 115, 143, 197. *See al-munâfiqûn.*

ibn al-sabîl, 54
Ibn Saʿd, biographer of the prophet Muhammad, 151

Ibrâhîm, 2, 63, 126, 164. *See* Abraham.
Iconium, 49. *See* Konya.
idol(s), idolater, idolatry, 7, 20, 33, 37, 39, 41, 53, 82, 89, 95–96, 107–9, 120, 126, 163, 172, 188, 196, 201–4, 206
Idumea(ns), 101n96, 162, 163. *See* Edom.
ʿ*ilm*, 99
ʿ*ilm al-kalâm*, 22
Injil, xi, 4, 8, 27, 96, 101, 127, 141, 153, 174, 176. *See* Gospel, New Testament.
ʿÎsâ, 5. *See* Jesus.
Isaac, 10, 23, 28, 30, 35, 48, 63, 74–75, 125, 131, 140, 147, 158, 160, 187. *See* Ishâq.
Isaiah, the prophet, 19, 20, 37–40, 44, 77–80, 82, 84, 87, 89n34, 95, 101–3, 201, 203
Ishâq, 2, 160n11. *See* Isaac.
Ishmael, 10, 43, 46, 48, 60, 94, 101, 125, 147, 158–64, 166, 187
Islamic art, 38
Islamic State, 106, 112

Jacob, 10, 23, 28, 35, 42–43, 48, 59–60, 63, 70, 74–75, 81, 86–87, 89–90, 125, 130–31, 133–35, 137, 140, 142–43, 144–47, 160, 165. *See* Yaʿqûb.
jahannam, 95, 204. *See gehenna*, hell.
Jeremiah, the prophet, 18n21, 35n83, 36, 95, 132n12, 186n10
Jerusalem, 3, 6, 19, 25, 38, 41–42, 52, 54, 72, 87–90, 92, 94, 96–97, 102, 114–15, 117, 119, 139, 152–53, 161, 165, 193, 201–4
Jesus, 2, 3, 5–10, 12, 14–15, 17, 22, 24, 26, 33, 35, 37–38, 41–42, 52, 55–57, 65, 73–74, 85–86, 90, 93, 95–96, 100, 103, 110–21, 129–30, 133, 147, 153, 155, 172, 174, 177, 192, 202–3, 208. *See* ʿÎsâ.
Jesus Sirach, 72
Jethro, 68, 124, 165, 185–86. *See* Shuʿayb.

SUBJECT INDEX

Jewish tradition, 52, 65, 70, 107
Jezebel, 29, 36. *See* Ahab.
Job, 48n5, 55, 56, 74, 186, 186n13.
John, (Apocalypse), 17, 199–200, 205–6
John the Baptist, 31, 44, 103, 110, 114, 129, 153, 184. *See* Yahyâ.
John the Evangelist, 42, 92, 119, 172
(Trans) Jordan, 64, 69, 87, 114, 185
Joseph, 6, 25, 43–44, 54, 81, 100, 109, 114–15, 128–54, 156, 169. *See* Yûsuf.
Jubilee, year of, 23
Jubilees, Book of, 163
Judah Maccabee, 117–18, 121
Judah, person and tribe, state, 79–80, 85–87, 90, 103, 132, 136, 144–45, 147, 150, 162, 185, 199, 204
Judaism (Rabbini), 9, 11, 12, 91–93, 127, 129, 131, 157–58, 166, 196
Judas, 116, 155
judgment, 24, 32, 65, 84, 96, 101n96, 107–8, 165, 168, 179n82, 201, 203, 207
judgment, hour of last, day of, 58, 110, 170, 173, 177–78, 205
Julius Ceasar, 113
Jupiter, 50–51. *See* Zeus.

Ka'ba, 9, 10, 24. *See* Mecca.
Kaysar, 96–97. *See* Byzantine.
Kenites, 185–87
Ketura, 95, 186. *See* Abraham.
Kiriath Arba, 175. *See* Hebron.
Kisrâ, king of the Persians, 96–97, 190
Konya, 49
Korah, 184, 189–91, 193–95, 209. *See* Qârûn.
Kores, 39. *See* Cyrus.

lamb, 61, 160n10, 207
law(s), 2, 4–8, 28n60, 40, 44–45, 48, 52–53, 65, 71, 85, 89–91, 105, 115, 118, 125, 164, 174, 187, 208
Levite, 18
Libya, 91, 189n22. *See* Cyrene.

light, 4, 5n11, 17, 25–27, 55, 110n24, 117, 149. *See* darkness.
lisân, 98n78, 99, 191. *See* tongue.
Lot, 47–48, 52, 55–57, 62, 64–73, 88, 96, 152–53, 167, 173, 186–87, 191, 193, 195. *See* Lût, Abraham.
Lourdes, 200
Lukmân, 192
Lût, 71, 152–53. *See* Lot.
Lystra, 49, 171

Maghreb, 92. *See* Morocco.
Maimonides, 92–93, 141n34
Mammon, 89, 204–5
manna, 57, 202, 207–8
Marib Dam, 24
Martin Luther, Reformer, xi, 2, 19
martyr(s), 9, 26, 167, 206
Masîh, 7, 181. *See* Messiah.
Mecca, Meccans, 10, 15, 20, 32, 46, 54–55, 68–69, 88, 94, 96–97, 103–4, 121, 124–25, 147, 151–56, 158–59, 161–64, 166, 172–75, 179, 189
Medina, 7, 9, 55, 94–96, 104, 125, 151–53, 155, 176, 179, 195
Menasse ben Israel, 59, 60n37. *See* Rembrandt.
Menoah, father of Samson, 57
Mercury, 50–51. *See* Hermes.
Mesopotamia, 9–10, 61, 69, 91, 184, 195
Messiah, messianic, 7, 19, 41–42, 59, 93, 116, 130, 181–82, *See* Masîh.
midbar, 161. *See* desert.
Midian, Midianities, 68, 73, 185–87, 191–92, 196
migrant, 23. *See* emigrant, wander.
milla, 108n12, 124–27
minbar, 95. *See* pulpit.
mishaf, 95
miskât, 27n55. *See* Al. Ghazzâli, niche.
Moloch, 89, 204
money, 4, 43, 54, 89, 115, 120, 139, 176, 193, 195, 201–2. *See* Mammon, rich, Qârûn, Korah.

monotheism, monotheistic, 4, 158
Morocco(n), 14, 92
Moses, xi, 4, 8, 12, 15, 18–19, 23–25,
    29, 34–37, 44, 54, 70, 73–74,
    81, 83, 86–88, 92–93, 96, 98,
    105, 109–11, 120, 123–25, 130,
    135, 138, 147, 152–53, 158,
    162, 164–65, 168–69, 174,
    184–88, 190–95, 198, 208–9.
    See Mûsâ.
mountain(s), mountainous, 24, 51, 73,
    102, 164, 166, 185
mount of transfiguration, 26, 73,
    96n62
Mount Carmel, 2, 30, 32, 35, 37. See
    Elijah.
Mount Horeb, mountain of God, 34
Mount Paran, 165
Mount Sinai, mountain of God, 24, 35,
    157, 164
mountain of Moses, 165
Muhammad, the prophet, ix, 3, 7,
    9–12, 15, 20, 26, 32, 35–36,
    38, 55, 63, 68, 75, 93–104, 111,
    115, 121–29, 131, 133–34, 141,
    146–47, 150–56, 163, 165–68,
    171–77, 179, 186–88, 191, 193,
    195
muhâjir(ûn), 69, 153
al-munâfiqûn See hypocrites.
Mûsâ, 4, 83, 165. See Moses.
Muslim tradition, 3–4, 19, 26, 31, 33,
    75, 94, 96, 98, 103, 111, 113,
    134, 145, 162–64, 166–67,
    172–73, 195. See hadith.
myth, mythical, mythological, 128–29,
    197, 205–6

Najrân, 9, 10, 104, 166
Naomi, 52
nasârâ (pl. *nasrâni*), 7
Negus, 97. See Ethiopia.
Nero, Roman emperor, 200, 202. See
    Caesar.
Nestorians, 9
New Testament, xi, 2, 5–6, 8, 11, 14,
    27, 32, 49, 74, 78, 96, 101, 167,
    176, 188, 196, 208

niche, 25. See al-Ghazâlî.
nightly journey of Muhammad, 152
Nimrod, 77, 96, 123. See Abraham.
Nineveh, 68, 77, 96–97, 146, 175–76,
    201, 210. See Jonah, Yûnus.
nomad(s), nomadic, 47–48, 63–64,
    74–75, 95, 101, 185–87
Noah, 24, 32, 86, 94, 124, 141, 173,
    186, 191–93. See Nûh.
nomads, 47–49, 63–64, 74–75, 95, 101,
    185–87
North Africa, 12

Obadiah, 30, 36. See Ahab.
Old Testament, 2, 11–12, 14, 27, 34,
    52, 78, 101, 103, 129, 131, 176,
    184. See Tanakh.
Orthodox Christians, 2, See Syrian
    Orthodox.
Ottoman Empire, 112n29

Palestine, Palestinian, 6, 79, 97,
    113–14, 131, 152, 160, 162,
    199–200, 205
parable(s), xi, 25–26, 45–46, 56, 99,
    169, 170–72, 177, 197
Paran, desert of, 158n7, 162–66, 188
Paris, 61, 105, 111–12, 121, 130, 189
Passover, 86, 90
Paul, the Apostle, 5–6, 8, 27, 46, 49,
    56–57, 74, 92, 100, 107–8, 117,
    171–72, 181, 188, 202
path, 4, 7–8, 20, 22–23, 43–44, 55, 72,
    99–100, 103, 111, 126–27, 155,
    174, 180, 185, 192, 196–97
Pentecost, 90–91
Pentateuch, 128
Peor, 188. See Baal.
Pergamum, 199–207
Persia(n), 7n18, 10, 19, 26, 39, 77,
    96–97, 166, 189–91, 199, 202
Persian Empire, 96
Pharaoh, 18, 23–25, 40, 70, 77, 81–82,
    86, 109, 120, 123–24, 130–31,
    134–39, 141, 152, 158, 162,
    168, 187–94, 198, 205, 209
Pharisees, 5, 56, 111, 114–15
Pilate, 114, 118–19, 130, 203

pilgrimage, pilgrim, 10, 69, 90, 97, 121–22, 156, 162, 164, 188–89, 200, 208, 210. See hajj.
plague, 70, 79, 81, 82n14, 162, 168, 186
power(ful), military, imperial, xi, 20–21, 33, 40–41, 80–85, 89, 92, 96, 103, 107, 109, 113–15, 119–21, 123, 128, 130, 134–39, 143, 145, 148, 156, 166, 168–76, 179, 183, 188, 198, 200–6, 208. See Moloch.
promised city, 188, 210
promised land, 43, 58, 69, 70, 74–75, 88, 152, 165, 186, 189, 208–9, 210. See Palestine.
propaganda, propagandist, 113, 119, 200, 206
prostitute, prostituting, 104, 201–2, 204
Psalm(s), psalmist, 27, 29, 32, 57, 85–90, 102n87, 105–8, 110–11, 121, 176, 204
Psalter, 27
Prophecy, prophecies, 27, 80, 95, 101–2. 193.
pseudepigrapha, 141, 163. See Jubilees.
pulpit, 10, 95. See minbar.

qahal, 8, 76. See ecclesia, church, umma.
Qârûn, 184, 189, 193–95. See rich, Croesus, Korah.
Queen of Sheba, 88, 167
Quraysh, 10, 151
Quss, 10

Rahmân, 95
rabbi, rabbinic, 11, 54, 59–60, 90, 94, 141, 146, 157, 162, 166, 177, 194, 208.
Raphael, 146. See Tobias.
Recab, Recabites, 186n10
religion(s), religious, xi, 3–4, 9, 11, 15, 19, 29–31, 40, 93, 97, 105, 110–14, 121–27, 147, 151, 157–58, 171, 175, 186–87, 197–98, 203. See dîn.
religion (of the desert), 157

religion and state, xi, 113, 121. See dîn wa dawla.
religion of Abraham, 108, See milla.
Rembrandt, xi, 52, 58–60, 211–12
retribution, 45, 169, 172, 184
revelation(s), x, xi, 3, 5n11, 11, 18, 20–21, 23, 26, 29, 34, 36, 46, 76, 90–91, 93, 98, 101, 135, 137, 147, 151, 153, 165, 169, 173, 175, 192, 199–200, 202. See Apocalypse.
revisionists, revisionism, 3
rich, riches, 44–45, 50–51, 56, 61, 64, 85, 107, 139, 167, 169, 170n50, 176, 190, 194, 205. See Croesus, Korah, Mammon.
Roman(s), 6, 17, 41, 56–57, 96, 97n70, 111–14, 118–19, 199, 202, 204–6. See Byzantines.
Roman Catholic, 15, 59, 112, 117
Roman Empire, 113–14, 116, 119, 199–200, 204–6
Rome, 5, 25, 56–57, 77, 91, 96–97, 100, 113–14, 116–17, 180, 185, 190, 200–3, 205. See Constantinople, Rûm.
Rûm, (second Rome), 96, 97n70, 190. See Byzantium.
Rûmî, Jalâl al-Dîn, 49

Saba', 24, 88, 169. See Seba.
sabbath, 194, 208
Sadr, Musa, Imam, 189n22
Saladin, 92
salafists, 113n30
Sâlih, Arab prophet, 68. See Thamûd.
Samaria, 29, 79. See Ahab.
Samson, 57
Santa Claus, 14
Sarah, Sarai, 43, 57, 60–64, 74, 158–62
Sassanid Persians, 97
satan, 46, 109–10, 115, 141–42, 147–48, 191–92, 200, 202, 204–6, 208
Saul, king, 56, 153, 185. See Tâlût.
Scrooge, Ebenezer, xi, 4, 42–43, 46
sea, 24, 31, 57, 83, 87, 167, 205. See bahr, yamm.
Seba, 24, 80. See Saba'.

seer, 17, 184, 193, 197–98, 200, 205.
    See John, Balaam.
Seir, 101n96, 102, 164–65
separation of church and state, xi,
    112–13, 116, 119
Septuagint, 72, 75, 101n96
Sermon on the Mount, 35, 177
serpent, 197–98, 200, 206. See satan.
shari'a, 8, 126
shaytân, 95. See satan.
Shu'ayb, 68, 165, 185–87, 192–93, 205.
    See Jethro.
Sinai, 24–25, 29, 34–35, 37, 53, 87–88,
    90–91, 157–58, 164–65, 185–
    86, 195, 199. See Sînay.
Simon the Maccabee, 41
Sînây, 25. See Sinai.
Sodom, 47, 61, 64–73, 96, 152, 167,
    175. See Gomorrah.
Solomon, King, 25, 40–41, 72, 88, 131,
    139–40, 151, 167, 204, 209
'son of the way', 54. See ibn al-sabîl.
South Africa, 189n23
St. Catherine Monastery, 165
St. Nicholas, 13–14, 42, 43
stranger, xi, 1, 13–14, 23–24, 28, 47–
    59, 61–67, 70, 73–75, 77, 132,
    139, 159, 178, 188, 190
sword, 30, 34, 95, 107, 119n44, 155,
    165, 196–99, 202–3
symbol, symbolic, 19, 27, 33, 40–42, 61,
    68, 96, 112, 134n22, 157, 186,
    188, 197, 200–201, 205, 207
Syria, Syrian, ix, 5, 26–27, 75, 96–97,
    112–31, 153, 187, 197–99, 202
Syriac, 166, 171
Syrian Orthodox, 9

Tabernacle, 25
tâghiya, 97n70. See tyrant.
Tahrir Square, 8
Tâlût, 153, 185. See Saul.
Tanakh, xi, 1, 27, 78, 96, 98, 101, 176,
    208
tawâf, 164. See circumambulation.
Tawra, 4, 27, 96, 101, 127, 141, 153,
    174, 176. See Tanakh, Old
    Testament.

Tema, 48, 95
terror(ism), terrorist, 24, 39, 79–80,
    83, 85, 106, 111, 119, 120, 122,
    136, 209
Thamûd, 68. See Sâlih.
Tiberias, 114, 166
Tiberius, Roman emperor, 114, 117, 120
Titus, Roman emperor, the Arch of, 25,
    200, 202
Tobias, 57, 146. See Raphael.
tohu wa bohu, 17
tongue(s), 18–19, 76–79, 81, 83, 85–87,
    89–91, 93, 95, 97–99, 101, 103,
    174, 177, 182, 197, 199, 203
Torah, x, 1–2, 4–5, 8, 11–12, 23, 28,
    52–54, 66, 87, 89, 91, 99, 105,
    111, 117, 120–21, 139–40, 153,
    162–64, 174, 194, 204, 208. See
    Tawra.
transform(ative), transformation, 32,
    85, 89, 103
tsaddîq, 141
Tûr, 37, 164. See Sinai.
Turkey, 5, 49, 199
tyrant, 97n70, 123, 190
Tyrus, 29

'Ukâz, 10
Umar ibn al-Khattâb, 96, 151
umma, 10–11, 75, 125n67, 126n76,
    127n82
'Urwa ibn, Masûd, 97n69
'Uthmân, 3

Vespasian, Emperor, 200
viceregent, 151, 156. See Joseph, caliph.
victory, victorious, 41, 141, 154–56.
    See Badr.
violence, 2, 54–55, 73, 106, 109,
    111–12, 119–21, 132, 169, 200,
    209–10
visit, visitation(s), visitors, xi, 5, 9, 14,
    42–47, 49–51, 53, 55, 57–59,
    61–63, 65, 67, 69, 71, 73, 75,
    88, 91, 94, 96–97, 104, 163,
    169, 178, 196, 207

Wahb b. Munabbih, 37, 163, 186
wander(ing(s)), wanderer, 2, 13, 23, 33, 50, 74–75, 114, 158, 160, 164, 180, 184–85
way of Cain, 184
way, people of the, 4–6
way of God, 58, 69n75, 111–12, 116–17, 121
way of the Lord, 103
way of love, 182
way of righteousness, 7
ways, two, 174, 180
wealth, 96, 107, 166, 170, 174, 176–77, 179, 194–95, 205–6. *See* Moloch, Qârûn, Korah, rich.
whore of Babylon, 200–201
wilderness, xi, 57–58, 70, 94, 103, 120, 161, 164, 183, 185, 187–88
Wilders, Geert, 4, 157n2
worship, 6, 15, 20, 31, 33, 52, 79, 84, 89, 93, 108, 110, 120, 168, 185, 188, 203–6

Xerxes, 190. *See* Ahasueros.

Yahyâ, 103, 153, 184. *See* John the Baptist, Zachariah.
Ya'qûb, 28
Yâqût, geographer, 162
yahûdha, 145. *See* Judah.
yamm, 24. *See* sea, *bahr*.
Yehud, 199
YHWH, 15, 23, 25, 27, 29, 35–36, 49, 86, 90, 135, 157, 178, 185–87
Yûnus, 210
Yûsuf, 130, 140, 166, 190

Zachariah, 31, 110. *See* John the Baptist, Yahyâ.
zabûr, pl. *zubur*, 27
zakât, 58, 110n23, 124n60, 195. *See* alms.
Zamaksharî, 26, 156
Zealots, 115–16, 118–19, 184
Zephaniah, 44, 89
Zeus, 49–50, 203. *See* Jupiter, Barnabas.
Zeus the Healer (Soter), 200
Zoar, 64, 72

Scripture Index

Hebrew Bible/Old Testament

Genesis

1:2	17	15:17–18	70
2:3	69	16:3	158
2:7	92	16:7	161
3:1–8	197	16:7–14	159
3:14, 15	198	16:8	159
4:8	183, 185	16:12	48, 48n5
4:11–16	158	16:13	43
4:15	184	17:2	159
4:17	31, 158, 185	17:6	130
5:32	94	17:8	74
6:3	176	18:1	62
10:7	95	18:1–15	61
10:8–9	123	18:2–15	57
10:25–29	93	18:13	63
11	91, 190	18:14	63
11:27, 31	64	18:16–33	61, 67
12:1	61	18:17	62
12:4–5	64	18:20	71
12:7	88	18:20–21	62
12:10	74–75	18:33	62
12:10–20	16, 21	19:1	62
12:36	131	19:1–4	57
13:1	64	19:3	56, 66
13:8–12	69	19:4–5	66
13:10–13	64	19:8	56
13:11	64	19:9	66
14:14–16	48	19:9–11	67
15:12–13	70	19:15	69
15:13	74	19:26	73
		19:30–37	64
		20:1	75

Genesis (continued)

21:4, 20–21	161
21:8–13	160
21:14	162
21:14–15	161
21:15–20	161
21:17–21	162
21:21	162
21:22–34	162
21:23–31	160
21:27–31	160n10
21:33	160
22:15–17	159–60
23:4	74, 186
25:3	95
25:4	186
25:14	101n96
25:29–34	28
26:3	75
26:7–14	75
26:32–33	160
27:35	28
27:36	144
28	59
28:15, 20	70
28:17	70
28:18	134
30:24	132
32:5	75
32:6	48
32:23–31	28
34:7	107
35:11	130
36:11–15	165
37–50	130
37:1	74
37:8	130
37:9–10	150
37:10	135
37:19	134
39:8–9	132
40:15	134
40:20–23	135
41:40–41	138
41:42	138
41:43	138
41:45	136, 138
41:46–49	139
41:55–56	139
43:32	131
44:16	136
44:33–34	136
45	135
45:5	136, 156
45:7	137
45:8	130, 137
46:4	146
49	125n70, 147
50:20	137, 142
50:24–25	43
50:25	43
50:26	131

Exodus

1–14	190
1:1–5	81
1:7	81, 139
1:8	135
1:14	82
2:11–14	73
2:11–15	187
2:12	185
2:22	73
3	164
3:1	186
3:2–6	35
3:7–8	83
3:12	187
3:13–15	23
3:15	24
3:16	44
3:19	24
4:10	18
4:22	120
4:30–31	44
5:5–19	139
6:26	87
7:14—11:10	81
8:20–24	168
8:22	81
10:2	86
12:14, 17	69

12:26	86	18:21	204
12:29–30	70, 82	19:18	5
12:29, 31	69, 82	19:28	30n67
12:29–33	81	19:33–34	53–54
12:38	95	21:5	30n67
12:40–41	86	23:15–16	90
12:41	87	25:35–38; 47–48	139
12:42	69		
12:49	74		
13:8	86		
14–15	40		

Numbers

10:29	185–86
11:12	120
12:1–2	188
12:8	35n83
16	190
16:3	193
16:22–24	184
16:32	193
20:15	75
22–24	188
22–25	195
22:8	196
22:9–14	196
22:19	196
22:20	196
22:20–35	197
23:19–20	84
24:22	185
25	188
28:26	90
30:15	23

15:13	88
15:22	188
15:24	188
16:6–9	207
16:17–18	208
18:1	186
18:2–3	187
18:10–12	186
19	29
19:4	120
19:16	34
19:17–18	91
19:18	34, 91
19:18–20	164
20:5	45
20:6	45
20:11	69
22:20	31, 66
23:9	53
24:9–11	186
24:16–17	91
25:31–39	25
31:17	69
32	19, 188
33:2	62
33:11	35n83
33:20	28
33:20–23	35n83
33:21–23	35
34	108
34:22	90

Deuteronomy

1:6–7	165
1:30–33	120
1:31	208
2:7	188
2:9, 19	64
4:1	208
4:29	36

Leviticus

11:15	33

Deuteronomy (continued)

4:34	24
5:2–3	165
5:4	35n83, 91
5:9	45n110
5:22	91
6:5	5
6:21	86
7:9	45
7:9–10	45n110
8:3–4	208
10:17–18	74
13:1–6	31n69
14:1	30n67
14:14	33
16:19	73
18:15–18	35n83
18:19–20	23
19:9	90
21:19	65
23:5	64
23:7	54
24:17	53
25:7	65
26:5	23n43, 75
27:19	53
32:9	85 n20
32:11	120, 164
33:1–2	101n96, 164
33:4	125n70
33:16	25
34:10	35

Joshua

18:15	175

Judges

1:16	185–86
2:11	56
3:7, 12	56
4:11	185
4:11–22	186
4:17	185
5:4	101n96
5:10	41
5:20	29n63
5:24	185
6:11–18	57
13:3–22	57
19	66
19:15	56
19:16–30	50
19:22–23	56
19:23–24	107
19:24	56

Ruth

1:16	52
4:1	65
4:13–17	65

1 Samuel

5:1—6:21	81
11:13	153
15:4–6	185
15:6	186
15:34	56
17:45	29n63
22:6	56
25	106n4
25:2–42	107

2 Samuel

18:24	65
20:24	140
23:2	18n21

1 Kings

1:33	42
1:38	41
5:6	40

5:14–17	140	**1 Chronicles**	
7:49	25		
8:44, 48	153	1:19–23	93
9:19	40	1:30	101
10:1	167	1:32	186
10:1–4	166		
10:1–13	88, 167		
10:14–15	95	**2 Chronicles**	
10:26	40		
10:28–29	40	9:12–14	95
11	209	24:20–22	184
11:7–13	104, 204	28:3	204
12:14	140		
12:18	140		
16:31–33	29	**Job**	
16:32	29		
17:1	29	1:15	166
17:4, 6	33	5:12	198
17:8—2 Kings 2:13		15:5	198
	29	22:13–14	107
18:1–16	30	31:31–32	56
18:15	29	38:41	33
18:19	33n78	39:5–8	48n5
18:26	29		
18:27–29	30		
18:36	29	**Psalms**	
18:36–40	30		
18:37	30	2	206
19:4	35	10:4	104, 106
19:4–9	34	10:11	106–7
19:8	35	14	106
19:9–12	34	19:8	4, 5n11
19:13	36	20:7	105
		23	85
		23:2–3, 6	57
2 Kings		24:6	36
		25:8–9	5
2:11–12	37	37	110
7:1	65	37:29	110n24
10:15–24	186n10	47	93, 96–99
10:19–20	29	58:4	197
15:5	81	64:1–5	177
16:3	204	68:8	90
18:26, 28	87	74:13	205–6
22	89	78:19–20	57
23:10	204		
23:1–14	89		

Psalms (continued)

78:24	57
78:25	207
78:52–54	58
78:54	88
83:1	29
83:18	29
90:10	176
94:9	177
95:10	188
96	206
97:2	206
104:14–15	58
105:12–15	74–75
105:40	207
106:19–20	108
106:37–41	204
113–118	86
113:3	88
114	86, 88–89
114:1–2	86
114:2	87–88, 90
114:2–7	87
114:8	89
119:105	5n11
121:2	69
121:3–5	69
121:4	69
140:3	197
146:3–4	41
147:9	33
149:7–9a	32
149:8	32

Proverbs

1:21	65
8:3	65
10:9	100
15:27	208n79
17:7	107
20:12	177
30:14	107
31:31	65

Ecclesiastes

12:1–7	176

Isaiah

1:2	120
1:9	68
1:10	71
1:23	193
3:9	71
5:7	71
6:1	62
6:1–5	78–79
10:1–3	44
11:4	203
15:3	81
17:1	203
19:1–4	82
19:2–4	82
19:4	81
19:16–25	79
19:18	77
19:21	84
19:24	85
19:25	85
21:5–9	38
21:8–9a	39
21:9b	39
21:11–12	102
21:13–15	95
23:16	201
28:10	2
28:11	17n15, 87
29:21	65
31:1, 3	40
32:5–6	107
33:19	87
34:5	203
40:9–10	102–3
41:2	19
44:6	135
44:6–20	20
44:28	19
45:1–2	19
45:6	135

45:13	20	23	201
45:15	19	25:13	96
46:3–4	120	27:15	95
48:14–15	19–20	27:22	166
52:7	102–3	35:5, 1–4	165
53:7	61	37:1–14	33n77
55:8	93	37:9	92
58:6–7	180	38:2—39:15	109
60:6	166	38:13	95
60:21	110n25		
63:9	120		
65:25	198		

Daniel

4:30	103
5:25	39n94
6:11	153
7	205
7:13	203

Jeremiah

2:2	200
2:34	201
17:19	65
21:12	65
23:1	71
29:7	132
29:10	44
29:13	36
29:14	37n88
31:9	120
31:12	58
31:20	120
35	186
50:2	39
50	132n12
51	132n12

Hosea

1:2–3	201
2:7	58, 201
2:13	188n19
2:21–22	207
3:3	201
4:12–15	201
9:1	201
11:1–3	120
11:9	84

Amos

5:4	36
5:10–15	65

Lamentations

5:14	65

Ezekiel

1:26	62
16	201
16:15	201
16:25–26	201
16:46	68
16:49	67, 71, 73

Jonah

1	176
3:4	68
4:2	210
4:4	114n35
4:11	176, 210

Micah

3:2–3	104
3:9–11	201
3:11	193
5:9	41
7:17	198

Nahum

3:1	201
3:4	201

Habakkuk

2:12	201
2:20	17

Zephaniah

1:7	17
2:7	44
3:9	89, 93
3:16	42n104

Zechariah

2:13	16, 17n14
3:9	25
8:16	65
9:9, 10	41–42

Malachi

3:1, 23–24	37

New Testament

Matthew

4:4	208
4:15	6
5:5	110n24
5–7	177
5:17	174
5:39	121
6:24	205
7:13–14	177
7:21	55
8:19–22	6
10:16	197–98
10:38	6
12:34	197
16:6, 11	115
17:1–8	73
21:2–7	42
22:37–40	5
23:35	184
25:31–46	177, 180, 207
25:35–45	178
26:15	116
26:30	86
26:52	119
26:52–54	155

Mark

1:2–4	103
1:3	103
1:9	114
1:13	115
1:15	103
3:18	115
5:6–10	114
5:15	114
8:11	115
8:15	115
9:2–8	73
10:2	115
11:15–19	115
12:13	116
12:13–14	111
12:15	115
12:17	112–13
14:26	86

16:10	198

Luke

1	133
1:68	44
1:78–79	44
4:4	208
4:24	114
9:28–36	73
9:30–31	96n62
10:19	198
10:42	85n20
11:31–32	167
12:1	115
12:13–21	170.n50
12:20	107
14:12–14	56
16:9, 11, 13	205
17:28–32	72
20:20–26	xiii
20:21	74
24:13–18	52

John

1:14	5
4:12	35
12:15	41–42
18:5	6
18:10–11	119
20:22	92
20:31	130

Acts

2:1–4	90
2:5–13	90
2:6	91
2:7–11	91
2:22	6
7:6	74
9:9, 23	7
10:34	74
11:26	5
13:9–10	100
13:17	75, 81
13:18	120
14:11–12	49
14:19	171
15:20, 29	53n16
16:17	7
18:26	7
20:16	90
21:27	90
24:5	7n18
24:14	6, 22, 74
24:22	6
24:24–26	6
25:11	202

Romans

1:21–22	108
1:22	107
1:23	108
2:11	74
5:5	92
6:4	5
8:1, 4	5
8:9, 11	92
16:17–18	100

1 Corinthians

5:7	115
10:6, 11	188
12:12–31	182
12:13–30	181
13	182

2 Corinthians

11:3	197

Galatians

2:9	74
4:26	88

Ephesians

2:12	75
3:19	27
6:9	74

Colossians

1:12	17
3:16	92
3:25	74

1 Timothy

3:2	57
3:16	46

Philemon

2:6–7	192
3:20	75

Hebrews

1:3	121
4:12	203
9:15	17
11:8–10	75
11:9	74–75
12:18	91
12:22	88
13:2	47

James

4:15–16	45

1 Peter

1:4	17
4:16	6
5:13	203

2 Peter

1:16–18	73
1:19	26
2:2, 21	7
2:6–7	73
2:15	196
2:15–16	185, 198

Jude

11	184

Revelation

1:16	203
2:12	203
2:12–17	202
2:14	196, 206
2:17	207
5:1	17
8:1	17
11:15	203
12:3	203
12:3, 9	206
13	205
13:2,3	205
13:11	205, 207
13:18	206
14:8	203
16:13	206
17	200
17:1, 5	201
17:9–10	200
19:15	203
19:20	206
20:7–10	109
20:10	206

Apocrypha and Septuagint

1 Maccabees

2:67–68	118
13:51	41

2 Maccabees

10:7	41

4 Maccabees

2:2	141

Sirach

48:9, 12	37

Tobit

3:11	153
11:1–8	146
12:1–20	57

Wisdom

10:6–8	72

Old Testament Pseudepigrapha

2 Baruch

4:2–6	88

1 Enoch

5:7	110n24
90:29	88

4 Ezra

7:30	17

Jubilees

20:9	163

The Qur'an

1:6	7	2:49–50	190
1:6–7	174	2:50	24, 153
2:1–3	21	2:51, 92–93	108
2:3	100	2:83	110
2:4	21	2:108	7
2:4–16	108	2:120	175
2:5	175	2:125	164
2:8–11	108	2:125, 127	162
2:12–13	108	2:126	164
2:30	109	2:127–28	164
2:31	99	2:128	125
2:32	99	2:130, 135	125
2:46–49	190	2:132	125

The Qur'an (continued)

2:133	125, 147	5:27–31	183
2:136	147	5:30–32	184
2:140	11	5:41	177
2:142	55	5:46	8
2:142–50	153	5:48	7, 11
2:177	54–55	5:56	110
2:181	153	5:82	192
2:205	109	5:112	95
2:206	204	5:116	22
2:213	11	6:7	165
2:215	58, 164	6:12, 54	210
2:220	110	6:19	173
2:243	33n77	6:37	115n40
2:258	123	6:48	173
2:271	58	6:55	7
2:273	58	6:59	22
3:2	153	6:63, 97	24
3:12	204	6:85	31, 110
3:13	153–54	6:91	175
3:14	170n49	6:123	125
3:19	122	6:126	7
3:45	95	6:161	125–26
3:50	9	7:13	191
3:52	197	7:20	198
3:67	7, 11, 125	7:48	205
3:68	125	7:55–56	175
3:95	125	7:73–79	110
3:96–97	164	7:75–76	192
3:99	100	7:80–81	71
3:104	11	7:85–93	186
3:123	154	7:88	192
3:155	198	7:88–89	125
3:167	177	7:101–2	190
3:179	21	7:103–57	190
3:196	175	7:107, 117	198
4:36	54	7:127	82, 109
4:36–38	205	7:128	110n25
4:38	58	7:130–34	81, 168
4:46	126	7:136	24
4:76	7, 148	7:137	88
4:119	110	7:138	24
4:125	125	7:146	7
4:172	192	7:150–51	19, 188
5:3	121–22	7:163	175
5:12	7	8:9–10	155
5:27–28	183	8:36	205
		8:54	24
		8:60	209

SCRIPTURE INDEX

8:61	210	12:38	125
9:40	55	12:41	140–41
9:41	55	12:43	190
9:100	179	12:44	141
10:9	24	12:46	141–42
10:37	101	12:47–49	142
10:47	10	12:50	149
10:72	124, 193	12:51–52	149
10:75	192	12:56–57	134
10:75–92	190	12:59	143
10:78	192	12:63	143
10:81	109	12:64	143
10:88	205	12:67	143
10:89	7	12:69	144
10:90	24	12:70, 76	144
10:94	101	12:76	149–50
10:98	175	12:77	144
10:98–99	176	12:78	150
11:2	98	12:79	145
11:69	62	12:80	150
11:69–74	67	12:82	175
11:71	63	12:83	144
11:71–72	63	12:84	144–45
11:74	67	12:85	144
11:74–83	175	12:86	144
11:77–79	67	12:87	144–45
11:81	69	12:89	145
11:84–95	186	12:90	145
11:87	205	12:92	156
11:120	32	12:93	145
12:3	130	12:95	145
12:5	147	12:96	146
12:5–6	140	12:99	147
12:8	143, 145, 149	12:100	142, 150
12:12	143	12:101	142, 150
12:16–18	148	12:102	150
12:18	144	12:104	193
12:19	133	12:111	133
12:24	154	13:9	165
12:25	133, 148	13:16	15
12:28	148	14:4	99
12:30	148	14:8	165
12:31	148	14:35	163
12:32	149	14:37	158, 163
12:33	134	15:51–53	63
12:33–34	149	15:53	63
12:36	140	15:71	67
12:37	140, 152	15:84	205

The Qur'an (continued)

Reference	Page
16:36	10
16:48–49	192
16:52	123
16:62	165
16:103	98–99
16:112–13	172
16:120	11, 125
16:125	8
17:1	88, 152
17:26	176
17:60	152
17:71	178
17:90–91	171
17:93	171
17:103	24
18	31
18:32–44	170
18:94	109
19:18–32	133
19:30–32	192
19:41	142
19:41–48	133
19:49	63
19:56	31, 142
19:97	98
20:10–14	25
20:12	164
20:24, 43	190
20:40	186
20:77	83
20:77–78	19
20:78	24
20:90–98	190
20:113	98
20:120	109
21:3	151
21:5	152
21:49	153
21:71	68
21:74	71, 74
21:81	88
21:85	31
21:87	176
21:92	10
21:93	10
21:105	110
22:44	186
22:78	125
23:20	165
23:52	10
24:22	55
24:35	26
25:1	153
25:63	192
26:29	123
26:63	24
26:63–66	24
26:127	193
26:145	193
26:160	68
26:164	193
26:176–91	186
26:180	193
26:195	98–99
26:195–99	98
26:214	173
27:2–44	89
27:12	81
27:69	172
27:82–85	207
27:91–92	124
28:2–50	190
28:4	109
28:8, 38	192
28:22–29	186
28:29	37
28:30	25
28:38	190
28:39	192
28:40	24
28:46	173
28:76–80	184, 193
29:26	69
29:27	69
29:29	71
29:31, 32	62
29:36–37	186
29:37	186
29:39	190–91
30	96
30:2–3	97
30:3	124
30:42	172
31:12–13, 16–19	192

SCRIPTURE INDEX

31:18	192	48:1	156
31:32	15	48:4	156
31:34	21	48:27	147, 155–56
32:15	192	49	147
34:15–17	169	51:24	63
34:16	24	51:24–30	67
34:28	10, 173	51:32	71
36:13–27	171	51:34	71
36:21	193	51:40	24
37:71–148	32	52:1	164
37:75–82	32	52:1–7	24
37:102	140	53:36	174
37:114–22	25	54:11–12	24
37:123–32	31–32	54:34	173
37:114–22	83	54:34–37	71
37:133	68	54:37	67, 71
37:147	176	55:2	99
37:148	176	56:7–10	179
38:32, 35	40	57:23–24	205
38:74–75	191	58:19	110
39:11	123	59:23	191
39:12	124	61:6	8
39:27–28	99	61:14	95
39:28	98	63:10	110
40:14	173	64:16	205
40:24	190	68:17–32	45–46
40:27	192	68:48	176
40:28	191	69:18–29	179
40:29	7	69:28	205
40:36	7, 190	69:33–35	179
40:66	124	69:34	58
41:3	98	71:1	173
41:13	32	71:7	192
41:15	192	72:2	173
41:26	100–101	72:26–27	21
41:41–44	100	73:1–2	36
41:44	98	74:38–47	179
42:5	175	79:15–24	124
42:7	98, 173	79:16	164
43:3	98	79:17	25
43:31	175	84:7	178
43:47–50	81	84:10	178n75
43:52	18	85:4–7	9, 167
44:23–24	83	85:12	167
44:24–25	24	89:15b–20	179n82
46:12	98	89:20	40
47:14	175	90:1	175
47:38	205		

The Qur'an (*continued*)

90:1–20	174–75	96:1	133
92:8	205	96:4–5	99
92:14	173	98:5	124
95:2	164	100:8	40
		104:1–3	205
		107	179n82

www.ingramcontent.com/pod-product-compliance
Lightning Source LLC
Chambersburg PA
CBHW050436240426
43661CB00055B/2408